P9-BZJ-054

365 DEVOTIONS

Savor

SHAUNA NIEQUIST

ZONDERVAN®

ZONDERVAN

Savor

Copyright © 2015 by Shauna Niequist
This title is also available as a Zondervan e-book. Visit www.zondervan.com.
This title is also available as a Zondervan audiobook. Visit www.zondervan.com.
Requests for information should be addressed to:
Zondervan, *Grand Rapids, Michigan 49530*

ISBN: 9780310344971

All Scripture quotations, unless otherwise indicated, are taken from The Holy Bible, *New International Version®*, *NIV®*. Copyright © 1973, 1978, 1984, 2011 by Biblica, Inc.™ Used by permission. All rights reserved worldwide.

Any Internet addresses (Web sites, blogs, etc.) and telephone numbers in this book are offered as a resource. They are not intended in any way to be or imply an endorsement by Zondervan, nor does Zondervan vouch for the content of these sites and numbers for the life of this book.

All rights reserved. No part of this publication may be reproduced, stored in a retrieval system, or transmitted in any form or by any means—electronic, mechanical, photocopy, recording, or any other—except for brief quotations in printed reviews, without the prior permission of the publisher.

Cover design: Connie Gabbert Design and Illustration
Cover and interior illustrations: Lindsay Letters
Back cover photography: Jennifer Blair
Interior design and typesetting: Mandi Cofer

Printed in China

15 16 17 18 19 20 / DSC / 11 10 9 8 7 6

For my grandparents Bob and Leah Barry,
who are still living a love story after all these years,
and teaching us all what it means to really savor life.

RECIPE LISTING

INTRODUCTION

What I want to do is savor this life—my life, my children, my community, this gorgeous world God created. That's what we all want, right? To soak up the goodness all around us, to be aware of holy fingerprints everywhere, to walk through each day expecting and noticing those glints and shimmers of the divine right in the daily—in a hug, a tomato sandwich, a quiet moment, a text from someone we love.

That's what I want, and so often I miss it. I lay in bed at night frustrated with myself that I allowed the minor annoyances of life to obscure the rich melody underneath it. I rush and push and don't even see the beauty all around me. I let my fear about the unknowns in our future or my desire to control everything and everyone around me cover over the deep beauty and grace and peace that are playing like a drumbeat under everything.

This collection is my attempt at paying attention, at clearing away space and noise, and inviting you to hear the drumbeat, too. God's always speaking, always. He's always moving, always present, always creating, always healing. The trick, at least for me, is paying attention. The trick is savoring.

I tend to live in my head—analyzing every word of that last conversation, regretting what I did, anticipating what's coming, worrying about what could go wrong. Whole plot lines unfold—beginning, middle, end—in the time it takes me to brush my teeth or for the toast to pop up out of the toaster.

I'm trying to get out of my head. And I'm trying to get right down into the raw soil of my own life. Because it's happening whether I decide to notice or not. These children are growing taller each day. I peeked in at Henry last night, and it seemed his legs stretched all the way down his bed, as though he's a teenager and not a seven-year-old.

Things will not always be as they are now—there will be new things, other things, good things. But I don't want to miss this, this right now, this sacred everyday. And I don't want to only see the surface. I want to see the depths—the work of God all around me, in conversation and prayer and silence and music. I want to connect with the God who made me from dust, on purpose and for a purpose. I want to walk through my days in a warm conversation through prayer, aware as I walk that he walks with me, that as I speak, he hears me, that as I rest, he carries me.

I forget so easily that there's a bigger picture. I'm easily seduced by the bustle of the day—lunch and laundry, deadlines and dinnertime. I forget that it's all held together by a holy, loving God, and that we get to be his partners in restoration and healing. I forget that there's more than I see, more than I can dream.

This book is my gift to you, my hand holding out to yours—let's remember these things together. Let's clear away space together, trusting that what we'll find in even small moments of prayer and silence will transform us. When I begin the day in prayer, I find that it's easier to continue that way. When I begin the day with God's word, with silence, with a grounding sense of his love for me, then I find it's easier to bring those things with me throughout the day, and it's harder for me to locate them if I didn't pause with them at the start.

So let's begin together. Let's savor this day, the beauty of the world God made, the richness of family and friendship, the good gifts of creativity and work. All the things that populate our days are worth savoring. Let's walk together.

365 Devotions

OUR STORIES

Don't you know that you yourselves are God's temple
and that God's Spirit dwells in your midst?

—1 Corinthians 3:16

These are my stories, the stories of life as it reveals itself in my field of vision, and the cast of characters are my friends and family and neighbors. I'm telling these stories because they're the only ones I know and the only ones I have the right to tell, believing that in them you will find your own stories, with your own beautiful and strange characters and plot twists. I believe that these love letters to my own quotidian life will unmask the tiny glimmers of hope and redemption masquerading as normal life in your corner of the world.

The world is alive, blinking and clicking, winking at us slyly, inviting us to get up and dance to the music that's been playing since the beginning of time, if you bend all the way down and put your ear to the ground to hear it.

You have stories worth telling, memories worth remembering, dreams worth working toward, a body worth feeding, a soul worth tending, and beyond that, the God of the universe dwells within you, the true culmination of super and natural.

You are more than dust and bones.

You are spirit and power and image of God.

YOUR STORY is worth telling—it's part of God's story, and his Spirit dwells within you. Take a few minutes to thank God both for your story and for his Spirit in you.

START WHERE YOU ARE

You prepare a table before me in the presence of my enemies.
You anoint my head with oil; my cup overflows.

—Psalm 23:5

My friend Laura's New Year's resolution is "start where you are." I love it. Whatever thing seems too intimidating, whatever new skill seems too far off to develop, whatever project has been hanging over your head forever: *start where you are.*

Each of us has been created by a holy God with love, on purpose and for a purpose. But so many of us feel afraid or unprepared. This is the secret, though: No one is prepared enough. No one is perfectly ready.

Let's choose together to take one step forward today, whatever that means—a phone call, an hour of writing, a day away to dream. Sometimes even just a half hour to brainstorm or plan gets us unstuck. No one lives out an exciting calling without just plunging forward at some point, full of fear and uncertainty.

The world is full of people who can talk your ear off about all the reasons they can't possibly just begin that thing they're longing to begin. Let's not be those people. Let's start where we are.

WHAT'S THE dream or vision or project you feel called to in this season of your life? What's one tangible way to start where you are?

BITTERSWEET

Shall we accept good from God, and not trouble?

—Job 2:10

The idea of *bittersweet* is changing the way I live, unraveling and reweaving the way I understand life. Bittersweet is the idea that in all things there is both something broken and something beautiful, that there is a sliver of lightness on even the darkest of nights, a shadow of hope in every heartbreak, and that rejoicing is no less rich when it contains a splinter of sadness.

Bittersweet is the practice of believing that we really do need both the bitter and the sweet, and that a life of nothing but sweetness rots both your teeth and your soul. Bitter is what makes us strong, what forces us to push through, what helps us earn the lines on our faces and the calluses on our hands. Sweet is nice enough, but bittersweet is beautiful, nuanced, full of depth and complexity. Bittersweet is courageous, gutsy, earthy.

So this is the work I'm doing now, and the work I invite you into: when life is sweet, say thank you and celebrate. And when life is bitter, say thank you and grow.

SPEND A few minutes thanking God even for the bitter parts of your life, trusting his love and goodness even in the midst of loss.

A PIECE OF A STORY

*That which was from the beginning, which we have heard, which
we have seen with our eyes, which we have looked at and our hands
have touched—this we proclaim concerning the Word of life.*

—1 John 1:1

When my friend Doug told me that the pattern of death and rebirth is the central metaphor of the Christian life, he was giving me the currency that he earned through his own brokenness. He was telling me something that God had written on his life as a part of his story. The reason I didn't understand it at that point was because I didn't need to, but then several years later, I did.

You tell what you know, what you've earned, what you've learned the hard way. You watch it fall on what seem to be deaf ears, and you mutter something under your breath, something about pearls before swine. But then ten years later you realize that one fragment of your story has now been woven into someone else's, as a bridge to a new way of understanding and living. I didn't need proof from a theologian or a tip from a church practitioner. I needed a piece of a story, something real and full of life and blood and breath and heartache, something that someone had lived through, a piece of wisdom earned the hard way. That's why telling our stories is so important.

WHOSE STORY has helped bring you to a new way of understanding and living? Who has been helped by hearing your story, your hard-won understanding?

THIS IS IT

I commend the enjoyment of life, because there is nothing better for a person under the sun than to eat and drink and be glad. Then joy will accompany them in their toil all the days of the life God has given them under the sun.

—Ecclesiastes 8:15

This is what I'm finding, in glimpses and flashes: this is it. This is it, in the best possible way. That thing I'm waiting for, that adventure, that movie-score-worthy experience unfolding gracefully. This is it. Normal, daily life ticking by on our streets and sidewalks, in our houses and apartments, in our beds and at our dinner tables, in our dreams and prayers and fights and secrets. This pedestrian life is the most precious thing any of us will ever experience.

I believe that this way of living, this focus on the present, the daily, the tangible, this intense concentration not on the news headlines but on the flowers growing in your own garden, the children growing in your own home, this way of living has the potential to open up the heavens, to yield a glittering handful of diamonds where a second ago there was coal. This way of living and noticing and building and crafting can crack through the movie sets and soundtracks that keep us waiting for our own life stories to begin, and set us free to observe the lives we have been creating all along without even realizing it.

EVERYDAY LIFE is an exquisite gift. What would it look like to really pay attention to that gift today?

January

6

WHAT MIGHT HAVE BEEN

Record my misery; list my tears on your scroll—are they not in your record?

—**P s a l m   5 6 : 8**

If you've been marked by what might have been, you don't forget. You know the day, the years. You know when the baby would have been born. You know exactly what anniversary you'd be celebrating, if the wedding had happened. You know exactly how old she'd be right now, if she were still alive. You'll never forget the last time you saw your child, or the last time *cancer* was a word about someone else's life, or the day that changed absolutely everything. It makes the calendar feel like a minefield, like you're constantly tiptoeing over explosions of grief until one day you hit one, shattered by what might have been.

I don't know what date it is for you—what broke apart on that day, what was lost, what memories are pinned forever to that day on that calendar. But I hope that on that day you hold yourself open and tender to the memories for just a moment. As one who also grieves, I grieve with you, for whatever you've lost, too, for what might have been.

H A S   Y O U R life been marked by what might have been? What meaningful traditions or moments have you practiced on those days? Today, allow the God who loves you to carry your sadness for you.

CIRCLING THE WAGONS

Love does not delight in evil but rejoices with the truth. It always protects, always trusts, always hopes, always perseveres.

—1 Corinthians 13:6–7

I believe friendship is God's greatest evidence of himself here on earth. Everyone needs a home team: a go-to, show-up, middle-of-the-night, come-in-without-knocking tribe that gets us through when things fall apart. I believe in circling the wagons—gathering your people around you to tell you the truth when all the voices out there are shouting bad news. And of course, I believe all this love and truth-telling and prayer and laughter happen best around the table.

That's why I love Thursday nights, because Thursday night is small group night. We always eat together. We pray together, to begin and end our time together. We create space for each person to be heard, to talk about what's good and what's hard, to ask for prayer and help. We take confidentiality and the safety of the table very seriously. We don't always do a study. Many times we read the Bible. Sometimes someone leads a liturgy or reading. Sometimes someone leads an exercise that helps us interact with a section of scripture or a set of ideas or spiritual practices. But every week, we gather around our table, and every week, my heart is so full and thankful.

WHO'S ON your home team? How do you nurture those connections and relationships?

AWARENESS OF HOLINESS

And he took bread, gave thanks and broke it, and gave it to them, saying,
"This is my body given for you; do this in remembrance of me."

—Luke 22:19

I believe that Jesus asked us to remember him during the breaking of the bread and the drinking of the wine every time, every meal, every day—no matter where we are, who we are, what we've done.

If we only practice remembrance when we take communion at church, we miss three opportunities a day to remember. What a travesty! Eugene Peterson says that "to eyes that see, every bush is a burning bush." To those of us who believe that all of life is sacred, every crumb of bread and sip of wine is a Eucharist, a remembrance, a call to awareness of holiness right where we are.

I want the holiness of the Eucharist to spill out beyond the church walls, out of the hands of priests and into the regular streets and sidewalks, into the hands of regular, grubby people like you and me, onto our tables, in our kitchens and dining rooms and backyards.

Holiness abounds, should we choose to look for it. The whisper and drumbeat of God's Spirit are all around us, should we choose to listen for them. The building blocks of the most common meal—the bread and the wine—are reminders to us: *He's here. He's here, and he is good.*

EVERY MEAL is an opportunity to remember Jesus, to honor him and celebrate holiness. Take a moment at your table today, and thank God for his presence and goodness.

BLESSINGS & CURSES

You intended to harm me, but God intended it for good.

—Genesis 50:20

When you realize that the story of your life could be told a thousand differ-ent ways, that you could tell it as a tragedy, but you choose to call it an epic, that's when you start to learn what celebration is. When what you see in front of you is so far outside of what you dreamed, but you have the belief, the boldness, the courage to call it beautiful instead of calling it wrong, that's celebration. When you can invest yourself deeply and unremittingly in the life that surrounds you instead of declaring yourself out of the game, once and for all, because what's happened to you is too bad, too deep, too ugly for anyone to expect you to move on from, that's a good, rich place. That's where the things that looked like curses start to stand up and shimmer and dance, and you realize that they may have been blessings all along. Or maybe not. Maybe they were curses, but the force of your belief and hope and des-perate love for life has brought a blessing from a curse, like water from a stone, like life from a tomb, like the story of God over and over.

WHAT EVENTS in your past felt like curses and turned out to be blessings? Is there something that seems more like a curse in your life right now? Ask God to show you the good that he will bring out of it.

January
10

THE PALM OF GOD'S HAND

He brought me out into a spacious place; he rescued me because he delighted in me.

—Psalm 18:19

I have discovered that I can make it through more than I thought, with less than I thought. I know better than to believe that the changes are over, or that the next ones will be easier, but I've learned the hard way that change is one of God's greatest gifts and one of his most useful tools. Change can push us, pull us, rebuke and remake us. It can show us who we've become, in the worst ways, and also in the best ways. It's not something to run away from, as though we could, and in many cases, change is not a function of life's cruelty but instead a function of God's graciousness.

Change is good, the way that childbirth is good, and heartbreak is good, and failure is good. By that I mean that it's incredibly painful, exponentially more so if you fight it, and also that it has the potential to open you up, to open life up, to deliver you right into the palm of God's hand, which is where you wanted to be all along, except that you were too busy pushing and pulling your life into exactly what you thought it should be.

ALTHOUGH CHANGE is so hard and scary, God often uses it in good and powerful ways. Are there any changes in your life that might be evidence of God's grace, even if they're difficult in the moment?

SHOULD IS A WARNING SIGN

He reached down from on high and took hold of me; he drew me out of deep waters.

—Psalm 18:16

We all have these weird rules about what we *should* love and what *should* make us happy and how things *should* work. *Should* is a warning sign, frankly. When you're using the word *should* more and more often, it's a sign that you're living further and further from your truest, best self, that you're living for some other set of parameters or affirmations that you think will bring you happiness.

Should never brings happiness.

During a particularly busy season, I felt like I *should* be happy because I was doing things I thought I wanted to do. When Mac was a baby, when he didn't sleep through the night for almost a year, I felt like I *should* never complain because I had longed for him so badly. I didn't let myself say I was tired and the math wasn't working and I was losing my ability to love and taste and experience my life, because that felt like failure.

Until all at once, I realized that I didn't care anymore about *should*.

I wanted a way of living that felt more like living and less like drowning.

And saying it out loud to myself was the first and most important step.

HOW OFTEN are you using the word *should*? Even in your thoughts? Where are you on that continuum between living and drowning? Be honest with yourself about that, and then with God, and with the people you love and trust.

ON WAITING

Encourage one another daily, as long as it is called "Today."
—Hebrews 3:13

I have always been waiting. Waiting to become something else, waiting to be that person I always thought I was on the verge of becoming, waiting for that life I thought I would have. I was always one step away, in my head. In high school, I was biding my time until I could become the college version of myself, the one my mind could see so clearly. In college, the post-college "adult" person was always looming in front of me, smarter, stronger, more organized. Then the married person, then the person I'd become when we had kids. For twenty years, I have waited to become the thin version of myself, because that's when life will really begin.

My life is passing, day by day, and I am waiting for it to start.

I don't want to wait anymore. I believe that there is nothing more sacred or profound than this day. There may be a thousand big moments embedded in this day, waiting to be discovered like tiny flecks of gold. The big moments are the tiny moments of courage and forgiveness and hope that we grab on to and extend to one another. The big moments are in every conversation, every meal, every meeting. That's the drama of life, swirling all around us.

WHAT ARE you waiting for? What keeps you on the sidelines of your own life? And what would you do if you decided to dive in and stop waiting?

Blueberry Yogurt Morning Cake

We spend summers in a tiny lakeshore town known for blueberries. We pick and freeze insane amounts, and I'm always on the lookout for new ways to use them. At the farmer's market in that little town, there's a woman who makes a morning cake I'm wild about—it's the perfect not-too-sweet morning treat. This cake is inspired by all those things: summers at the lake, blueberries, that farmer's market morning cake. The tartness of the yogurt is a good balance for the sweet juicy berries. You scatter them on top of the batter, but they end up everywhere, bursting and tender.

½ cup butter, softened, plus more for the pan

1 cup sugar, plus 2 tablespoons for the berries

3 eggs

1 ½ cup plain yogurt

¼ teaspoon almond extract

2 cups all-purpose flour

1 ½ teaspoons baking powder

1 teaspoon baking soda

2 cups pound blueberries

» Preheat oven to 350 degrees. Butter a 10-inch springform pan, and line it with buttered parchment paper.

» In a large mixing bowl, combine butter, sugar, eggs, yogurt, and almond extract. Mix well. Add flour, salt, baking powder, baking soda, and mix by hand until combined. Be careful to not overmix. Pour the batter into the springform. Toss the berries with the 2 tablespoons sugar, and then scatter them over the top of the batter.

» Bake for 45 to 55 minutes, or until a toothpick inserted in the center comes out clean. Let cool for 10 minutes, then transfer to a cake plate.

NEXT RIGHT STEP

A feast is made for laughter.

—Ecclesiastes 10:19

I'm learning, slowly, a rhythm of feasting and fasting that brings a rich cadence to my year. I use the word *fasting* loosely, as an opposite term to *feasting*—permission and discipline, necessary slides back and forth along the continuum of how we feed ourselves.

The weeks between Thanksgiving and New Year's Day are a feast. I love the traditions and tastes of the season—sweet potato biscuits with maple butter, Aunt Mary's raisin bread, toasted and topped with melting sharp cheddar slices.

And then in January, fasting gives me a chance to practice the discipline of not having what I want at every moment, of limiting my consumption, making space in my body and spirit for a new year, one that's not driven by my mouth, by wanting, by consuming.

Fasting, I find, starts as a physical act, but it quickly becomes spiritual: Am I slave to my appetites? Am I ruled by my hunger? Do I trust that God meets my needs, or am I impatient and ravenous, needing to meet them all myself? The rhythm of flavor and feast and celebration during the holidays, tempered by limitations and structure in the new year, draws me closer to God, more dependent, more connected, more grateful for his presence.

WHAT ARE the rhythms, the patterns of your year? What changes do you make to keep yourself healthy from season to season?

SLEEP & PRAYER

In peace I will lie down and sleep, for you alone, LORD, make me dwell in safety.
—**Psalm 4:8**

I believe in God partly because I have to, because I need something to pray to with my rabid, sweeping mix of fear and love. When Henry was a baby, I would have blown a fuse in my brain every night if I couldn't have entrusted him to God for safekeeping while I slept. It's hard enough for me to sleep, and I believe very desperately in God. I'd never sleep a wink if I didn't.

Those first nights, I prayed out loud every night, asking God to keep Henry alive through the night. I had no reason to believe that anything would happen to him. He was healthy and normal, although at the beginning healthy and normal seem relative, because they are so tiny and wiggly and alien. So I prayed out loud, fervently, like I was at a revival. Dear God, *please please please* keep our baby healthy and alive through the night. *Thank you thank you thank you* for him, and *please please please* keep him safe through the night. I wasn't creative in my language, but what I lacked in vocabulary, I made up for in intensity.

WHAT ARE you praying for right now in your life, in that fervent and desperate way? Remember that God carries us as we sleep, that it's not all up to us, that his protection and power are real.

January
15

WHAT WE LOVE

From heaven the LORD looks down and sees all mankind; from his dwelling place he watches all who live on earth—he who forms the hearts of all, who considers everything they do.

—Psalm 33:13–15

Lynne Rossetto Kasper, the host of *The Splendid Table* on NPR, says there are two kinds of people in the world: people who wake up thinking about what to have for supper and people who don't. I am in the first camp, certainly.

I wake up in the morning and I think about dinner. I think about the food and the people and the things we might discover about life and about each other. I think about the sizzle of oil in a pan and the smell of rosemary released with a knife cut. It could be that that's how God made me the moment I was born, and it could be that that's how God made me along the way as I've given up years of secrecy, denial, and embarrassment. What matters is that one of the ways we grow up is by declaring what we love.

I love the table. I love food, what it means, what it does, and how it feels in my hands. It's morning and I'm hungry. I'm thinking about dinner, not just tonight, but the next night and the next. There are two kinds of people, and I'm tired of pretending I'm the other.

WHAT IS it that God has made you to love? How do you declare that love and live it out?

ANTI-FRANTIC

Make it your ambition to lead a quiet life.

—1 Thessalonians 4:11

I think I've been in a hurry for almost seven years. Seven years ago, I found out I was pregnant with Henry. Later that week I was offered a contract to write *Cold Tangerines*. And since then, it seems, I've been running against the clock. I've been stacking things up, plan upon plan upon plan. I've been cramming things in—pushing, hustling, scurrying. I've been strategizing, multitasking, layering commitments one upon another like bricks.

Frantic is when your mind has to work seven steps ahead instead of just being where you are, because this deadline's coming, and the laundry has to get done before that trip, because you can't forget to pack snowpants for school, and you need to beg for more time on this project. Again.

I'm not alone. So many of us are really, really tired of the hustle, and the next right thing is to slow down, to go back to the beginning, to stop. I'm done with frantic. The new baseline for me: *will saying yes to this require me to live in a frantic way?* The word that rings in my mind is anti-frantic. Present with my kids. Present to my own life. Anti-frantic.

ARE YOU tired of the hustle, the frantic? What would it look like for you to slow down, to stop? How does it feel to even contemplate that question?

ON BUILDING A MARRIAGE

My beloved spoke and said to me, "Arise, my
darling, my beautiful one, come with me."

— S o n g   o f   S o n g s   2 : 1 0

I chatted with a new friend in Nashville last week. She asked my advice on marriage. She's a newlywed with a busy career, and she was telling me that she wanted to be a good wife, but it was so hard to keep the house clean and learn to cook, etcetera. I said, *Hold on: Don't worry so much about cooking and cleaning. Cooking and cleaning never built a marriage. But listening and memory-making and looking each other in the eye will. Make time to be together, to go on dates and bikes rides and listen to each other.*

When Aaron and I are stressed, what puts us back together is intentional, connected time together. It's dates, where I put on heels and perfume, and he wears a tie, and we hold hands and talk and talk and talk. Making that time and pushing ourselves out of the house even when we're tired is so good for us, because it reminds us that we're living a love story, not running a small business together. It reminds us that part of love is taking the time to listen to the tiny details of someone else's life and genuinely care about them.

IF YOU'RE married, how do you make time to reconnect with your husband? What does that look like for you? Are you getting enough of that time together lately?

January
18

WHY I PRAY

When my life was ebbing away, I remembered you, LORD,
and my prayer rose to you, to your holy temple.

—Jonah 2:7

I pray because I need to. Because I need to remind myself that there is something up there and that it is good. I pray to be heard, certainly, but practically speaking, what the act of prayer does in my life is profound in its own right. The act and posture of prayer connects me back to something I lose so often, something that gets snipped like a string. Prayer ties up the string one more time. Prayer says *I know you're up there. I believe you. I can make it. I know you are good.* To pray is to say that there is more than I can see, and more than I can do. There is more going on than meets the eye.

Prayer heals all the muscles that I've been clenching for a long time, while I'm holding it together, gritting my teeth, waiting for impact. Prayer, like yoga, like singing, brings soft from hard, pliant from brittle, possible from impossible, warm from cold, breath from breathless. And no matter what gets you there, it is better to be there than not.

SPEND A moment in prayer, and let the act of it remind you who God is and what he does in our lives.

RUSSIAN DOLLS

However many years anyone may live, let them enjoy them all.

—Ecclesiastes 11:8

My grandma is eighty-two, and I love to look at old photographs of her and my grandpa. She told me that getting old is like carrying all these selves with you. She remembers just how that thirteen-year-old in the picture felt, and how that nineteen-year-old bride felt, and how that thirty-year-old on the back of a motorcycle felt. She said you carry them inside you, collecting them along the way, more and more and more selves inside you with each passing year, like those Russian dolls, nesting within themselves.

The other night I dug out an old photo of Aaron and me. We were at a wedding, right after we had started dating, and you can tell by the way his arm is around me so tightly, by the way I'm huddled into him so closely, that if I could have climbed on to his lap, I would have, that if we could have kissed throughout the entire reception, we would have.

When I look at that photo, I see a girl who was wild about a boy, and a boy who loved that girl right back. It makes me happy to know they're still in there, still inside us, like Russian dolls.

WHEN YOU look at old pictures or think back over your life, what "younger selves" come to mind? How has God changed you along the way?

APOLOGY TO MY BODY

I praise you because I am fearfully and wonderfully made;
your works are wonderful, I know that full well.

—Psalm 139:14

I owe my body an apology. Technically, I owe my body thousands of apologies, for the thousands of times I've accused it, pushed it, pulled it, starved it, stuffed it, made fun of it, lied about it, hid it, hated it. But now I owe it another one, and I also owe it my gratitude.

I'm sorry for taking you for granted, for wishing you were different, and for abusing you because you looked different than I wanted you to. I'm sorry. Thank you for, despite my persecution, being strong and able in the most important way. Thank you for carrying and bearing and nourishing my son.

What bodies can do during childbirth will take your breath away. I am a scared, squeamish person who faints at the sight of blood, but if I could relive Henry's birth every day, I would. It felt sacred and overwhelming and full of beauty and prayer. It silences all those voices that have been yelling at my body for years.

This body might not look like much, but it did what it came to do on that day, and for that, I am grateful, and I offer it my most sincere apologies.

TAKE A moment to thank God for the way he made your body, for breath and strength and health.

THE MIDDLE

When the hour came, Jesus and his apostles reclined at the table. And he said to them, "I have eagerly desired to eat this Passover with you before I suffer. For I tell you, I will not eat it again until it finds fulfillment in the kingdom of God."

—Luke 22:14–16

You don't know what the story is about when you're in the middle of it. All you can do is keep walking.

At the beginning, you have buoyancy and a little arrogance. The journey looks beautiful and bright, and you are filled with resolve and silver strength, sure that you will face it with optimism and chutzpah.

And the end is beautiful. You are wiser, better, deeper. The end is revelation, resolution, a soft place to land.

But, oh, the middle. The middle is fog, exhaustion, loneliness, the daily battle against despair and the nagging fear that tomorrow will be just like today, only you'll be wearier and less able to defend yourself against it.

All you can ask for, in the middle, are sweet moments of reprieve in the company of people you love. For a few hours, you'll feel protected by the goodness of friendship and life around the table, and that's the best thing I can imagine.

LIFE HAS so many rough passages along the way, and we need to offer each other the haven of friendship and community. Is there someone in your life who needs rest and reprieve in the middle of a difficult season? How could you provide that?

January
22

ENTRUSTING CHILDREN TO GOD'S CARE

Hannah replied, "I am a woman who is deeply troubled. . . . I was pouring out my soul to the LORD. . . . I have been praying here out of my great anguish and grief."
—1 Samuel 1:15–16

At one point when Mac was in the PICU at ten days old with a high fever, my dad sent me out of the room. He told me to stretch my legs, to get some fresh air and something to eat. He said there was a chapel and suggested I walk down there.

I'd sent a text to my friend Emily, and in her reply, she said that when she's scared about her baby, her mom reminds her to pray to Mary, the Blessed Mother, the one who understands, certainly, what it's like to worry about a child. She said she'd pray the Hail Mary for me and for Baby Mac.

Mary, then, was fresh in my mind, and it didn't seem surprising that there was a tall, slender statue of her in the chapel. I knelt near her, and I prayed for our baby. *Dear God, we need your help*, I said. *Help my baby. Help my baby. Help my baby.* No longer a prayer, now more a keening, a low wail. *Help my baby. Help my baby.* The statue of Mary, pale and silent, reminded me that I was one of a great line of mothers who entrusted their children into God's care, terrifying as it is.

IF YOU have children, how have you entrusted them into God's care? If you don't have children of your own, are there children in your life, perhaps nieces and nephews and family friends, who you love and pray for?

Lemon Dill Soup

I made this soup over and over this winter—it's got that perfect combination of warm, comforting winter textures, and bright, almost surprising flavors. Guests always want seconds, and it's easy to make for vegans, too.

• •

2 cups chopped onion

1 cup chopped celery

1 cup chopped carrots

olive oil

3 cloves garlic, minced

6 cups chicken or vegetable broth

½ cup brown rice

2 cups chicken, cooked
and shredded (optional)

¼ cup juice from fresh lemons

4 sprigs fresh dill, finely chopped

salt and pepper

• •

» In a Dutch oven, sauté the onion, celery, and carrots in olive oil until soft, then add garlic. Add broth and rice, and allow rice to cook most of the way through. Five minutes before rice is cooked through, add chicken (if using), and lemon juice and dill. Add salt and pepper to taste.

FRIENDSHIPS ARE LIKE BREAKFAST

Though one may be overpowered, two can defend themselves.
A cord of three strands is not quickly broken.

—Ecclesiastes 4:12

Good friendships are like breakfast. Walk across the street, or drive across town, or fly across the country, but don't let really intimate loving friendships become the last item on a long to-do list. You think you're too busy to eat breakfast, but then you find yourself exhausted and cranky halfway through the day, and you discover that your attempt to save time totally backfired. In the same way, you can try to go it alone because you don't have time or because your house is too messy to have people over, or because making new friends is like the very worst parts of dating. But halfway through a hard day or a hard week, you'll realize in a flash that you're breathtakingly lonely, and that the Christmas cards aren't much company. Get up, make a phone call, buy a cheap plane ticket, open your front door.

There really is nothing like good friends, like the sounds of their laughter and the tones of their voices and the things they teach us in the quietest, smallest moments.

REALLY CLOSE friendships nourish us and strengthen us, and they must be cultivated with time together. Are you investing the time these friendships require? If not, why not?

NUMBERED DAYS

Teach us to number our days, that we may gain a heart of wisdom.

—Psalm 90:12

When my brother and I were small, there was a family from church who encouraged my parents to take family vacations. My parents had very little time and even less money, but we began a tradition of family vacations. And they were great.

When the husband and father of the family who urged us toward those vacations died far too young, we sat with his family at his funeral. There were hundreds of photographs and bits of video from family vacations, funny and sweet.

After the service my dad began to cry, the chokes and coughs of a man who seldom finds himself overcome by tears and unable to stop them. He pulled us into a circle, stretching his arms around us.

"We've got to be like them," he choked. "We've got to take the time right now because there's nothing more important than this." He bent his head and cried. "We've got to be like that."

Our family vacations since then have carried the weight of that day, and the weight of knowing that one day, our family will mourn the way their family did, and that we want to have the depth and breadth of memories they do.

FAMILY VACATIONS are priceless investments in our love and our relationships. How can you make this kind of time together a priority in your family life?

CRYING JUST A LITTLE

My eyes fail from weeping... my heart is poured out on the ground.
—Lamentations 2:11

Today all I can think about is what might have been. Today would have been my due date, had my pregnancy been a healthy one. Someday we might have another child. But we'll never have a child born on January 31, 2009. That baby will never be. And it seems worth stopping for today, just for a moment.

Of course I knew women who had miscarried. But when it happens to you it's like waking up to a conversation you've heard before and only now grasp, and you realize what they were trying to find the words to describe.

It was deeply moving to me that my body nurtured and nourished Henry, delivering him safely into the world, and this miscarriage has forced me to ask some questions: Did my body fail me? Did I somehow fail it? We've had a tenuous relationship in the past, my body and I; was this a breach of trust?

On most days, it's all right. I understand that God is sovereign, that bodies are fragile and fallible, that grief mellows over time, and that guarantees aren't part of human life. But on this day, I'm crying just a little for what might have been.

HAVE YOU ever cried for a loss of a baby, for a due date gone unfulfilled? Allow yourself to be loved and cared for by the God who adores you.

THE ACT OF PRAYER

Is anyone among you in trouble? Let them pray.

—James 5:13

Prayer helps me. When I pray, something freaked-out and dazed inside me finds a place to lay down and rest. When I pray, I don't feel so alone in the universe. I feel like there is a web, a finely spun net, holding it all together, keeping it spinning. I feel powerless, and prayer reminds me that I may be powerless, but there is power, and the one who holds the power is good. Prayer reminds me that the universe is not powerless against evil and loss.

I imagine a huge choir, hundreds of voices, and they're singing something unquestionably, remarkably beautiful, and if you look at each person, you can see their intensity, their attention to detail and precision, their extreme focus on sounds and phrases. And you can see their love for music and their passion to sing. You could never pick out an individual voice, out of those several hundred, but that's not the point. They are not singing to be heard individually. They are singing for the act itself, for the love of music and tone and melody. That's one of the reasons I pray, for the act itself.

PRAY FOR a few minutes, joining your voice with the voices of Christians all over the world who pray with great passion and expectancy.

MORE LOVE, LESS HUSTLE

There is no fear in love. But perfect love drives out fear.

—1 John 4:18

This year is the year of *more love, less hustle*.

When I say *hustle*, what I mean is that voice that tells you to *get up off the couch* as soon as you sit down for even a second. That voice that says *with these ten minutes you should be able to accomplish these seventy-six things*. That voice that says *you're never done, you have to push harder, think ahead, plan ahead, hold it together, go, go, go*.

Hustle isn't about your job, necessarily, or my job, necessarily. I know people who work more than I do, longer than I do, with a lot more success and pressure, and they don't hustle. And I know people who have very few demands on their time or very little financial pressure or whatever, and they're always, always hustling.

It's about your to-do list, but more than that it's about what it is inside you that made you sign up for all that.

I've said *no* to some big and small things in this season—so hard for me to say, of course, for a million reasons. But saying *no* lets me say *yes* to those I love: my husband, my boys, our family and community, our church.

LET THE fearful voice of hustle be overwhelmed and silenced by love.

January
28

ASKING FOR GRACE

Carry each other's burdens, and in this way you will fulfill the law of Christ.

—Galatians 6:2

I've been working on the idea of *more love, less hustle* for a long time: writing about it, circling around it, messing up and trying again. I suspect I'll be working on it for a long time to come, that this is one of my *things* that will never quite get solved. That's okay. I'm still trying.

What I'm learning is that it's okay to ask for help and ask for grace, even if it's embarrassing, even if you disappoint people, even if in the process people find out (gasp!) that you're not a super-person, but just a regular person, a person who gets sick and tired and emptied out sometimes. That's the *less hustle* part of the deal.

I wanted to start this year strong and organized, focused and rested. Instead I'm starting it sick and wobbly, wrapped in a blanket, with Christmas cards that still haven't been sent, asking for help and grace, undoing and staying in, because life is a teacher and God is good—and also hilarious. This year so far has been slow and strange, full of surprises and full of love, so I feel like we're off to a very good start.

More love and less hustle, indeed.

GIVE OTHERS the gift of accepting their help when you need it. So often, people would love to help us. What would it look like for you to let yourself be helped?

January
29

ROOM FOR SILLY

Then young women will dance and be glad, young men and old as well. I will turn
their mourning into gladness; I will give them comfort and joy instead of sorrow.

—Jeremiah 31:13

I used to be spontaneous and silly, warm and whimsical. I used to dance in
the kitchen and eat cake for breakfast with my kids. And then for a while
things got complicated and busy and in order to keep up with my life and
schedule and commitments, I had to hustle, multitask, always staying five
steps ahead, always planning, always ticking things off a list.

There wasn't room in the system for spontaneous and silly. The life I
signed myself up for required a level of strategy and structure that made me
feel, over time, like I was running a military operation, not living a life.

So now I'm working toward a new way of living. I'm a better person than
I was, a better parent, a better partner. I'm less angry. I dance in the kitchen
again. I'm remembering what it's like to not be tired all the time.

I believed that if I walked away from some things—things I thought I
really wanted—in exchange for those things, I would recover my own self.
I would, possibly, rediscover that silly, warm person. And it's working.

ARE YOU living in such a way that your own favorite qualities
have a chance to shine? If not, what sort of adjustment would make
room for them again? Is there anything you might need to give up
in exchange for that?

January
30

ARRIVING & BECOMING

He guides me along the right paths for his name's sake.

—Psalm 23:3

My dad used to have one of those cars where you could plug in your destination and the woman's voice would tell you when to turn and when to stop to get you there. And when you got there, she'd say, in this totally dramatic, slightly sexy, slow voice, "You. Have. Arriiiiiiived." We burst out laughing the first time we heard it. We wanted her to say it again. We wanted to plug in more places, and then go to them, just so that she would tell us again that We. Have. Arrived. It was the greatest car in the world. You knew, cognitively, that she was a computer, and that she was only talking about arriving at the dry cleaner, but another part of you just melted when she said it. "Me? Me? I've arrived? Thank you! Say it again!"

I want to arrive. I want to get to wherever I'm going and stay there. That's why I used to be such a ferocious planner of my life. But I've learned to just keep moving, keep walking, keep taking teeny tiny steps. In those teeny tiny steps and moments I become who I am. We don't arrive. But we can become. And that's the most hopeful thing I can think of.

IN THE passing moments of our lives, in the small steps we take, we are shaped into who we are becoming. What small steps have you taken recently? How have they shaped you? Who are you becoming?

ZERO DEGREES

Each of you should give what you have decided in your heart to give, not reluctantly or under compulsion, for God loves a cheerful giver.

—2 Corinthians 9:7

It's literally *zero* degrees in Chicago today. It's scary weather, where gas freezes in tanks and where a failing furnace quickly becomes an emergency situation. All over Chicago there are people who can't feed their families, so they're going to work anyway. They're bundling up their kids in whatever they have, and it's probably not enough.

The chill I feel today reminds me that the needs in our communities aren't theoretical or abstract: we're talking about mothers and babies, empty bellies, painfully cold fingers and toes, coughs that don't quit.

Part of our purpose here on earth is to use everything God has given us—our days, our talents, our finances, our dreams, our homes, our very selves—with great wisdom and passion, to heal and help.

So I'm boxing up canned goods and dropping them off at a nearby food pantry, tucking a check with the cans. Local needs, local solutions, from mother to mother. As I drive, I'm praying for moms just like me, in this town, and I'm praying that what God has given our family can help another family, too.

GOD HAS given to us so that we can give to those in need. With whom are you sharing your resources? What needs do you feel called to meet in this world?

MY DRUG & MY DEFENSE

Martha was distracted by all the preparations that had to be made.

—Luke 10:40

Sometimes I stay busy because I hate having to face the silence and feel things I don't want to feel. What if this book doesn't connect with people at all? What if something happens to one of the kids? What if I've made the wrong choices, and I'm missing something important, something I could have been or should have done?

And I use my busyness as an excuse for why I might not succeed, or accomplish the things I want to, or have the relationships I want to have. *I'm juggling a million things here, of course the book's not perfect. Where am I supposed to find time to work out and become some gorgeous supermodel when I have like seven thousand things on my plate? I probably didn't get invited because they knew I'd be out of town anyway, right?*

The busyness is a drug to keep me numb and a defense to keep me safe. And it works. But *numb* and *safe* aren't words for the life I want to live. I want to be present and whole and have nothing to hide, no excuses to be made, because I did my best, and because that's enough.

WHY DO you keep yourself busy? What would it look like for you to lay down *busy*, both the drug and the defense?

YOUR STORY IS ENOUGH

Has anything like this ever happened in your days or in the days of your ancestors? Tell it to your children, and let your children tell it to their children, and their children to the next generation.

—Joel 1:2–3

When I worked at a church a few years ago, it was my job to help people tell their stories on Sunday mornings at our gatherings. And a funny thing happened. When we were at the coffee shop, when it was just me and them and their story, their story came out in fits and starts, unvarnished and raw. We cried and laughed and every time I was amazed at what God had done in this person's life.

And then almost every time, when they arrived on Sunday, they looked a little less like themselves. They were kind of a distant, polished, fancy version of themselves, and when they walked up on that stage, they sounded a lot less like themselves. They stopped believing that their story was enough, and they started saying all the phrases and quoting all the verses we've all heard a thousand times. They did it because we as a community have trained ourselves to believe that a story isn't enough.

I could not disagree more. We dilute the beauty of the gospel story when we divorce it from our lives, our worlds, the words and images that God is writing right now on our souls.

WHAT IS the story that God is writing in your life and on your soul these days?

Fregolotta

Italian Jam Tart { Adapted from *Food 52* }

I'm a terrible baker—I'm not exact or patient enough for
it—but this beautiful tart is so easy even I can make it. I adore
this recipe.

• •

12 tablespoons unsalted butter,
   softened

½ cup sugar

¼
   teaspoon pure almond extract

1 ½
   cups unbleached all-purpose

flour

⅛
   teaspoon salt

½ cup jam (I especially love fig
   or raspberry, but use your
   favorite kind)

⅓ cup sliced natural almonds

• •

» Preheat the oven to 350 degrees.

» In a large bowl, beat butter and sugar with an electric hand
mixer. Beat on medium speed until very light in color,
three or four minutes. Scrape down the sides with a rubber
spatula. Add the almond extract and blend again.

» Add flour and salt, and mix on low speed until thoroughly
combined. Remove one cup of the dough, shape it into a
ball, wrap it in plastic wrap, and put it in the freezer. This is
for the top, and it crumbles more easily when it's chilled.

» Press the remaining dough into a 9-inch tart pan or

springform pan. If the dough is too sticky, chill it briefly.

» Spoon the jam onto the dough, and use the back of the spoon to spread it in an even, thin layer, leaving an inch around the edges for a crust.

» Remove the reserved dough ball from the freezer, and crumble it in small pieces over the jam layer. Sprinkle the almonds over the top.

» Bake for 40 to 50 minutes, or until the topping is golden brown. Remove from the oven and place on a rack to cool completely.

So good.

NOISE & PRAYER & COUNSELING

Truly my soul finds rest in God; my salvation comes from him.

—Psalm 62:1

One thing I'm learning about myself is that when it's go-time, I turn up the volume, literally and figuratively. I blast hip-hop in my car, and I wipe away tears and take a deep breath and keep pushing. I become ravenous in my appetites—when I do have a free moment, I watch a show on TV while shopping online while flipping through a magazine, building a fortress of noise to keep out the sadness, the fear, the mess.

Instead of cranking up the volume and frantically avoiding honesty at all costs, I need prayer and counseling. Prayer and counseling are both about honesty, and they're both about admitting need. I need help sifting through all my feelings and expectations and bruises. I need help and strength and a sense of God's presence. I need to allow myself to be instructed by God's Spirit and voice and not my own fear and weakness, so that I can make different choices. When the pressure's on, my instinct is to abandon both prayer and counseling for a freer season down the road. But when do I need the grounding of both things more than in the whirling, intense seasons?

WHAT DO you notice about the noise level in your life? Where do you find help to sift through your feelings and expectations and bruises? How do busyness and stress affect your praying? What are the things you need most during intense seasons?

FOOD & DISCIPLINE

The flesh desires what is contrary to the Spirit, and the Spirit what is contrary to the
flesh. They are in conflict with each other, so that you are not to do whatever you want.

—Galatians 5:17

My impulse, when things feel scary or busy or heavy, is to eat like a truffle pig and drink like it's my only solace. I push myself like I'm a college football player doing two-a-days, and then after all that pushing, I think that the only way to nurture and nourish myself is with mindless eating, because I can't possibly be asked to do one more hard thing, like feed myself with health and kindness. I think that it's simply too hard to impose any more structure in my already structured-to-the-max days, that I can only blast through the work and then flop down on the couch with cheese and red wine at the end of the day.

What I really need, though, is discipline. Instead of using food and drinks as desperate ways to backfill all the needs I've been neglecting, I'm learning that discipline and healthful choices set me free and get me through stressful seasons. I thought that discipline would make an already difficult season unbearable. Instead, when I feed myself healthy food, when I drink lots of water, when I take the time to eat well, it gives me more energy and more clear-mindedness.

WHAT HAS been your experience with discipline? Have you ever found discipline to be surprisingly freeing?

FILTERS

The wisdom that comes from heaven is first of all pure; then peace-loving,
considerate, submissive, full of mercy and good fruit, impartial and sincere.

—James 3:17

Some people take all criticism equally. They don't differentiate between internet reviewers and actual critics—people who are educated and experienced in evaluating a particular kind of work. They hear the words of a best friend and the words of a nasty blog commenter at equal volume. They have no filter, no protective skin, and everything travels straight to their heart.

I know people at the other extreme: they never read reviews, and they shut out critical words from family and strangers alike. They alone understand their art, and everyone who disagrees is a fool who doesn't "get it."

I don't think either extreme is helpful or healthy—either all the voices bulldoze us, or we spend our energy building a wall against all of them. Either way, we're still driven by the voices.

The only way, I'm finding, is to develop a set of filters: Whose voices are the ones that matter to me? Which ones matter more than any others, and which ones matter just a little?

WHOSE VOICES really matter to you? How might you filter out or turn down the volume on the voices that don't matter as much—or at all?

NOT WEAK

I am poured out like water, and all my bones are out of joint.
My heart has turned to wax; it has melted within me.

—**Psalm 22:14**

One winter, I got the kind of tired that you can't recover from, almost like something gets altered on a cellular level, and you begin to fantasize about what it would be like to just not be tired anymore. You don't fantasize about money or men or the Italian Riviera. All you daydream about is not feeling exhausted, about neck muscles that don't throb, about a mind that isn't fogged every single day. I was talking to my husband about it, complaining about being tired, but also bringing up the fact that lots of women travel and work and have kids. Everybody has a house to clean. Why couldn't I pull it together?

He said, gently, ostensibly helpfully, something along the lines of "you know, honey, just because some other people can do all that, it doesn't mean that you can or have to. Maybe it's too much for you."

One tiny, almost imperceptible beat of silence. And then I yelled, viscerally, from the depths of my soul, as though possessed, "I'M NOT WEAK!"

As soon as the words came out, we looked at each other in alarm. It seemed, perhaps, we'd hit upon the heart of something.

GOD HAS compassion on our limitations—whether we do or not. What is it that you don't want to admit about yourself? Pray for a few minutes, and let that identity go.

"DO EVERYTHING BETTER"

*"Martha, Martha," the Lord answered, "you are worried and
upset about many things, but few things are needed."*

—Luke 10:41–42

I'm a list-keeper. I always, always have a to-do list, and it ranges from the mundane: go to the dry cleaner, go to the post office, buy batteries; to the far-reaching: stop eating Henry's leftover Dino Bites, get over yourself, forgive nasty reviewer, wear more jewelry.

At one point, I kept adding to the list, more and more items, more and more sweeping in their scope, until I added this line: DO EVERYTHING BETTER. It was, at the time, a pretty appropriate way to capture how I felt about my life and myself fairly often. It also explains why I tended to get so tired I'd cry without knowing why, why my life sometimes felt like I was running on a hamster wheel, and why I searched the faces of calmer, more grounded women for a secret they all knew that I didn't.

Do everything better captures the mania of modern life, the anti-spirit, anti-spiritual, soul-shriveling garbage that infects and compromises our lives. And I'm the one who wrote those words on my very own to-do list. I'm in a lot of trouble with my own self for that, because the "do everything better" way of living brought me to a terrible place: tired, angry, brittle, afraid, hollow.

WE ARE not called to infinite achievement; we are called to love. Spend a few minutes in prayer, resting in unconditional love.

THE POISONS OF "DO" & "BETTER"

"Not by might nor by power, but by my Spirit," says the LORD *Almighty.*

—Z e c h a r i a h   4 : 6

Do: we know better than *do*, of course. We know that words like "be," and "become," and "try," are a little less crushing and cruel, spiritually and psychologically, a little friendlier to the soul. But when we're alone sometimes and the list is getting the best of us, we abandon all those sweet ideas, and we go straight to *do*, because *do* is power, push, aggression, plain old sweat equity. It's not pretty, but we know that *do* gets the job done.

    Better is a seductress. It's so delicious to run after *better, better, better. Better* is what keeps some women decorating and redecorating the same house for years on end, because by the time you get the last detail of the finished basement home theater just right, your countertops are ever so slightly outdated, and so you start again. *Better* is what makes us go to a spinning class—or maybe two, or three today. *Better* is what makes us get "just a little work done," after the last baby, or just to look a little bit fresher and more well-rested. *Better* is a force.

GOD WANTS us to rely on his Spirit, not on our own strength and accomplishments.

THE POISON OF "EVERYTHING"

What you are doing is not good. . . . The work is too
heavy for you; you cannot handle it alone.

—Exodus 18:17–18

Everything is just a killer. *Everything* is the heart of the conversation for me, my drug of choice. Sure, I can host that party. Of course, I can bring that meal. Yes, I'd love to write that article. Yes, to *everything*.

One of my core fears is that someone would think I can't handle as much as the next person. It's fundamental to my understanding of myself for me to be the strong one, the capable one, the busy one, the one who can bail you out, not make a fuss, bring a meal, add a few more things to the list. For me, *everything* becomes a lifestyle. *Everything* is an addiction.

Deciding what I want my life to be about isn't that hard. But deciding what I'm willing to give up for those things is like yoga for the superego, stretching and pushing and ultimately healing that nasty little person inside who exists only for what people think.

G O D   I S the only one who can handle *everything.* Pray for a few moments, and give over to God the many things you've been carrying.

VEGETABLES

*It is for freedom that Christ has set us free. Stand firm, then, and
do not let yourselves be burdened again by a yoke of slavery.*

—Galatians 5:1

My friend Ginger came over the other day, and I was making lunch for
Henry and her daughter, Samantha. I gave them each Dino Bites and or-
ganic fruit leather, and I was trying to find something vegetable for them.
I was looking in the freezer and in the pantry. Ginger was coaching me,
"Maybe some peas? Or little baby carrots?" Finally Ginger said, "You know
what? Even if you put them on her plate, she won't eat them. I don't actually
give her a vegetable every single day at lunch." And I said, "Me neither! Me
neither! I do it at dinner, I swear, but I don't always give him a vegetable at
lunch." You would have thought in that moment that we were confessing our
deepest, darkest secrets to one another.

I've known Ginger since I was thirteen. We were in each other's weddings. She knows all the things I did in high school that my parents still
don't know about. Why were we faking each other out about vegetables
for two-year-olds? Because we both believed, in that moment, that moms
should be perfect. That somehow everyone else is able to pull it off, even if
we can't. But that's a lie, and it was a relief to break free of it.

ARE THERE areas in your life where you think everyone
else is achieving perfection? Name that illusion for what it is: an
illusion. Ask for God's help in recognizing reality.

WITH OR WITHOUT A SIGNIFICANT OTHER

*See what great love the Father has lavished on us, that we should
be called children of God! And that is what we are!*

—1 John 3:1

Our culture is weirdly obsessed with romance and couples and being part of a matched set. Some of the people I love most are single—either because they haven't yet found their person, or because their marriage has ended. I've reached that age when I hear more divorce announcements than wedding bells. Sometimes I wonder if there would be fewer divorce announcements if we weren't so hung up on marriage as a status symbol or accomplishment.

I *love* being married to Aaron. He's my person, and every day I'm thankful for the life we're making together. But being married doesn't mean my life is any more significant than the lives of my single friends. It breaks my heart when they feel like they're less or half or waiting around for their real lives to start. That's garbage.

Some of the worst people I know are married, and some of the best people I know are single. I don't know how it happens. But it's not about the fundamental value of the person in question. Your value is not riding on a cultural obsession with romance and tulle and diamonds.

You are significant with or without a significant other.

YOU ARE significant, you have value, you are loved by God—no matter your marital status.

COMPASSION

The Lord longs to be gracious to you; therefore he will rise up to show you compassion.

—Isaiah 30:18

Do you have a word right now that catches you every time you see it? You're drawn to it, and you want to hold it in your hand like a coin? That's how I feel about the word *compassion* right now—when someone uses it, I lean in close. When I read it in Isaiah, something in me yearns for it.

I've always thought about being compassionate to other people—quick to give grace, happy to give a second chance, eager to show kindness. But the idea of God showing his great, tender compassion toward me? That's not something I've thought a lot about, and now that I do, I find it so welcome, so healing, so deeply moving.

Our God, holy and perfect, loving beyond measure, doesn't force himself to show us compassion—he longs to do it. He's looking for ways to show his tender, healing love.

So often I think of God as an angry boss I've failed again or a stern parent I've disappointed again. But Isaiah reminds me what is true: our God longs to be gracious and compassionate. And I'm longing for that grace and compassion, an entirely different way of living than the one I'm used to.

WHEN WAS the last time you truly experienced God's graciousness and compassion? What myths or images of God sometimes stand in the way? Spend a few minutes in silence, allowing yourself to feel his deep compassion for you.

WHAT I CAME TO DO

For we are God's handiwork, created in Christ Jesus to do good works, which God prepared in advance for us to do.

—Ephesians 2:10

There are a thousand things I do just because I'm human and I have to, and when I do them I certainly don't feel any spark of having been created for something very specific and tender.

But every once in a while, when I write, I feel that feeling of a thousand slender threads coming together, strands of who I've been and who I'm becoming, the long moments at the computer and the tiny bits of courage, the middle of the night prayers and the exact way God made me, not wrong or right, just me. I feel like I'm doing what I came to do, in the biggest sense. That's why I write, because sometimes, every once in a while, I feel entirely at home in the universe, a welcome and wonderful feeling. I could cry at that feeling, because it happens so rarely. Doing the hard work of writing makes me feel like I'm paying my rent on a cosmic level. Writing wakes me up, lights me on fire, opens my eyes to the things I can never see and feel when I'm hiding under the covers, cowering and consumed with my own failures and fears.

GOD HAS purposes and plans for you and for your gifts. When have you felt like you were doing what you came to do?

FULL CIRCLE

But I am like an olive tree flourishing in the house of God;
I trust in God's unfailing love for ever and ever.

— Psalm 52:8

Here I am, deeply, wholly committed to God and to his church, demonstrating that God is in fact very gracious and kind of a jokester. I tried as hard as I could to find a better way to live, to move past or through or beyond this tradition and set of ideas and practices that had defined my life. I separated myself from the language and the circles and the people who represented that world, and I couldn't wait to find that other thing, that better thing. And as I traveled and pushed and explored, I started realizing with a cringe that the road was leading me dangerously close to the start, and I was finding myself drawn against all odds, against my intentions, to this way of living, this way of Jesus, this way of passion and compassion that I had grown up in.

I'm immeasurably thankful to have been born into a community of faith. And I'm even more thankful that that community of faith allowed me the space and freedom to travel my own distances around and through the questions I needed to answer. I'm thankful for the patience and grace I was given, for the forgiveness I was extended and the guidance I needed.

WE CAN'T walk the journey of faith for anyone else. Sometimes the greatest gift we can give—or receive—is room to travel. Who in your life could benefit from your encouragement as they continue on their journey?

Pumpkin Banana Anything Muffins

These muffins are the perfect healthy-but-still-yummy breakfast treat. They have no sugar (or other sweetener), grain, dairy, or oil. The pumpkin-banana part of the recipe always stays the same, and then you can add a cup of fresh or frozen fruit and a cup of dry mix-ins—chocolate chips, dried fruit, or nuts.

- 3 bananas (the browner the better), mashed
- ½ can pumpkin puree (about 1½ cups)
- 2 eggs, beaten
- 2 cups almond meal (not almond flour)
- 1 teaspoon salt
- 1½ teaspoons baking soda
- 1 cup frozen blueberries (or another fresh or frozen fruit)
- ½ cup walnuts
- ½ cup dark chocolate chips (or, instead of walnuts and chocolate chips, use 1 cup of whatever other dry mix-ins you like)

» Preheat the oven to 350 degrees. Grease a muffin pan with nonstick cooking spray.

» In a large bowl, mix together the bananas, pumpkin, and eggs. In another bowl, mix the almond meal, salt, and baking soda. Then add the dry ingredients to the wet ingredients. Add the blueberries, walnuts, and chocolate chips to the mixture. Mix well, and then spoon batter into 12 greased muffin cups, and bake for 30 minutes, or until a toothpick inserted in the center of a muffin comes out clean.

FASTING

I put on sackcloth and humbled myself with fasting.

—Psalm 35:13

When we were preparing to move back to Chicago from Grand Rapids, we wanted to arrive sharp, healthy, and focused, but at the rate we were going, we'd arrive totally off our rockers, cranky and more caffeine-addicted than ever, wild-eyed and bloated. Something had to change.

Aaron said he needed to fast. Fasting is a way of trusting God's provision and creating silence and space for prayer. I said I'd join him, as did our friends Steve and Sarah. We decided to have nothing but juice or broth for one week, and to pray in the morning and the evening, all at the same time, wherever we were, whatever we were doing.

The fast was embarrassingly hard at first. We were vaguely angry about everything and tried to alternately blame each other and find loopholes. But we were also surprisingly clearheaded. It seemed like my mind and spirit were wiped clean and working well for the first time in forever. I felt able and bright-minded. I slept like a rock and woke up easily. When I prayed, my prayers were full of peace, expectation, confidence. I didn't feel the panic and anxiety that had been marking my days. I felt hungry but clean and strong.

PRAYER AND fasting can awaken us to our dependence on God. Have you ever fasted? What did God show you during that time?

A DUSTY WELL-WORN PATH

We fasted and petitioned our God about this, and he answered our prayer.

—Ezra 8:23

Fasting is more about desperation than anything else. I was feeling totally untethered to God or anything else and wanted to find a way to connect once again to the things that matter to me. Fasting was a move of desperation.

I found the rhythm of set prayer times to be an undergirding to my day. I made progress on things I'd been dragging my feet on for weeks. It was a week of complaining and hunger and silence, but it was also a grounding, exciting week, opening us to a better way of living. When I do something that people have been doing for thousands of years, like reading the Bible or fasting or set prayer times, at first I think I should tell a lot of people about this new, wonderful thing.

Then I realize that it's not a new practice or the next big idea. It's an enduring way of living that has been shaping and reshaping people for years. When I fasted and prayed on a set rhythm, I felt humble, one more set of footprints on a dusty well-worn path, discovering something new that's not new at all, and I was thankful.

GOD'S PEOPLE before us have left clear paths to follow. What spiritual disciplines have been meaningful for you as you've grown in your faith?

February
17

ALONG THE WAY

Trust in him at all times, you people; pour out your hearts to him, for God is our refuge.

—Psalm 62:8

One night in Minneapolis, I asked the musician I was touring with how she felt about traveling and touring. She said she loved winning over a new audience, being charming for an evening. She didn't like being home for long and was sometimes nervous and bored between trips. I felt just the opposite. I missed my friends and my family.

That night I got back to my room late after the last event. I sat on the hotel floor and ate a club sandwich and French fries and drank a glass of Chardonnay. I knew in some wordless way that I needed that sandwich more than a person should need a sandwich. I had to find a new way to live and a new way to nourish myself. When we eat, drink, shop, or watch TV for comfort, we never end up truly comforted. Along the way I'm learning that rest and relationships nourish me in a way a club sandwich never could.

WHEN YOU'RE in need of comfort, where do you turn? What would be a healthier choice?

ONLY YOU CAN TELL YOUR STORY

*For you, LORD, have delivered me from death, my eyes from tears, my feet
from stumbling, that I may walk before the LORD in the land of the living.*

—Psalm 116:8–9

If you've been sitting quietly, hoping that someone will start speaking a
language that makes sense to you, may I suggest that you are that person?
If you've been longing to hear a new language for faith, one that rises and
falls like a song, may I suggest that you start singing? If you want your community to be marked by radical honesty, by risky, terrifying, ultimately
redemptive truth-telling, you must start telling your truth first.

I've spent my life surrounded by deeply gifted pastors, great leaders,
and brilliant preachers. I understand the temptation to simply let them
continue telling God's story. I settled myself into the back row, certain
that a girl like me had nothing to contribute, and that everything in the
world that needed to be said was being said by people like them — extremely talented, polished people who never seem scared, who know the systems
and the forms and the formulas like the backs of their hands.

But there is one thing that those pastors and preachers and leaders cannot do, one thing they can never do. They cannot tell my story. Only I can
tell my story. And only you can tell your story.

NO ONE else has your voice or your story. Your story is
worth telling. In what ways are you telling your story?

TREASURE

I will sing of your strength, in the morning I will sing of your love;
for you are my fortress, my refuge in times of trouble.

—Psalm 59:16

Our morning routine is fast, loud and messy, running circles to get back-packs packed and diapers changed, water bottles filled and coffee made.

After too many days of being the worst kind of cranky mom—where I snapped at everyone and set the bowls down on the counter for cereal with a *thunk* that made everyone jump, I thought to myself, *There has to be a better way to do this. There has to be a way to live these mornings with more soul and patience.*

I began praying in the morning, sometimes even just for thirty seconds, right after I heard Mac yell for the first time, until the yelling became more insistent. And the word I prayed was *treasure. God, these children are my treasures. I treasure our time together. Help me to steward the treasure you've given me—every moment, every hour.*

We still have our meltdowns, of course. I'm still committed to copious amounts of strong coffee along with the praying. But the prayer reminds me what the morning time is: a chance to make the three boys in my life feel loved and ready to face the world.

WHAT'S ONE word you could use as a prayer in the morning that would remind you of the way you want to live, the way you want to steward the opportunities you've been given?

CHOOSING JOY

Rejoice in the Lord always. I will say it again: Rejoice!

—**Philippians 4:4**

I believe in a life of celebration. I believe that the world we wake up to every day is filled to the brim with deep, aching love, and also with hatred and sadness. And I know which one of those I want to win in the end. I know that Death knocks at our doors and comes far too early for far too many of us, but when he comes for me, I want to be full-tilt, wide-open, caught in the very act of life.

It's rebellious, in a way, to choose joy, to dance, to love your life. It's much easier and much more common to be miserable. We could just live our normal, day-to-day lives, saving all the good living up for someday, but I think it's our job to live each day like it's a special occasion, because we've been given a gift. We get to live in this beautiful world. When I live purposefully and well, when I dance instead of sitting it out, when I let myself laugh hard, when I wear my favorite shoes on a regular Tuesday, that regular Tuesday is better.

MUCH OF the time, if we don't consciously choose celebration, we'll be swept along by the mundane and miserable things in life. Where have you found joy in everyday life lately? Look for opportunities to celebrate today, and grab hold of them.

February
21

NEW LIFE

The desert and the parched land will be glad; the wilderness will rejoice and blossom.
Like the crocus, it will burst into bloom; it will rejoice greatly and shout for joy.

—Isaiah 35:1–2

I don't know where you are these days, what's broken down and what's beautiful in your life this season. I don't know if this is a season of sweetness or one of sadness. But I'm learning that neither lasts forever. There will be something that invades this current loveliness. It won't be sweet forever. But it won't be bitter forever either. If everywhere you look these days, it's wintery, desolate, lonely, practice believing in springtime. It always, always comes, even though on days like today it's nearly impossible to imagine, ground frozen, trees bare and spiky. New life will spring from this same ground.

Anything can happen in a year. Broken down, shattered things can be repaired in a year. Hope can grow in a year, after a few seasons of lying dormant. I didn't like who I was or how I was living a year ago, but I didn't know any other way to do it. I recognize the face that stares back at me in the mirror these days. When I look into my own eyes, I recognize a person I thought was lost, and I feel whole, for the first time in years.

THE PASSING of time brings new seasons, both on the earth and in our hearts. Even when we're in cold, dark days, we can anticipate the next surge of new life.

NOURISHMENT OF MANY KINDS

Share with the Lord's people who are in need. Practice hospitality.

—Romans 12:13

One February, my friend Kelly and I decided to have a party because life felt sort of snowy and dim and the bad kind of quiet. I proposed Italian food—warm, heavily flavored, comforting, sprawled out over a table, unfussy. Melissa from my book club made fantastic Italian hummus, and Kelly and Lacey brought bread and cheese and wine. The table was gorgeous and full—pastas and risotto and salads and roasted asparagus with garlic aioli. We told stories and passed bowls and laughed at Julie's punch lines. After dinner, we sat around the coffee table eating Stefany's flourless chocolate cake with crème anglaise and champagne, little clusters of conversations, occasional bubbles of laughter in the dim light.

We asked them to bring money, whatever amount felt right, for the church in our neighborhood that feeds people from a truck a few times a month. I put my little red tomato pot next to the wine and glasses, and at the end of the night it was full. It felt right to think about other people's hunger as we were thinking about our own—hunger for food and for friendship, for nourishment of many kinds.

THERE ARE many ways to meet each other's needs, and sometimes our own needs are met at the very same time. What are some ways you can meet the relational needs in your community while meeting practical needs as well?

February
23

THAWING THE ICE

Jesus said, "Feed my lambs."
—John 21:15

After the dinner party that cold, dim February night, I stayed up long after the guests left, letting the candles burn down, remembering how the table looked and how each bite tasted. I felt nourished on an impossibly deep level, thankful and full and proud and humbled all in the same moment. It felt like we'd been a part of something important, something larger than a meal, like we'd managed to thaw the ice just for an evening and traverse bridges normally impassable. The next morning, Aaron kept remarking that I seemed unusually buoyant. It may have been that I had Stefany's chocolate cake for both breakfast and lunch, but in any case, I fairly glided through the day, bouncing on the bright feelings of the night before as I put away the wineglasses and counted out the money we'd collected for my neighbor, the pastor of the food truck church.

Sometimes the most spiritual things we do are the most physical, the most tactile. Feeding people is one of those things, whether we're helping to feed hungry people, or feeding the hunger in each one of us on these dark and heavy winter nights.

FEEDING PEOPLE is spiritual work, important work, holy work.

TASTING GRACE & PATIENCE

Be completely humble and gentle; be patient, bearing with one another in love.

—**Ephesians 4:2**

I have always been on the round side of average. I was a round-faced, chubby baby, a little girl with soft, puffy cheeks, a teenager who longed to be skinny and never was, who routinely threw all her pants on the floor and glared at them like enemies. A woman who still longs to be skinny and who still, from time to time, throws all her pants on the floor and glares at them like enemies. The heaviest thing isn't the number on the scale but the weight of the shame I've carried all these years—*too big, too big, too big.*

I used to think the goal was to get over things—to deal with them once and for all. But there are some things you don't get over, things you just make friends with at a certain point, because they've been following you around like a stray dog for years.

Being a Christian means practicing grace in all sorts of ways, and my body gives me the opportunity to demonstrate grace, to make peace with imperfection every time I see myself in the mirror. On my best days, I practice grace and patience with myself, knowing that I can't extend grace and patience if I haven't tasted them.

WHAT ISSUES have followed you through the years? Have you ever considered making friends with them? What would that look like? How can you practice grace and patience with yourself around these things?

February
25

THE TASK AT HAND

Whatever your hand finds to do, do it with all your might.

—Ecclesiastes 9:10

When you work on a team and you have a boss and projects and deadlines, when you get to the end of something, someone says, "Good job." Or "Thank you." Or "Wow, that was smart and helpful." But Henry never looks up at me when I'm changing his diaper and says, "Good move with the wipes, Mom. Very thorough." He doesn't look up at me when I'm trying to get him to go back to sleep in the night and whisper, "Fabulous technique with the shushing and rocking. You're a genius."

It doesn't matter to Henry one little bit that I can speak French or explicate sentences or cook really good roasted salmon. What matters is that I can be there with him as long as he needs me. What matters to him is that I play with Froggie, his favorite toy, one more time, one more time, one more time.

All my life I've been multitasking. I'm good at it. I don't want to be braggy, but I'm kind of a champion multitasker, really. And all of a sudden, what's valuable is not the multitasking, but the single task—being with him, only him, doing nothing else.

WHAT'S MOST valuable in your life right now? What are the most important roles or tasks at hand?

ON VULNERABILITY & CATS

*Who knows a person's thoughts except their own spirit within them? In the
same way no one knows the thoughts of God except the Spirit of God.*

—1 Corinthians 2:11

We like the idea of vulnerability, but it's harder to do than we think it will
be. I'm learning to create the space for it, and then wait, like you're waiting for a cat to come out from behind the couch, sort of acting like you
don't even care, but you really do.

For our small group, there's something about a messy table, crumpled
napkins, me puttering around the kitchen, opening and closing cabinets,
making tea and slicing cake. If I suspect that sneaky old cat is going to
wander out any second, I get up from the table and bang around in the
kitchen a little—I can still hear because it's only like five feet away, but it
breaks that pressure-y spell and the words start coming out.

Doing anything shoulder-to-shoulder helps. My darling brother is a
motorcycle guy, and there's not enough money in the world that could make
him, say, go to coffee with one of the other motorcycle shop guys and stare at
each other over a latte. But in the shop, shoulder to shoulder, tinkering and
fixing, the truth comes sliding out, like a stubborn, beautiful cat.

HOW HAVE you learned to make space for vulnerability in
your life? Are there particular people that you long to share more
vulnerability with? How might you make space for that to happen
in the future?

THE BASS PLAYER'S BIRTHDAY

*There is a time for everything, and a season for every activity under
the heavens...a time to be silent and a time to speak.*

—Ecclesiastes 3:1, 7

We love to do birthday toasts. Each person comes ready to say something about what that person has brought to their life in the last year or a prayer for the year to come, and after dinner, we toast with those thoughts.

Our friend Nathan, the bass player in Aaron's band, has a warm, easy-going presence, and people love to be around him. But he's more comfortable encouraging others than being the center of attention. I felt his nervousness, like he wanted us to stop. But we stayed with it. We talked about what he teaches us, what he adds to the band, to our church, to each of our lives.

The heart of hospitality is creating space for these moments, protecting that fragile bubble of vulnerability, truth, and love. It's all too rare that we tell the people we love exactly why our lives are richer because they're in it. That night we risked the awkwardness of saying tender, meaningful things out loud in front of our friends, trusting that those words would travel down to a deep part of someone we cared about. I watched Nathan's face move from slightly nervous and uncomfortable to overwhelmed in the best possible way.

DO YOU have any special birthday traditions? How can you use words as gifts to celebrate the people in your life?

Melody's Sausage & Egg Strata

I love having friends over for breakfast or brunch—lazy, coffee-soaked, kids running around. This is a staple for days like these, especially because you can make it the night before.

• •

1 pound ground sausage (I like hot sausage, but any kind will do)

6 eggs

2 cups milk

1 tablespoon mustard (I use Dijon)

½ teaspoon salt

½ teaspoon pepper

6 slices bread, cut into cubes

2 cups shredded cheese (I like sharp cheddar)

• •

» Cook sausage in a pan over medium-high heat until browned, breaking up large chunks as much as possible. Remove from heat and drain well.

» Beat eggs, milk, mustard, salt, and pepper in a large bowl with a whisk or hand mixer on medium speed until mixture is smooth.

» Add bread, cheese, and sausage to the egg mixture and stir/fold until solids are coated with the egg mixture and the cheese is mixed in. Spray the bottom and sides of a 13 x 9-inch baking dish with cooking spray and pour in the mixture. Cover with plastic wrap and refrigerate overnight.

» Bake uncovered at 400 degrees for 30 to 40 minutes, or until a knife inserted in the center comes out clean. Allow to cool for 5 minutes before cutting and serving.

PEACE FROM YOUR TOES

Do not be anxious about anything, but in every situation, by prayer and petition,
with thanksgiving, present your requests to God. And the peace of God, which
transcends all understanding, will guard your hearts and your minds in Christ Jesus.
—Philippians 4:6–7

I have glimpses every once in a while of an achingly beautiful way of living that comes when the plates stop spinning and the masks fall off and the apologies come from the deepest places and so do the prayers. I want that spirit or force of happiness that is so much deeper than happy—peace that comes from your toes, that makes you want to live forever, that makes you gulp back sobs because you remember so many moments of so much un-peace. I search for those moments the way I search for beach glass, bits of glitter along a desolate expanse of sand, and I want those moments to stretch into hours, into days.

I have been surprised to find that I am given more life, more hope, more moments of buoyancy and redemption, the more I give up. The more I let go, do without, reduce, the more I feel rich. The more I let people be who they are, instead of cramming them into what I need from them, the more surprised I am by their beauty and depth.

WHEN HAVE you felt this kind of peace and hope and buoyancy and redemption?

March

1

HOSPITALITY IS ABOUT LOVE

*There, in the presence of the L*ORD *your God, you and your families shall eat and shall rejoice in everything you have put your hand to, because the L*ORD *your God has blessed you.*

—Deuteronomy 12:7

As Christians, we are called to hospitality. But there's no one right way to practice hospitality, so find a way to entertain that works for you. Hospitality is about love, not about performance. If there's a time crunch, leave the food till the last few minutes. Guests don't mind helping in the kitchen, but it's no fun to leave them in the living room while you put on makeup. No matter how unimpressive the food is or how messy the house is, if you greet your guests at the door with happiness and warmth, they'll feel glad they came.

At the same time, the food can be flawless and the napkins fashioned into origami, but if the host is so nervous it's clear she's counting the minutes till you leave, nothing can save that party. It's easy to get carried away with an ambitious menu, and then spend the whole night flinging things around your kitchen and being annoyed with your guests for having the audacity to try to talk with you. Everyone would rather have a simpler meal and a happier host. The warmth and love you show your guests is the key ingredient in any gathering.

HOW HAVE others shown you love through their hospitality? How have you shown love through hospitality?

THE WHOLE STORY

I consider that our present sufferings are not worth comparing
with the glory that will be revealed in us.

—**R o m a n s 8 : 1 8**

I believe that God is making all things new. I believe that Christ over-came death and that pattern is apparent all through life and history: life from death, water from a stone, redemption from failure, connection from alienation. I believe that suffering is part of the narrative, and that nothing really good gets built when everything's easy. I believe that loss and empti-ness and confusion often give way to new fullness and wisdom.

But for a long season, I forgot all those things. I didn't stop believing in God. It wasn't a crisis of faith. I prayed and served and pursued a life of faith the way I had before that season and the way I still do now. But I realized all at once, sitting in church on a cold dark night, that the story I was telling was the wrong one—or at the very least, an incomplete one. I had been telling the story about how hard it was. That's not the whole story. The rest of the story is that I failed to live with hope and courage and lived instead a long season of whining, self-indulgence, and fear. This is my confession.

WE NEED both halves of the story: the suffering and the redemption. Either part by itself is incomplete.

A SMALLER STORY

We live by faith, not by sight.

—2 Corinthians 5:7

Looking back on a particularly difficult time in our lives, I'm able to see now that what made that season feel so terrible to me were not the changes. What made that season feel so terrible is that I lost track of some of the crucial beliefs and practices that every Christian must carry with them.

More than anything, it was a failure to believe in the story of who God is and what he is doing in this world. Instead of living that story—one of sacrifice and purpose and character—I began to live a much smaller story, and that story was only about me. I wanted an answer, a timeline, and a map. I didn't want to have to trust God or anything I couldn't see. I didn't want to wait or follow. I wanted my old life back, and even while I read the mystics and the prophets, even while I prayed fervently, even while I sat in church and begged for God to direct my life, those things didn't have a chance to transform me, because under those actions and intentions was a rocky layer of faithlessness, fear, and selfishness.

GOD ASKS us to live by faith because he wants more for us than our human eyes can see. Has there been a season in your life when you stopped seeing the big story and started living a much smaller story?

March
4

A TRICKY JOURNEY

*Praise the LORD, my soul, . . . who redeems your life from the
pit and crowns you with love and compassion.*

—Psalm 103:2, 4

I believe that faith is less like following a GPS through a precise grid of
city blocks, and more like being out at sea: a tricky journey, nonlinear and
winding, the wind kicking up and then stalling. But what I really wanted
during a difficult season was dry land and a computer-woman's soothing
voice leading me through the mess.

I prayed the way you order breakfast from a short-order cook: this is what
I want. Period. I didn't pray for God's will to be done in my life, or, at any
rate, I didn't mean it. I couldn't make peace with uncertainty—but nothing in the biblical narrative tells us certainty is part of the deal. I prayed for
the waiting to be over, instead of trying to learn something about patience
or anything else. I prayed for it to get easier, not that I would be shaped in
significant ways. I prayed to be rescued, not redeemed.

I don't like the person I became, and I'm not proud of the contagious
fear and ugliness I left in my wake. This is my confession, and my promise: I want to live a new way, the way I've always believed, but temporarily
lost sight of.

WHAT ARE you praying for? Are you praying to be taught,
transformed, and redeemed? Or just to be rescued? What would
it look like to pray for something deeper and less predictable?

HOW TO BE A WOMAN

By wisdom a house is built, and through understanding it is established;
through knowledge its rooms are filled with rare and beautiful treasures.

—Proverbs 24:3–4

My professor Heather was and is one of the clearest real-life pictures of the kind of person I want to be. When I was eighteen, I took her class in my first semester of college at Westmont. She was beautiful, strong, and tall with blonde hair. She was impossibly articulate and intelligent. She pushed us and made us want to impress her and please her, so we studied hard, wrote voraciously, and read carefully, hoping to bring her something of value to each class meeting, like small children cupping fireflies and salamanders in their hands. She became my advisor, and then my friend. We talked about books and about telling the truth in your writing.

When I moved out of my mother's home, Heather gave me another image of how to be a woman. I needed my mother's image, but I also needed a few more images with which to piece together a future self. Heather is one of the most significant of those images. She pushed me, as a writer, as a person of faith, and as a woman. There were times when I failed her, and when I did, her disappointment crushed me, and then her grace healed me.

WHO ARE the people who have given you different images of how to be a woman? Who are the clearest real-life pictures of the sort of woman you want to be? What have you learned and how have you grown through knowing them?

AT MY BEST & AT MY WORST

This is what the Sovereign LORD, *the Holy One of Israel, says: "In repentance and rest is your salvation, in quietness and trust is your strength."*

—Isaiah 30:15

When I spent a semester in Britain during college, my very favorite professor, Heather, taught the semester course. One evening, we sat on a bench, looking out over the black branches in the fading light. She was worried about me, she said. She loved to hear my stories, about taking trains, staying out all night, drinking with strangers, and swimming in fountains, but she feared I was losing my ability to be contemplative. She told me that I was a leader, and the other students would follow me, and she didn't think I was leading them anywhere worth going.

I wrote her words in my journal, and while they were accurate then, they were also prophetic: as I grow older, I see that same pattern throughout my life. When I am at my best, I can see and think and feel at a deep level, and when I am at my worst, I'm a tap-dancing, tipsy show-off, with funny stories and painfully little else.

She was brave with me, telling me the truth about myself, and I was a little bit brave with her, withstanding her disappointment and letting it reach down to the deepest parts of me and draw me up to a better self.

WHAT QUALITIES describe you when you're at your best and your worst? Who are you willing to listen to when you need to hear the truth about yourself?

ON PLAYING DUMB & FRAGILE

Honor her for all that her hands have done, and let her
works bring her praise at the city gate.

—Proverbs 31:31

I think the current cultural messaging that tells women it's attractive to play dumb and fragile and hope that they're saved by their beauty is incredibly destructive. And I don't consider men the only problem. Every woman who plays cute instead of smart, who is known for her body more than for her brains, or who depends on her pout to get what she wants is part of the problem.

If you get what you want by batting your eyelashes, faking fragility, or making the most of your push-up bra, and then you wonder why you're not taken seriously in your career or given responsibility in your church, I think you may have believed the reigning cultural lie about what makes us attractive.

Let's set a new example for a generation of young women who are watching us closely. Let's teach them by our example to be women who work hard, who pay attention to their dreams, who give themselves to making the world a better place, women who believe that there are a whole lot of things more important than being the prettiest princess in the room.

HAVE YOU ever been tempted to depend on your looks rather than on your strengths and skills? How does that serve you? What effect do you see that having on your daughters, younger sisters, and other women around you?

March

8

LENT

*Even if I am innocent, I cannot lift my head, for I am
full of shame and drowned in my affliction.*

—Job 10:15

Aaron and I stopped watching TV and movies for the six weeks of Lent. We had watched ourselves turn from thoughtful, creative, curious people to people who lay on the couch for hours on end, watching just one more episode. We knew it would be good for us but also extremely painful.

Unfortunately for me, I left my job in the middle of Lent, and all the attending fear, sadness, anxiety, and brokenheartedness landed with a thud in the silence of our TV-free living room. To make matters worse, I was pregnant. I'm not a heavy drinker, but if I had not been pregnant, the pain of that season might have been eased by, say, ninety glasses of wine and an *E! True Hollywood Story* marathon. But neither of those were options, so I drank sparkling water and cried in the cavernous, echoing silence.

Why was this happening to me when I had nothing to protect myself with? I was helpless and exposed. I felt like I was in a winter storm with bare legs and bare arms, nothing to buffer or protect me. I felt, sometimes, like I had no skin, and everything struck bone and vein directly.

DO YOU observe a Lenten tradition, or have you ever given something up during Lent? If so, what has that experience been like for you? What effect has it had in your life over time?

SPACE FOR GOD

"Surely I am with you always, to the very end of the age."
—Matthew 28:20

When Aaron and I gave up TV and movies for Lent, the pain when I left my job was excruciating. Although I have not had this impulse before or since, if I'm being completely honest, I wanted to be self-destructive. I wanted to act out physically what was boiling over inside me. But I couldn't even think about doing anything that would hurt the baby. So I waddled around and took my prenatal vitamins, I ate eggs and cheese and drank cranberry juice, and I shuffled through that season clear-minded, wide awake, unmedicated, unshielded.

What I believed at the outset that I needed from Lent was to create a space for God's voice and presence in my life. God bloomed into my quiet house and my broken heart like yeast in bread, leavening and changing everything. If I had known that my life would be sliced open so deeply, I would never have chosen the quiet. But that's the magic of Lent, that you sign yourself up for something, hoping that God will slide something new into your life, and when he does, it's never what you thought, and never what would have been easy, and always just the right thing.

GOD HAS a way of surprising us when we open ourselves to him and give him room in our lives. How has he surprised you in the past? How might you create silence and new space for him in this season?

WRITING IN PENCIL

In their hearts humans plan their course, but the LORD establishes their steps.

—Proverbs 16:9

I should have written in pencil. I should have viewed the trajectory of my life as a mystery. I should have planned lightly, hypothetically, and used words like "maybe" and "possibly." Instead, every chance I got, I wrote in Sharpie. I stood on my future, on what I knew, on the certainty of what life would hold for me, as though it were rock. Instead, it's more like a magic carpet, a slippy-slidy-wiggly thing, full of equal parts play and terror. The ground beneath my feet is lurching and breaking, and making way for an entirely new thing every time I look down, surprised once again by a future I couldn't have predicted.

I'm going to start writing in pencil.

Life with God at its core is about giving your life up to something bigger and more powerful. It's saying at every turn that God knows better than we know, that his Spirit will lead us in ways that we couldn't have predicted. I have known that, but I haven't really lived that.

There is a loosey-goosey feeling to the future now, both a slight edge of anxiety like anything can happen, and a slight bubble of hope and freedom that, well, anything can happen.

DO YOU tend to write your future in pencil or in Sharpie? How do you feel about trusting your future to God? Is there something in your life right now that you need to offer back to God, trusting him with that unknown?

EVERYTHING IS INTERIM

You make known to me the path of life; you will fill me with joy in
your presence, with eternal pleasures at your right hand.

—Psalm 16:11

I went for a walk one day with my friend Rosa. She's an elder at our church and has four kids. Her husband owns a successful dental practice. The last few years they've been traveling, helping churches all over the world, and they've decided to move to North Africa.

I commented that this season, while they're selling their house and getting ready to move, must feel like an interim season. "You know, Shauna," she said, "everything is interim. Every season that I thought was stable and would be just how it was for a long time ended up being a preparation or a path to the next thing. When you decide to be on this journey with God, everything is interim."

Life is like that, twisty and surprising. But life with God is like that exponentially. We can dig in, make plans, write in stone, pretend we're not listening, but the voice of God has a way of being heard. It seeps in like smoke even when we've barred the door, and it moves us, to different countries and emotional territories and ways of living. It keeps us moving and dancing and watching. And with the surprises comes great hope.

HOW ARE you hearing the voice of God in this season? How is it moving you? How are you responding?

Frisée, Hazelnut & Goat Cheese Salad with Dijon Vinaigrette

This is a simple, flavorful French salad, perfect in combination with a heavier entrée—cassoulet or stew. In a jar, shake together the vinaigrette. Assemble the ingredients for the salad, then toss with the vinaigrette. Serve immediately.

FOR THE SALAD

3 bunches Frisée, trimmed and washed

1 Granny Smith apple, julienned

¼ cup hazelnuts, toasted and lightly crushed

½ cup goat cheese, crumbled

FOR THE VINAIGRETTE

1 shallot, minced

¼ cup red wine vinegar

1 tablespoon Dijon mustard

1 teaspoon honey

½ cup extra virgin olive oil

salt and pepper to taste

KNEES OR BUNS

I...delight to see how disciplined you are and how firm your faith in Christ is.
—**Colossians 2:5**

When Henry was three, he liked to stand on his chair at the dinner table so he could lord his tallness over the rest of us. It's dangerous, not to mention annoying, to be lorded over by a toddler while you're trying to eat. So we gave him a choice: knees or buns. He had to sit, but he got to decide whether to sit on his knees, kneeling, or on his buns.

Writing is a lot like dealing with a toddler. It's helpful to feel as though I have choices, and for those choices to be extremely narrow. When I'm writing, I am free to sit anywhere in our house: at my desk, in the brown chair by the window, on the couch in the kitchen.

However, I cannot get out the tape measure to see what size rug to order for the living room, and I cannot wander from room to room collecting assorted members of the Justice League and throwing them back in the toy box.

Writing isn't hard, but sitting down in the chair is really, really hard. I can sit anywhere I like, but I have to sit down, and then the hardest part is over.

THE FIRST step is often the most difficult. Once we've begun, we may find we can do our work with less struggle than we expected. In what area of your life do you need to take a first step today?

DRYER LINT

Envy rots the bones.

—Proverbs 14:30

When you're stuck creatively, it absolutely does not help to google yourself or check your blog comments every six minutes. Even if, say, nine out of ten reviews on Amazon are lovely, that one less-than-glowing review will dive into your psyche like a virus you can't shake.

Don't read about other people online, either. If you're feeling scared and small, your twisted-up mind will make them into heroes and paragons of talent and virtue. All you'll notice are the fun things they're doing and how skinny they are in their pictures. All the status updates and tweets, when you're feeling jittery and terrified, somehow line up in this vein: "Just got back from 45 days in Hawaii." "My new army of housekeepers is cleaning my house top to bottom." "Sifting through awards and invitations from journalists and reviewers who think I'm a genius." It's not really like that, of course. Mostly people are talking about how badly they need a coffee and what they thought about the new Vampire Weekend album and how frustrated they are that their kids won't nap. But when you're stuck, all you see are the ones that make you feel tiny and gray, like dryer lint.

BE KIND to yourself. Don't compare the minutiae of your daily life to the highlights reel someone else has posted online.

NO SUCH LUCK

Wounds from a friend can be trusted.

—Proverbs 27:6

I e-mailed my friend Kirsten while I was supposed to be writing. I sent her a rambling, complaining email about how hard writing is, how I'm no good at it, and how I'm so not in the right space, mentally. Finishing the book was so not the right thing for me to do; it was stressing me out and making me cranky.

Kirsten is a tender, imaginative soul. She lives in San Francisco, land of karma and wine and hippies, so I thought she would cut me a little slack in the name of not feeling it.

No such luck. Almost immediately she responded with an email two pages long, single-spaced. She said "Get to work" and "It's not mystical or magical. Just do the writing." She asked me to consider how I'd feel about myself, walking away from this opportunity.

I wanted to be coddled, babied. I wanted someone to buy my excuses and sanction my desire to quit. But she loved me enough to tell me the truth about myself, about life, and about what matters. One of the best things great friendship does is tell us the truth about ourselves when we need it most.

FRIENDSHIP DOESN'T always mean being partners in crime; sometimes, at its best, it requires exactly the opposite—an honest word, a push, a loving correction.

TIME & LOVE & STIRRING

We count as blessed those who have persevered.

—James 5:11

Creativity isn't easy, and it isn't something you turn on like a light switch. My inbox will tell you that the world is full of writers who don't write, painters who don't paint, dancers who don't dance. They want me to tell them something, ostensibly a secret something that will get them up and moving again, creating again. My reply is always disappointing: I don't know what to tell you. But then I tell them: do it for the feeling you'll have when you're done. Making art doesn't have the instant payoff that most things in our modern lives do, but like all things that really matter, the big payoff is invisible and comes much later.

Yesterday my friend Meredith came over and we made meat sauce together. We talked and diced and stirred and tasted and made adjustments, and then let the sauce simmer for a long time. You could taste the time it took, the layers of flavor—red wine, rosemary, garlic, a couple different kinds of tomatoes. That's how it is when you give yourself to something: it takes time and love and stirring, but at the end, no one would mistake it for quick sauce.

RICH, BEAUTIFUL work takes time and effort and persistence, and it shows.

ON REST

May God himself, the God of peace, sanctify you through and through. May your
whole spirit, soul and body be kept blameless at the coming of our Lord Jesus Christ.

—1 Thessalonians 5:23

I went to a retreat several years ago, and the woman who led it, in her opening remarks, said, "Oh, by the way, while you're up here, if at any time you want to rest or sleep, by all means do—sometimes it's the most spiritual and obedient thing we can do."

We all laughed nervously—who doesn't need a nap, right?

And I've been thinking about her words for years. How often do we push and rush and produce and achieve, and then find ourselves depleted and short with the people we love? And then how often do we blame ourselves for being weak or unorganized?

Lately, I've been aiming to live what the woman at the retreat taught. I'm learning that to rest is not to be weak. To rest is to prepare yourself to be used by God—because imagine what he can do in a person who is fully rested, able to think well and feel deeply?

I'm learning to see naps as holy gifts, going to bed early as an investment in my relationships, and admitting my tiredness as a sign that I'm committed to caring for myself well: body, soul, and mind.

ARE YOU in the practice of resting your body well? What's one concrete step you can take to rest well?

WATERWORKS

Those who sow with tears will reap with songs of joy.

—Psalm 126:5

My friend Eve told me once that the ability to cry is a sign of health, because it means your body and your soul agree on something, and that what your soul is feeling, your body is responding to. I tell my husband that every time my own personal waterworks turn on. Sign of health, honey.

In the same way that tears are a gift and a sign of health, I'm coming to learn that pain is, among other things, an opportunity to learn something about our bodies, a chance to listen to them and learn what they have to teach us. And pain is an opportunity to be comforted, something I always resist, greatly preferring immediate solutions or independence.

My friend Mindy pushed and worked and overworked and kept running past all the signs she should have paid attention to, until one morning she found she had vertigo so bad she couldn't get out of bed. Our bodies know what they're doing, and they know how to get our attention. It's like a toddler asking the same question over and over and over until you think you might lose your mind.

WE WERE created to cry and feel pain. These processes come with a purpose, and it's healthy to listen to the wisdom they carry. For a few minutes, allow yourself to feel the sorrow and loss you carry with you.

TWO KINDS OF PAIN

There is a time for everything, and a season for every activity under the heavens
...a time to weep and a time to laugh, a time to mourn and a time to dance.

—Ecclesiastes 3:1, 4

There are two very different kinds of pain. There's the anxiety and fear I felt when we couldn't sell our house. And then there's the sadness I felt when my grandma passed away. The first kind invites us to grow. The second kind invites us to mourn.

God's not trying to teach me a lesson through my grandma's death. When we lose someone we love, when a dear friend moves away, when illness invades, it's right to feel deep, wrenching sadness.

But then there's the other kind of pain. My friend Brian says that the heart of all human conflict is the phrase "I'm not getting what I want." When you're totally honest about the pain, what's at the center?

It's sloppy theology to think that all suffering is good for us, or that it's a result of sin. All suffering can be used for good, over time, after mourning and healing, by God's graciousness. But sometimes it's just plain loss, not because you needed to grow or learn any kind of lesson. The trick is knowing the difference between the two.

PAIN IS sometimes a call for growth—and sometimes a companion of mourning. Spend a few minutes praying through the losses in your life. Which of them call for growth? Which call for mourning?

WHEN MY HEART BREAKS

*My sacrifice, O God, is a broken spirit; a broken and
contrite heart you, God, will not despise.*

—Psalm 51:17

I used to think that the growth we experience through pain, physical or not, was a consolation prize. I used to think it was like having a good personality. Who wants a good personality when you can have legs for days or a face that launches a thousand ships? I thought that what we really want are easy lives, and if we can't have those, then we can at least become deep, grounded people who grow through heartbreak.

But I don't know anyone who has an easy life forever. Everyone I know gets their heart broken sometime, by something. The question is not, will my life be easy or will my heart break? But rather, when my heart breaks, will I choose to grow?

Sometimes in the moments of the most searing pain, we think we don't have a choice. But we do. It's in those moments that we make the most important choice: grow or give up. It's easy to want to give up under the weight of what we're carrying. It seems sometimes like the only possible choice. But there's always, always, always another choice, and transformation is waiting for us just beyond that choice.

THROUGH PRAYER, invite God into the midst of your pain. Invite him to carry you through toward transformation.

OUT OF THE WRECKAGE

"See, I am doing a new thing! Now it springs up; do you not perceive it?
I am making a way in the wilderness and streams in the wasteland."

—Isaiah 43:19

My friend Steve says that God doesn't speak to everyone the same way, but that he generally speaks the same way over and over again to each person. I think that's absolutely true. God generally speaks to me through grand gestures. Actually I think he speaks to me first in whispers, and that I don't listen until he's shouting. I regret this, and I think certain seasons of my life could have been a little easier had I been a better listener.

But I'm learning. It's human to struggle. It's human to nurse a broken heart, to wonder if the pain will ever let up, to howl through your tears every once in a while. And the best, most redeeming, exciting thing I could imagine, from the smashed-up, broken place I've been, is that something beautiful could blossom out of the wreckage. That's the goal.

This is what I know: God can make something beautiful out of anything, out of darkness and trash and broken bones. He can shine light into the blackest night, and he leaves glimpses of hope all around us. An oyster, a sliver of moon, one new bud on a black branch. New life and new beauty are all around us, waiting to be discovered, waiting to be seen.

GOD SPEAKS to us, and his words are of beauty and new life. What might he be whispering to you today, out of the wreckage of a painful part of your life?

TWO OPTIONS

We also glory in our sufferings, because we know that suffering produces perseverance; perseverance, character; and character, hope. And hope does not put us to shame, because God's love has been poured out into our hearts through the Holy Spirit, who has been given to us.

—Romans 5:3–5

There are things that happen to us that give us two options. Either way, we will never be the same, and we shouldn't. These things can either strip us down to the bone and allow us to become strong and honest, or they can be the reasons we use to behave poorly indefinitely, the justification for all manner of broken relationships and broken ideals. It could be the thing that allows everything else to turn, the lock of our lives to finally spring open and allow our pent-up selves to blossom. Or it can be the reason we use to justify our anger and the sharp tones in our voices for the rest of our lives.

We become who we are in these moments. I have a friend who falls back, whenever things are too hard, to an event that happened over a decade ago. It's the thing that she uses to justify cruel behavior. But wouldn't it be great, wouldn't it be just like God, if that terrible thing could be the thing that lifts her up and delivers her to her best, truest self? It can. It happens all the time.

WHAT ARE the events in your life that have shaped you in defining ways? Who have you become as a result?

JUST PAST THE HEARTBREAK

*You turned my wailing into dancing; you removed my sackcloth
and clothed me with joy, that my heart may sing your praises and
not be silent. LORD my God, I will praise you forever.*

—Psalm 30:11–12

I would never tell you that every bad thing is really a good thing, just waiting to be gazed at with pretty new eyes, just waiting to be shined up and—
ta-da!—discovered as fantastic. But for me, and for a lot of the people I
love, we're discovering that, not every time, maybe, but more often than
not, there is something just past the heartbreak, just past the curse, just
past the despair, and that thing is beautiful. You don't want it to be beautiful, at first. You want to stay in the pain and the blackness because it feels
familiar, and because you're not done feeling victimized and smashed-up.
But one day you'll wake up surprised and humbled, staring at something
you thought for sure was a curse and has revealed itself to be a blessing—a
beautiful, delicate blessing.

Nothing good comes easily. You have to lose things you thought you
loved, give up things you thought you needed. You have to get over yourself,
beyond your past, out from under the weight of your future. The good stuff
never comes when things are easy. It comes just when you think it never will.

IS THERE a heartbreak anywhere in your past that later
ended up yielding joy for you? Spend a minute thanking God for
turning your mourning into dancing.

STITCHING OUR HEARTS BACK TOGETHER

David asked, "Is there anyone still left of the house of Saul to whom I can show kindness for Jonathan's sake?"...Ziba answered the king, "There is still a son of Jonathan; he is lame in both feet."...So Mephibosheth ate at David's table like one of the king's sons.

—2 Samuel 9:1, 3, 11

There will be a day when it all falls apart. My friend lost her mom this year. Another friend's marriage ended. A friend I hadn't talked to in ages called late one Sunday night to ask me how to get through a miscarriage. "The bleeding," she said, "has already begun."

These are things I can't change. Not one of them. Can't fix, can't heal, can't put the broken pieces back together. What I can do is offer myself, wholehearted and present, to walk with the people I love through the fear and the mess. That's all any of us can do. That's what we're here for, the presence, the listening, the praying with and for on the days when it all falls apart, when life shatters in our hands.

The table is where we store up for those days, where we log minutes and hours building something durable and strong that gets tested in those terrible split seconds. And the table is where we return to stitch our hearts back together after the breaking.

WHAT IS falling apart in your life? In the lives of the people you love? How are you offering yourself to walk through the mess with them?

Lindsay's Green Chile Strata

8 corn tortillas

1 ½ cups chopped green chiles
(3 4-ounce cans)

8 ounces Monterey Jack cheese,
shredded (about 4 cups)

6 eggs

1 ¾ cups milk

¾ teaspoon salt

» Preheat the oven to 350 degrees. Generously coat a 13 x
9-inch baking dish with cooking spray or olive oil spray.
Cover the bottom of the dish with 4 tortillas. Sprinkle with
half of the chopped green chiles, then half of the cheese.
Repeat layers once more, ending with the cheese.

» In a medium bowl, beat the eggs. Add milk and salt and
whisk until combined. Pour over the layered ingredients
in the baking dish. Refrigerate for at least 30 minutes or
overnight.

» Bake for 50 to 60 minutes—the strata should be slightly
puffed and bubbly, and turning golden. Let cool for 5 to 10
minutes before serving.

THANKFUL

Give thanks to the LORD, for he is good; his love endures forever.

—Psalm 107:1

When I left my job, in the swirling pain and confusion of that season, a few people told me that at some point, I would be happy for this, thankful, even. That didn't sit well with me, and it felt even worse than the clichés about closing doors and opening windows. It felt cruel: not only was I supposed to not be sad, I was supposed to be thankful? It felt inauthentic and creepy, and I swore to myself that even if I healed someday, even if the pain abated, even if I was happy again, I would never ever be thankful for this.

Then, months later, I went with my family to the house of some wonderful, generous family friends. The last time I had been there was the day after I left my job. Being there again brought me back to that place, and showed me, to my surprise, the distance I had traveled in the intervening months. I looked back through my journal, and I looked out at the ocean at the same times of day, to see the same colors on the same sky, and I realized I am different. And not only different, but better, and not only better, but thankful.

HAVE YOU ever been surprised to find yourself thankful for something that had initially been very painful? How did you realize that change had happened?

A NEW GRATITUDE

He has sent me . . . to bestow on them a crown of beauty instead of ashes, the oil of joy instead of mourning, and a garment of praise instead of a spirit of despair.

—Isaiah 61:1, 3

About a year after I left my job, I realized that I was thankful for the breaking of things that needed to be broken, that couldn't have been broken any other way, thankful for the severing that allowed me to fall down to the center of my fear and look it in the face, thankful for being set free from something I didn't even know I was enslaved to. There is a quality in my life that I sense now, like a rumbling bass line, or thunder faraway, and it is the feeling of having nothing to lose. I was embarrassed and ashamed in a deep way, and to my surprise, I'm still here. I'm happy in a new way, free in a new way.

I am all the clichés that made me so mad several months ago. I believe in the gift of pain. I believe that loss deepens us. I am grateful for God's graciousness toward me that he would teach me these things. As much as I hate to admit it, I've found a new gratitude, and it's gratitude for the way God has redeemed darkness and pain, for the way he brings something beautiful out of something horrible.

IF YOU are in a dark place, take heart. You are in the midst of a process that takes time, and God is there with you. You're not alone.

THE HEALING EFFECTS OF A BARBECUE

Jesus turned and saw her. "Take heart, daughter," he said, "your faith has healed you." And the woman was healed at that moment.

—Matthew 9:22

About six weeks after I left my job at the church in Grand Rapids, I had a little tiny bit of energy and readiness to move forward. The best way I could figure out to do that was to throw a party two months to the day after I left my job.

We filled our red wheelbarrow with ice and beer, and we cooked steaks and set out cupcakes and frosting and sprinkles for the kids. I waddled my pregnant self around and chatted with people I used to work with and missed terribly. We told stories, and when the sun dipped down, I passed out all our sweatshirts and fleeces, so we could stay out on the porch a little longer.

After everyone left, Aaron looked at me and said, "You're back." And now I'm a fervent believer in the healing effects of a barbecue, because that one brought me back to life a little bit. In the moments that I thought would be the loneliest, I had brothers and sisters sitting on the porch with me, telling me the truth as they saw it, which was a lot more beautiful than the truth as I saw it then.

GOD LONGS to heal us of our wounds, and he will use whatever we offer him.

DIVIDE & CONQUER

Over all these virtues put on love, which binds them all together in perfect unity.

—**C o l o s s i a n s 3 : 1 4**

Our parenting strategy for the last several months has been "Divide and Conquer." When I was pregnant and sick, I stayed home basically all the time, and Aaron took Henry to school and to the park. Every night these days, I put on Mac's jammies and feed him while Aaron's reading to Henry and tucking him in. Then Aaron rocks Mac while I clean up the kitchen. Back and forth, divide and conquer.

Because we both travel for work, I'm home when Aaron's working and traveling, and he's home when I'm working and traveling. It's a complex shuffle of schedules, and it works for us, generally. Back and forth, divide and conquer. But this summer we realized that it had left us a little too divided.

Aaron surprised me with a weekend in New York City. He'd arranged for our moms to watch the boys. We had a fantastic time. A glorious, wonderful, laughing-and-kissing, wandering little neighborhoods, *cheesy-romantic-comedy-montage* great time. We came back resolved to spend our time and our money and our childcare more carefully, and to give time alone together a higher priority. We may still divide and conquer with the kids. But now we know better than to let it divide us.

IF YOU'RE a wife and mother, how do you and your husband manage the responsibilities of parenting? How do you work into the mix time together as a couple, to nurture your relationship?

March
28

TELLING THE STORY OF WHO GOD IS

We will tell the next generation the praiseworthy deeds of the
LORD, his power, and the wonders he has done.

—**P s a l m   7 8 : 4**

There are two myths that we tend to believe about our stories: the first is that they're about us, and the second is that because they're about us, they don't matter. But they're not only about us, and they matter more than ever right now. When we, any of us who have been transformed by Christ, tell our own stories, we're telling the story of who God is.

I bet God has done something in your life that would make our hair stand on end if you told us about it. I bet the story God has written in your life and your home gives voice and breath and arms and legs to the gospel every bit as much as a church sermon ever did. Preaching is important, certainly. But it can't be the only way we allow God's story to be told in our midst.

There's nothing small or inconsequential about our stories. There is, in fact, nothing bigger. And when we tell the truth about our lives—the broken parts, the secret parts, the beautiful parts—then the gospel comes to life, an actual story about redemption, instead of abstraction and theory and things you learn in Sunday school.

WHO HAS God revealed himself to be in your story? What has he healed and redeemed in your life?

LOVE STORY

Come away, my beloved, and be like a gazelle or like a
young stag on the spice-laden mountains.
—Song of Songs 8:14

Confession: when I'm stressed, the to-do list becomes king. Cooking and cleaning are tangible ways for me to care for my family, and I default to those things—if everyone's in clean clothes and well-fed, I must be holding things together, right? But marriage isn't about a well-executed to-do list, and Aaron would much rather eat takeout and hunt around for a clean basket of laundry if that means I put down the list and really listen to him.

All of the above, of course, would be lovely—cooking and cleaning *and* listening and memory-making. Maybe we'll get there someday. But along the way, I'm learning that being connected in a deep way is so much more valuable than being well-organized, efficient, buttoned-up, and tidy. I default to tidy when what my husband wants and needs more than anything is laughing, listening, and playing, being *with* instead of being efficient.

Marriage isn't a business, co-owned and managed. It's a love story. The most important things we can give our marriage are time and romance, kissing and laughing. Laundry can wait, but a love story needs to be written a little bit every day.

> **WHEN WE'RE** stressed, it can be a challenge to remember and find time for what we need most. If you're married, how do you write your love story a little bit every day?

CONTROL & GRACE

And God raised us up with Christ and seated us with him in the heavenly realms in Christ Jesus, in order that in the coming ages he might show the incomparable riches of his grace, expressed in his kindness to us in Christ Jesus.

—Ephesians 2:6−7

When I'm in a really busy season, I want control. Woe to the people who mess up my house, because when everything else is swirling, my impulse is to control whatever I can. And what I can control, basically, is my countertops. The people who mess up my house, of course, are the three people I live with, two of whom are little boys whose whole existence, basically, is messing stuff up. That's how it should be. You'd think that when the pressure's on, I'd relax about things like hanging up coats and putting away shoes. In some super-awesome twist-of-crazy, however, the more demands on my time and mental space, the more mental space I want to put toward neatness.

Instead of control, I need grace. *GraceGraceGrace.* Grace for my tired self, grace for my kids, grace for my messy house. And I'm learning, slowly, surely, to soften my grip, to ease up on the control, and instead, to dwell in grace.

SOMETIMES WHEN one part of our life feels completely out of control, we find a strange relief in being hyper-controlling in another area. Reflect a little bit. Is this dynamic at play anywhere in your life right now?

ON LISTENING IN MARRIAGE

My dear brothers and sisters, take note of this: Everyone should be
quick to listen, slow to speak and slow to become angry, because human
anger does not produce the righteousness that God desires.

—James 1:19–20

Aaron and I had a really hard season. We said terrible things to one another, gripped tightly to unrealistic expectations, and failed to forgive, even when we promised we would. But we're inching our way back, and I'm so grateful. We began listening to each other at what seemed like the last possible moment. We were heading for a crash and we both knew it, and turned to one another in the nick of time—*Okay, tell me again. Really, tell me.*

In our best, gutsiest, most honest moments of the last year, we said things to each other that we never imagined saying out loud to anyone, things we were afraid of, things we couldn't bear. And those ugly honest confessions bloomed into a new intimacy, a new protectiveness, a new promise to walk together, and better than before.

Marriage is more than a contract. It's a messy, beautiful, living, breathing thing, full of dreams and history and patterns and memories. You can make your point all day long, and you can even be right about your point, but if you stop listening, if you stop really hearing and seeing that other person, something fundamental will be lost.

LISTENING IS so necessary to a vibrant marriage. What helps you listen to each other and really hear and see each other?

SOUTH BEND

As far as the east is from the west, so far has he removed our transgressions from us.

—Psalm 103:12

One cloudy Sunday some years ago, Aaron and I went to South Bend. I had a TV interview there on Monday morning, but the most important thing that happened there had nothing to do with the interview.

Aaron and I struck an important agreement. We decided to leave a tangled-up mess of six months of *you-did, you-should-have, you-said* right there in South Bend. We had been injuring one another for months, in the name of honest discussion, beating the same dead horses to dust. We were deeply tired of fighting the same fight so many times, of apologizing for the same things, accusing one another of the same things. From then on, we were free to fight about anything we wanted, but not if it was something we left in South Bend, because it could not be resurrected. There had to be a statute of limitations.

If God removes our sin as far as the East is from the West, then for Aaron and me to leave our offenses in South Bend was a good start. The absence of all the things we left there created space for new things, good things, new patterns to be built, new moments of warmth and connectedness.

> **IS THERE** an ongoing conflict in your life that needs to be laid down? What's one concrete step you can take toward forgiveness?

A RESTORED CONNECTION

Forgive and comfort him, so that he will not be overwhelmed by excessive sorrow.

—2 Corinthians 2:7

I was not afraid during that dark season that Aaron and I were going to split up. I didn't think either of us were going to cheat or leave. But I was afraid that the damage would be irreparable, and that we would slide into being one of those couples who has closed their hearts to one another in the deepest way. We'd continue to live together and raise a child together and watch TV together at night after long days. But we'd lose that deep trust and connection, that willingness to be vulnerable and to try again and risk being hurt again. That's what I was afraid of.

Of all the things I'm thankful for now, the restored connection between us might be at the top of the list. We made it through and into a new, better place. That's what I want to tell you, if you're married and you think the damage is done. I thought that, too, a couple times over the last few years. But our hearts are more elastic than we think, and the work of forgiveness and transformation and growth can do things you can't even imagine from where you're standing now.

WHAT DOES it look like in your marriage right now, in terms of connection and vulnerability? How open are your hearts to each other? Even if you're not where you'd like to be, there is hope.

THE PLACE OF HEALING

While Jesus was having dinner at Matthew's house, many tax collectors and sinners came and ate with him and his disciples. When the Pharisees saw this, they asked his disciples, "Why does your teacher eat with tax collectors and sinners?" On hearing this, Jesus said, "It is not the healthy who need a doctor, but the sick. But go and learn what this means: 'I desire mercy, not sacrifice.' For I have not come to call the righteous, but sinners."

—Matthew 9:10–13

We tend to believe that what we've done is too bad—that our sins and mistakes are beyond repair, and our faults and failures too deep and ugly. That's what shame tells us. But if we take a chance and come to the table, and if there we are treated with respect and kindness, then that voice of shame recedes for a little while, enough to let the voice of truth, of Christ himself, get planted a little deeper each time. The table becomes the place of healing.

When the table is full, heavy with platters, wine glasses scattered, napkins crumpled, dessert plates scattered with crumbs, candles burning low—in those moments I feel a deep sense of God's presence and happiness.

When you offer peace instead of division, faith instead of fear, when you offer someone a place at your table instead of keeping them out because they're different or wrong somehow, you represent the heart of Christ.

JESUS CALLS us all to his table. What keeps you from joining him there?

FIRE ESCAPE

The boundary lines have fallen for me in pleasant places;
surely I have a delightful inheritance.

—Psalm 16:6

Aaron and I are deliberate about creating experiences and memories alone together. Our schedules don't allow for a set date night every week, but we grab date nights whenever we can—driving to the city for dinner, going for a run together, staying in for a movie.

One of my favorite writers told a story about how now that they have kids, sometimes instead of getting a sitter and going out, they have a drink together on their fire escape, a mini-date looking over Manhattan. That idea stuck with me, and some nights when the kids are in bed, instead of watching TV or working on our computers, one of us will say to the other, "Fire escape?"

We open a bottle of wine or brew a pot of tea, and we sit on our front step together, looking out onto our quiet suburban street, talking and listening. It's not a fire escape looking over Manhattan, but it's our spot where we sit shoulder to shoulder looking out at the moon rising, the trees, the airplanes to and from O'Hare zigzagging across the sky.

OUR OWN places grow sweeter to us when we invest time in enjoying them and sharing them with those we love. When was the last time you laid down your work to spend time with someone you love?

SWEET SLOW SEASON

*The L*ORD* gives strength to his people; the L*ORD* blesses his people with peace.*

—P s a l m   2 9 : 11

Like every couple, we have our ups and downs, and we've had our sweet seasons and our dark ones. Sometimes it's hard to get a handle on what causes what, but I'm paying close attention these days, because I want to learn how to live for longer stretches in these sweet seasons. Looking closely, I think some of the hard choices we've made in the last year have cleared a path for this season.

One of those hard choices was to slow down. I suspect that I'll be talking and writing about this issue for the rest of my life, because it's so easy for me to get too busy, and for the fallout of that to have negative effects on the rest of my life. This is what I know: my life works better a little slower. Our family life works better a little slower. And our marriage works better a little slower, when there's space to listen and laugh, when we read together on the couch after the kids are in bed, when we don't have to be fast-paced business partners and just get to be us.

WHAT COULD you say no to this week to allow more space and slowness in your life?

Ravinia Pasta Salad

From my friend Heather

Ravinia is a beautiful outdoor concert venue, but the main event is not the concert; it's the picnic. When I go with my friend Heather, she brings a table with linens, flowers in a vase, and this incredible pasta salad—truly next level.

•••

2 cups sundried tomatoes, softened and chopped

3 tablespoons olive oil

3 cloves garlic, minced

salt and pepper

1 pound pasta, cooked

2 cups chicken, cooked and shredded

4 cups fresh spinach, torn

¾ cup grated Asiago cheese

½ cup grated Parmesan cheese

1 cup pine nuts, toasted

•••

» Combine tomatoes, olive oil, garlic, salt, and pepper. In a separate bowl, combine pasta, chicken, spinach, and cheeses. Toss with the tomato and olive oil mixture. Season with extra salt and pepper as needed. Top with pine nuts.

» Can be served hot or cold.

April

6

SUPPORTING MARRIAGES

Everyone who does evil hates the light, and will not come into the light for fear that their deeds will be exposed. But whoever lives by the truth comes into the light, so that it may be seen plainly that what they have done has been done in the sight of God.

—John 3:20–21

I'm so deeply thankful to be standing with Aaron in a spot of light and love and richness in our marriage these days. One of the things that has helped yield this loveliness is talking about our marriage with close friends, together and separately. When Annette and I catch up on the phone, she always asks me about my marriage, and I always ask about hers. I stood in their wedding and she stood in ours, and I'm so thankful to be a part of a community that takes that ongoing role seriously. Annette didn't just support me on the day of our wedding—she continues to support our marriage all these years later, and I'm honored to do that for her, too. Our small group and the Cooking Club girls and a few other friends are always ready to listen and help when we get stuck, and their voices of encouragement and honesty are such gifts. Secret-keeping takes its own toll, so even when things are hard, we tell the truth to our community.

OUR MARRIAGES are strengthened when we encourage each other and tell the truth about our marriages. Who in your life knows the good and the hard parts of your marriage or dating life?

ON SPRINGTIME

For as the soil makes the sprout come up and a garden causes seeds to grow, so the
Sovereign LORD will make righteousness and praise spring up before all nations.

—Isaiah 61:11

In my little corner of the world, I think spring officially started on Friday night. Aaron and I walked behind Henry on his tricycle as we made our way to the park. We held hands and sat on a park bench while we watched him slide and swing and climb, and then we walked home in the soft evening light. The grass is all glowy and technicolor at that time of day, lending a sense of magic to everything. Henry and I snuggled up in the hammock while Aaron grilled, and then we sat at the patio table and ate ripe melon, strawberries, hummus, and grilled chicken. It felt just like spring.

Sometimes a change in season around us is just what we need to prod us out of our own internal winters, to shake off the dust and darkness we've become accustomed to. I've been winter-y for a long time—sick, discouraged, a little isolated. I'm turning from fear to prayer, trusting that God can create new life and beauty from anything. I'm inviting the springtime around me into my own life, hoping it takes root and begins to show signs of new life in me, even small ones.

WHAT ARE the signs that spring has officially arrived in your corner of the world? What would it look like for you to move from winter to spring—or from fear to prayer—in your life?

SOUP FROM BONES

The LORD answered Moses... "Take in your hand the staff with which you struck the Nile.... Strike the rock, and water will come out of it for the people to drink."

—**Exodus 17:5–6**

This week I made soup from bones, which is essentially making a meal out of things that would otherwise become garbage. As a little girl, I loved the *Little House on the Prairie* books. I got them for my sixth birthday in a yellow cardboard box set and reread them every year. Making soup from bones seemed like something that Ma would do in the winter, while Pa was breaking the icicles from the cows' noses so they didn't freeze.

I chopped garlic, onions, carrots, and celery. I boiled the bones in my big red soup pot. I added some leftover turkey and a handful of rice, and all of a sudden, soup!

That plain old turkey soup made me feel like a miracle worker or a magician, bringing something from nothing. There's a particular beauty to that idea for me because I've spent so long feeling like a pile of bones, and the idea that these old bones can make something lovely and sustaining moves me. That's the heart of the story of God and people and his hands in the world. All through history, he's making soup from bones, life from death, water from rocks, love from hate.

WHERE DO you notice God making life from death and love from hate in your community? In your church? In your family? How about in your very own heart and life?

April

9

COMING TO LIFE ANEW

"I tell you," he replied, "if they keep quiet, the stones will cry out."

—Luke 19:40

What if, all at once, all the shabby, tired, used-up bodies and minds start to wriggle and pop, like they've been dropped into a deep-fryer, sizzling and dancing, transformed into motion? And something that has been deadened and distracted by the tension and noise of this world comes to life anew, wakes up and wiggles like a fritter in a frying pan, anointed, and taught to dance. Because we were made for motion, for arching up toward God with all the energy and passion of a thunderstorm, lightning slicing through a sleepy world to remind us that we serve a fast-dancing God, a God who set this world whirling and crashing through space so that we could live from our toes and drum out the pulse of a billion veins carrying lifeblood to a billion hearts, temples to a God that got his hands dirty making us from dust. Let's get dirty, in his name. Let's sizzle and pop in his name. Let's dance and shimmer and scrawl out our stories across the sky, like he taught us to. Let's echo his words, and let our lives speak those words: It is good.

WHAT SHIMMERS and dances in your life when you are most connected to God? What is the story that your life is telling right now? How does your life echo God's words that "It is good"?

April

10

COMMUNION ANYWHERE

But you are a chosen people, a royal priesthood, a holy nation, God's
special possession, that you may declare the praises of him who
called you out of darkness into his wonderful light.

—1 Peter 2:9

Body of Christ, broken for you. Blood of Christ, shed for you. "Every time you eat the bread and drink the wine," Jesus says, "remember me." Communion is connection, remembrance.

In our tradition, we take communion as a part of the church service every month or so. We pass a plate of bread, and another with tiny cups of wine—juice, actually. We also celebrate communion in less formal places—at a camp, or on a retreat. It isn't terribly uncommon to take communion together in a makeshift way, in a home or a backyard or on a beach, one person reading the scripture, another passing the bread and wine around a circle of friends, a small group, or a team that serves together.

I believe the bread and wine is for all of us, for every person, an invitation to believe, a hand extended from divine to human. I believe it's to be torn and handled, gulped. I believe that we can practice the sacrament of communion anywhere at all, that a forest clearing can become a church and any one of us a priest as we bless the bread and the wine.

WHEN WAS the last time you received communion? What do the bread and the wine mean in your life?

DEATH & REBIRTH

*"Unless a kernel of wheat falls to the ground and dies, it remains
only a single seed. But if it dies, it produces many seeds."*

—John 12:24

Years ago, my friend Doug told me that the central image of the Christian faith is death and rebirth. I'd heard that before, but when he told me, I really thought about it for the first time. And I didn't agree.

What I didn't understand until much later is that he wasn't speaking to me as a theologian or a pastor or an expert, but rather as a person whose heart had been broken and who had been brought back to life by the story God tells in all our lives. When you haven't yet had your heart really broken, the gospel isn't about death and rebirth. It's about life and more life. It's about hope and possibility and a brighter future. And it is, certainly, about those things.

But when you've faced some kind of death—the loss of someone you loved dearly, the failure of a dream, the fracture of a relationship—you start understanding that central metaphor. Rebirth and new life then become very, very important to you.

Now I know Doug was right. I know that death is real, and I trust that rebirth is real, too.

THE GOSPEL of Jesus Christ overflows with the promise of rebirth. What needs to come to life anew for you?

ISLAND

In six days the Lord made the heavens and the earth, the sea, and all that is in them, but he rested on the seventh day. Therefore the LORD blessed the Sabbath day and made it holy.

—Exodus 20:11

For many years, we've been going to a tiny little island for our family vacations. We love it there, and there are a million reasons why. It's the jumble of the waves and the sand and the goats tied to stakes in people's yards and the glittering green-blue of the water and the smell of conch fritters dipped in their mysterious sauce that I finally discovered is just ketchup and mayonnaise—it's those things that make it magic, that have made it the backdrop of our family's memories for over a decade.

It's all those things, and something that our family becomes when we are there. We're the best version of our family there, relaxed and connected and without agenda or schedule. We have conversations that unfold lazily and resolve over days instead of minutes. We tell stories that everyone's already heard, and it doesn't bother us. We make up plans as we go, and we've been going there long enough to have patterns just like worn spots in carpet, patterns that have become traditions, things you do without thinking, that feel familiar and meaningful.

WHEN HAVE you felt most connected to the people you love? How can you create meaningful memories and traditions with the people in your life?

WHAT YOU'RE WILLING TO GIVE UP

Let us throw off everything that hinders and the sin that so easily
entangles. And let us run with perseverance the race marked out for
us, fixing our eyes on Jesus, the pioneer and perfecter of faith.

—Hebrews 12:1–2

I love the illusion of being able to do it all, and I'm fascinated with people who seem to do that, who have challenging careers and beautiful homes and vibrant minds and well-tended abs.

Out to lunch one day with my friend Denise, I asked her about it. Denise is a mother of four, and a grandmother, and she works and writes and travels and cooks, and—most important to me at that time—she seems settled in some fundamental way. There's something she knows about herself that I didn't yet know about myself, certainly.

And this is what Denise told me: she said it's not hard to decide what you want your life to be about. What's hard, she said, is figuring out what you're willing to give up in order to do the things you really care about. Her words from that day have been rattling around inside me for years. Since that time we've worked together, traveled together, cried together, but when I think of her, I will always think of that day, and the clarity and weight of those words.

SOMETIMES IT'S not sin that's most difficult to throw off— it's the otherwise good stuff that gets in the way of our becoming who God is calling us to be. What do you need to let go of today?

THINGS I DO

"Teacher, which is the greatest commandment in the Law?" Jesus replied:
"'Love the Lord your God with all your heart and with all your soul
and with all your mind.' This is the first and greatest commandment.
And the second is like it: 'Love your neighbor as yourself.'"

—Matthew 22:36–39

After my conversation with Denise, I started keeping two lists: things I do and things I don't do.

The first list came pretty easily.

Above all else, I try to keep my faith in Christ at the center of my life, the heart and source of everything.

I do everything I can to make my marriage a deeply connected partnership.

I give the best of my heart and energy to raising our sons.

I work hard to become a better writer, to tell the truth as best I can, the story of who God is and what he does.

I read a lot: novels, essays, magazines, cookbooks, and the Bible.

I live in daily, honest, intimate community with a small group of people. I give my time, energy, and prayer to my family and close friends.

> **TAKE A** minute to list the top five or six things you feel called and committed to in this season of life. Seeing them written on paper, in order, can help us orient ourselves and make decisions that spring from those priorities.

THINGS I DON'T DO

One thing I do: Forgetting what is behind and straining toward what is ahead, I press on
toward the goal to win the prize for which God has called me heavenward in Christ Jesus.
—Philippians 3:13–14

The second list—the things I don't do—is the more important list. What am I willing to *not* do in order to do the things I believe in?

I don't garden or do major home improvement projects or scour flea markets for the perfect home accessories. No expectation for perfect housekeeping either. I don't make our bed. I don't scrapbook or make photo albums, although I take a lot of pictures of my kids. I only blow-dry my hair on special occasions, and I don't paint my fingernails.

I don't spend time with people who routinely make me feel like less than I am, or who talk mostly about other people's money or what's wrong with everyone else.

This list sets me free. Time is finite, as is energy. One day I'll stand before God and account for what I did with my life. There is work that is only mine to do: children that are ours to raise, stories that are mine to tell, friends that are mine to walk with.

WHEN WE know what's essential in our lives, everything else is negotiable. What are some things you don't do? What things could you intentionally leave undone so that you can focus more deeply on the things you feel called to and passionate about?

HOMEMADE

Then the LORD God formed a man from the dust of the ground and breathed into his nostrils the breath of life, and the man became a living being. Now the LORD God had planted a garden.... The LORD God made all kinds of trees grow out of the ground—trees that were pleasing to the eye and good for food.

—Genesis 2:7–9

More than the food I've eaten in restaurants, I remember the food I've prepared with my own hands. I have a terrible habit of not using recipes. Sometimes my mother has to leave the kitchen when I'm cooking, because things get a little chaotic, and my lack of technique leaves a bit to be desired, but I really believe that every person should be able to feed themselves and the people they love. Preparing food and feeding people brings nourishment not only to our bodies but to our spirits. Feeding people is a way of loving them, and it is a way of honoring our own createdness and fragility.

When we stop to gather around the table and eat a meal made by someone's hands, we honor our bodies and the God who created them. And in that moment we acknowledge that even though life is fast and frantic, we're not machines and we do require nourishment, physically and otherwise.

MEALS CAN be so much more than just refueling stops. When we slow down to enjoy the food and the company and think about what we're doing, meals can nourish our spirits as well as our bodies.

FEEDING MUSICIANS

The trumpeters and musicians joined in unison to give praise and thanks to the LORD.

—2 Chronicles 5:13

I've been feeding musicians since I met Aaron nearly thirteen years ago, and I find them to be some of my favorite people to feed. Some, of course, absolutely live the stereotype of "starving artist," so I've gotten used to packing up every last bit of leftovers and sending them with skinny guitar players and drummers, feeling maternal, knowing it's likely I'll never see that container again. And musicians tend to be sense-oriented people, so they notice texture and smell and flavor—the most fun people to feed, of course.

I love that we have a steady stream of musicians in our home, a community of people who believe that art and creativity and soul really matter, that making something out of nothing and telling your story—through lyrics or essays or anything at all—is noble work.

Sometimes food is the end and sometimes it's a means to an end, and sometimes you don't know which it is until it happens. The food and the table and the laughter help to create sacred space, a place to give someone the gift of words. That's what some of the best nights are about—sacred space and words of love.

WHO ARE the people that you love to feed and create space for? What are the threads that link you into a community?

Curried Chicken Salad Tea Sandwiches

{ Adapted from *Southern Living* }

People love these sandwiches because they're an unexpected twist on chicken salad. The toppings totally make it, so be sure to do the coconut, almonds, and green onions—yum!

Calling them tea sandwiches makes them sound so fancy—they're perfect for a special event. But they're also great for everyday meals. For me, they make a plain old lunchtime so much better.

1 (8-ounce) package cream cheese, softened

2 tablespoons mango chutney

1 ½ teaspoons curry powder

¼ teaspoon salt

¼ teaspoon pepper

2 cups diced, cooked chicken

24 thin slices whole wheat baguette

½ cup chopped almonds, toasted

½ cup flaked coconut, toasted

¼ cup green onions, diced

» Mix together cream cheese, mango chutney, curry powder, salt and pepper until well combined. Fold in chicken.

» Spread a heaping tablespoon or so of chicken salad on each baguette slice, and top with a sprinkle of almond, coconut, and green onion.

PERMISSION TO BE TIRED

"Be still, and know that I am God."

—Psalm 46:10

A few years ago, I traveled and spoke quite frequently over a three-month period. As the weeks wore on, I found myself feeling frayed, tired, scraped away. The question I couldn't answer was what it looked like to take care of myself during that season of heavy travel. When I was home between trips, I cooked, threw parties, called/texted/e-mailed, read, went out for dinner, shopped. But I didn't really stop, listen, feel. When I did, it scared me a little.

I felt like my rough edges were showing all the time. I didn't like how my anger was flaring out like an automatic weapon at the smallest inconveniences. I was unbelievably productive, but even when I was tired, I was still consuming—wine, shows, magazines, books. I lost my ability to slow down.

When I'm hungry, lots of times what I want more than food is an external voice to say, "You've done enough. It's okay to be tired. You can take a break. I'll take care of you. I see how hard you're trying." The work I'm doing now is to speak those words for myself, to give myself permission to be tired, to be weak, to need.

WHAT ARE your signposts in your heart or mind or behavior that tell you it's time to rest? How easy or difficult is it for you to admit that you're tired? To take the rest you need?

GRAPPLING WITH OUR WORTHINESS

Whatever were gains to me I now consider loss for the sake of Christ. What is more, I consider everything a loss because of the surpassing worth of knowing Christ Jesus my Lord, for whose sake I have lost all things.

—Philippians 3:7–8

Sometimes I pretend that writing is very cut and dried. I'm a writer. He's a plumber, she's a teacher, I'm a writer. Everybody has a job. That's a way of distancing myself from the uncomfortable side of it: sharing your work is scary, and it's an invitation to grapple with your own worthiness.

If you're not careful, you'll hang your entire self-worth on getting published or getting a certain amount of page views. We might feel like failures if we don't get them. *But it's equally dangerous if you do get them.* Little by little it's easy to start needing them—the comments, the reader e-mails, the Amazon rating, the positive reviews, the Twitter mentions or the Facebook likes.

Remember why you started writing in the first place. You write because you have a story to tell, because you sense that you can find words for things that might matter to someone else, that might set them free, that will make them feel less alone, like they've made a friend, like they're not crazy, like they're not wrong just for being who they are. You write because you think it might matter to someone, the way other people's words mattered to you.

WHAT DO you hang your self-worth on? Does that ever get in the way of what you truly want to be doing, what you feel called to do?

MADE TO BE THE THINGS THAT HE IS

Then God said, "Let us make mankind in our image, in our likeness."

—Genesis 1:26

I was on iTunes making a playlist the other day, looking for inspiration anywhere I could find it, and as I scrolled through all the options, I felt like I hadn't heard of practically any of the bands. And I thought to myself, how many bands *are* there? How many bands does the world need?

Yikes. That's the wrong question, the worst ever, most art-killing question there is. So much of life, really, comes down to asking the wrong questions. This is the thing about art: it's not about market demand. It's not like trying to figure out if this town needs another grocery store or dry cleaner. The general world population will survive without one more stage production and one more gallery showing.

This is the thing, though: you might not. We create because we were made to create, having been made in the image of God, whose first role was Creator. He was and is a million different things, but in the beginning, he was a creator. We were made to be the things that he is: forgivers, redeemers, second chance-givers, truth-tellers, hope-bringers. And we were certainly, absolutely, made to be creators.

LET THE creativity within you bloom. You were made for it.

HENRY'S SONG

Be filled with the Spirit, speaking to one another with psalms, hymns, and songs
from the Spirit. Sing and make music from your heart to the Lord, always giving
thanks to God the Father for everything, in the name of our Lord Jesus Christ.

—Ephesians 5:18–20

When Henry was born, we brought music into the delivery room, and the song playing *just* after he was born was "Needle and Thread" by Sleeping at Last. It's about God and angels and hospitals and love, and in that moment, it became our song, Henry's song.

A few months later, Aaron and I went to a Sleeping at Last show, and when they played that song, we held hands, and I cried, and thought about our boy, the night he was born, and the rich and miraculous thing it is to be his mother. I wanted to tell the songwriter how deeply his song traveled through the most tender parts of our life.

I didn't tell him, but if I had, this is what I would have said: Thank you, and keep going. Please keep writing songs. We need the sounds and words and rhythms of hope and longing and beauty. We need the haunting twist of your voice. We need the poetry of your lyrics and the spirit and force of your sounds. We're desperate for great music, and there's never, ever enough.

WHAT DO you feel called to make in your life—whether art or social change or community? There are a million ways to express our God-given passions—what passions are you living out right now?

LESS

*"I am the true vine, and my Father is the gardener. He cuts off
every branch in me that bears no fruit, while every branch that does
bear fruit he prunes so that it will be even more fruitful."*

—John 15:1–2

One of my key words for this season is *less*—less everything. Our house is feeling a little cramped, so I'm on a "get rid of it" spree. I'm simplifying, clarifying my contributions to various teams and projects. I'm inching out of all sorts of things, redrawing the lines, making things smaller. And it feels so much better to live in an uncluttered mind. Less, less, less.

There's a season for more—frankly, most of my seasons are seasons of *more*. More meals, more music, more laughter, more playing, more people. More books, more flip-flops, more champagne. *More, more, more.*

But being a grown-up is stretching yourself into new ways of living, bending into new postures, training new muscle memory instead of slipping into the same old story.

My nature is *more*, but this season is *less*. Paring down to barer bones, making space, scraping away. We love big stories, ones that involve passports, mountains, and photo-ops. But sometimes being courageous means less, quieter, stiller, smaller.

Clearing away all the excess makes space for what needs to come to life.

IS THERE anything you need to clear away, in order to make room for something new to come to life?

LADYBUGS

There are different kinds of service, but the same Lord. There are different kinds
of working, but in all of them and in everyone it is the same God at work.

—1 Corinthians 12:5–6

I was good at working, good at the buzz and busyness of leading people and managing events and ideas. What made me good at it was my ability to hold so many things in my head, like a handful of ladybugs. And now my work, writing, is about letting all the bugs crawl away and being able to focus on a totally blank page, a totally empty hand.

I thought that my single tasks, caring for our baby and writing, both would make my world very small. What I have found is that they make my world impossibly big, that they open up something in my head and in my heart.

In my grandparents' house when I was small, there were crystals hung on fishing line over the kitchen sink. When the sun came through the glass in the mornings, the whole kitchen was filled with bright wiggling rainbows of light, and we were mesmerized by the beauty and magic of it. That's how it is now, like this tiny child and this blank screen have turned the living room into a wonderland, bouncing and brimming over unexpectedly with beauty and color and bands of light.

HAVE YOU ever made a change in your life that required a completely different set of skills? What did you learn from that transition?

TRICKS & DISCIPLINE

Two are better than one, because they have a good return for their
labor: If either of them falls down, one can help the other up.

—Ecclesiastes 4:9–10

I'm paying close attention to the change of seasons, because I need a change to move me forward, and I'll take anything I can get. Today I need to end a season of time wasting, fear, obsessive blog-reading, and totally non-essential Wikipedia research. First step: I met a friend at a coffee shop. I left the house a mess, choosing to believe that writing is, for this morning, more important than cleaning up toys. Writing is a mind game, and I'm not above some tricks to get me out of this terrible stuck place I've been for about six weeks.

As I write I'm sitting with my friend Margaret, a screenwriter. We're not talking, mostly, but we're doing the most important work one artist can do for another: we're keeping each other in the chair and off the internet. I can keep working if she can, and she can keep working if I can. Some days it all comes down to tricks and discipline.

Learn your tricks, find a friend, leave the dirty dishes in the sink for a while. Do the work, learn the skills, and make art, because of what the act of creation will create in you.

WE CAN help each other in so many ways—sometimes even just by sitting together. Who are the people in your life who help you get unstuck?

MADE TO CREATE

No discipline seems pleasant at the time, but painful. Later on, however, it produces a harvest of righteousness and peace for those who have been trained by it.

—Hebrews 12:11

If you were made to create, you won't feel whole and healthy and alive until you do. My husband is a pianist and songwriter, and you can set a timer by his need to play and create. If it's been too long, I can feel it in our house, like something gone bad in the refrigerator or a dead mouse in the walls. He was made to play, to sing, to create with sounds and notes and words, and when he doesn't, he's not himself.

I know there are some artists who create around the clock, who feel art coursing through their very veins, who can go without sleep and food and human interaction for days while they revel in the rich universe of their own minds. But I think those artists are very rare, or maybe that they're fibbing. For most of us, it's hard work, fraught with fear and self-consciousness, and it's much easier to make dinner or mow the lawn or reply to emails.

Get up. Create like you're training for a marathon, methodically, day by day. This is your chance to become what you believe deep in your secret heart you might be.

DISCIPLINE IS not antithetical to creativity; it's vital to it. What structures help you create well?

THE BIG MOMENT

"Whoever can be trusted with very little can also be trusted with much."

—Luke 16:10

I love movies about "The Big Moment"—the game or the performance or the wedding day or the record deal that changes everything. I always wanted a movie-worthy event. I believed that the rest of my life would fade into the background, and that my big moment would carry me through life like a lifeboat.

The Big Moment, unfortunately, is an urban myth. Some people have them when, say, they win the Heisman. But even that football player is living a life of more than that one moment. Life is a collection of a million tiny little moments and choices, like a handful of luminous pearls. Strung together, lined up through the days and the years, they make a life. It takes so much time, and so much work, and those beads and moments are so small, and so much less fabulous and dramatic than the movies.

The Heisman Trophy winner knows this. He knows that his big moment was not when they gave him the trophy. It was the thousand times he went to practice instead of going back to bed. It was the miles run on rainy days, the healthy meals when a burger sounded like heaven. That big moment represented and rested on a foundation of moments that had come before it.

EVERY DAY contains countless big moments. Walk through your day today looking for those moments, hunting for them, mining them like gold.

END OF DAY RITUAL

From the rising of the sun to the place where it sets, the name of the LORD is to be praised.

—Psalm 113:3

Working from home is wonderful in many ways, but there's no commute at the end of the day to let the mind unwind. I've had to create my own ritual to mark the end of the work day and the beginning of the family evening.

I close my laptop, and I go to the kitchen. The first step, always: set out the knife and the cutting board. I can feel my stress level sinking already, my shoulders climbing down from my neck little by little. A swirl of oil into a pan, and while it begins to shimmer and thin, a quick rough chop of an onion. By the time the onion is on its way and the vinaigrette is made, I can feel the tension of the day slipping off my shoulders. These moments are some of the sweetest of my day, moments that are about texture and heat, knife and aroma.

God made a world of extraordinary beauty, and sometimes the most important thing we can do is slow ourselves down enough to see it, hear it, smell it, taste it, enter into it. When I stand before the cutting board, knife in hand, it's just another way, really, of praying.

WHAT'S THE best moment of your day? What are your meaningful daily rituals or routines? How do you do mark the switch from work time to non-work time?

CHURCH GIRL

"But what about you?" he asked. "Who do you say I am?"

—**M a r k   8 : 2 9**

Growing up, I loved going to church until about halfway through high school, when I got tired of being a church girl, of being one of the only church girls in my group of friends at school, the only one on my pom squad, the only one at the party who never had to worry about taking a Breathalyzer. When I played Powder Puff football, I missed the day we chose nicknames for our jerseys, and my friends chose mine for me. All their names were thinly veiled drinking references or allusions to scandalous dating experiences. When I picked up my jersey, it said, "Church Lady."

I knew they loved me and that they knew I was more than a *Saturday Night Live* sketch, but it hurt me. I didn't want to be that person anymore. I was tired of being different, and underneath that, I wanted to know why it was worth being so different. I was different because that's the way I had grown up, and I needed to see if it was what I would have chosen on my own.

W H E N   D I D you begin to move from the faith legacy you were given to the one you're living now? In what ways is your faith different from your parents' faith? In what ways is it similar?

April

29

FIGHTING FOR SPACE

"The LORD does not look at the things people look at. People look at the outward appearance, but the LORD looks at the heart."

—1 Samuel 16:7

During my college years, all I could see about faith were the things that offended me, the things I couldn't connect with, the things that had embarrassed me in high school. But there was this tiny hope inside me, not like a flame, more like a lighter that's almost out of juice, misfiring, catching for just a second, this tiny hope that maybe there was a way of living this faith that I just hadn't found yet. I thought about God, even though I didn't talk about him. It wasn't really about God, for me. I didn't have big questions about theology. Essentially, I wanted to know if there was room in the Christian world for someone like me. Because it didn't always seem like there was.

There's a lot of pressure on pastors to coerce their kids into looking the part, or to distance themselves from kids whose mistakes reflect poorly on their churches. My parents did just the opposite: they flew across the country several times a year to be with me, to demonstrate that no matter how ferociously I fought for space in a world that felt like it had no room for me, they would be right next to me, helping me fight and helping me make peace.

IF YOU'RE on a spiritual journey right now, keep going! This is a sacred, valuable part of your story, and all of heaven is cheering you on. Pray a prayer of complete honesty today—admitting exactly where you are, asking for help to take the next step.

Monica's Goat Cheese Toasts

Monica is one of my college friends, and generally one of the most knowledgeable, competent people I know. She could teach you how to drive a stick shift, point you to a great hotel in London, remove a splinter without making you cry, give sage advice about marriage, and pass on a killer appetizer recipe. Everyone should have a friend like Monica.

I needed an appetizer for a Christmas party, feeling tired of all my old staples. Monica sent this one, and I've been making it ever since. It's easy and quick, but elegant, and easy to do in large quantities if necessary.

1 baguette

8 ounces goat cheese

¼ cup honey

½ cup chopped walnuts

1 tablespoon chopped fresh rosemary

» Preheat the oven to 350 degrees. Slice the baguette into ¼-inch diagonal slices. Spread goat cheese on each slice. Arrange on a rimmed baking sheet. Bake until edges are slightly golden and cheese is soft, about 10 minutes. While they're baking, warm the honey in a saucepan, and toast the nuts on a foil-covered rimmed baking sheet or in a dry pan on the stove. Arrange baguette slices on a platter, then drizzle with the honey, sprinkle the nuts, and finish with rosemary.

OUR BEST SELVES

The wise woman builds her house, but with her own
hands the foolish one tears hers down.

—Proverbs 14:1

Aaron and I are working hard to be healthy individuals—spiritually, emotionally, all of the above. A mentor of ours says that healthy marriages can only be made between two healthy people. To be perfectly honest, looking back, we've never had a sustained difficult season between us when we were both at our best personally. Another way to say it: personal pain or brokenness or struggle leads to pain and brokenness and struggle in our marriage.

We're learning that one of the best things we can do to build our marriage is to build our own healthy selves, whether that's making rest and sleep a priority, or seeing a counselor or spiritual director or meeting with a mentor, or going for a run or saying no to something.

When Aaron and I can bring our best selves to our partnership, the partnership thrives. Of course, the opposite is true: when all I bring is fear and fragments and exhaustion and anxiety, there's not a lot to build on. That's why I'm committed to bringing my best self to our marriage.

MARRIAGE IS like so many other things: we get out of it what we put into it. Married or not, what are you bringing to the people you love? What would it look like to bring your best self in this season?

MY JOURNEY BACK

I am laid low in the dust; preserve my life according to your word.

—Psalm 119:25

The journey back toward faith came in flashes and moments, and entirely through pain. I wanted to build my life on my own terms. I felt like having faith was like having training wheels on your bike, and I wanted to ride without those training wheels even if I fell. For a while, I loved it. I felt creative and smart and courageous.

And then everything fell apart, over the course of a year. I was heartbroken and confused and very much alone, and I started doing the craziest things. If you're a really sensible, stable person, and somebody breaks your heart, you might do something wild, like go out dancing and drinking all night, but that's what I did on normal days. So I dug out my Bible. I have no idea why, really. I sat alone on my bed on a Saturday afternoon with the light slanting through my window. I was a literature major, so my room was crammed with books, and underneath a tall stack of books on the windowsill, I found my Bible. I just held it. I don't think I even read it that day. I just held it on my lap with both hands, like it was a cat.

SOMETIMES WE just have to take the next step, even when it doesn't entirely make sense. What would the next step in your spiritual journey look like? What's keeping you from taking that step?

THE SUREST PLACE TO FIND HIM

By the word of the LORD the heavens were made, their starry host by the breath of his mouth. He gathers the waters of the sea into jars; he puts the deep into storehouses.

—Psalm 33:6–7

There was something inside me that was pushing me toward God, pushing me toward the church. And it was like learning to walk after an accident—my body recalling so much, feeling so familiar, but entirely new this time. I started going to church, but that didn't work right away, because when I went, I could still only hear the things that distanced me or the things that made me mad, the clichés and assumptions that had pushed me away in the first place.

I wanted to connect with God somehow, so I decided that I would go to the beach every night at sunset. It was the most sacred thing I could think to do. I wasn't ready yet for church, but I was ready for God, and I have always believed that the ocean is one of the surest places to find him. I started praying a little bit more honestly and listening a little bit more closely.

There was something inside me, some hopeful, small, faltering voice that said, "There's room for you." I don't know why, but I trusted that voice.

WHERE DO you go to connect with God? When was the last time you were in a space that made you feel connected to him or aware of him?

ON WRITING

Sing to him a new song; play skillfully, and shout for joy.

—Psalm 33:3

My friend Steve leads a junior high ministry. He asked me to come one night so that he could interview me. We talked about being a writer and what that's like, and after it was over, one girl came up to talk to me.

"I write, too." She said it like it was a confession or a secret. "Do you have any advice for me?"

"Thank you, and keep going," I said. "Thank you for writing, for taking the time and spirit and soul to write, because I *love* to read, and I'm so thankful to writers like you, for writing things for me to read. And keep going, even when people make you feel like it's not that important. It might be the most important thing you do. Keep going."

So to all the secret writers, late-night painters, would-be singers, lapsed and scared artists of every stripe, dig out your paintbrush, or your flute, or your dancing shoes. Pull out your camera or your computer or your pottery wheel. Create something particular and honest and beautiful, because we need it. I need it.

Thank you, and keep going.

DO YOU have a creative outlet? Or did you in the past? What would it look like for you to keep going? What would it be like for you to share it with someone?

ON FINDING YOUR OWN FAITH

Jacob replied, "I will not let you go unless you bless me."... Then
he blessed him there. So Jacob called the place Peniel, saying, "It is
because I saw God face to face, and yet my life was spared."

—Genesis 32:26, 29–30

Most people need a season of space, a time to take a step back and evaluate the spiritual context of their youth. I didn't go to church for a long season in college, and that space and freedom gave me the perspective I needed to find my own faith. But it's easy for a season of space to turn into several years without any kind of spiritual groundedness. And then you find yourself unable to locate that precious, faith-filled part of your heart and history, because it slowly disintegrated over months and years. Do whatever you have to do to connect with God in a way that feels authentic and truthful to you.

Stop every once in a while, sit down with your journal, and ask yourself some good questions like, *Am I proud of the life I'm living? What have I learned about God this year? What parts of my childhood faith am I leaving behind, and what parts am I choosing to keep with me for this leg of the journey? Do the people I'm spending time with give me life, or make me feel small? Is there any brokenness in my life that's keeping me from moving forward?*

WHAT HAS your journey been from the spiritual context of your youth to finding your own faith? Take some time to pull out your journal and reflect on where you are and what your faith journey has been like in recent seasons.

May

5

ONE PERFECT BLOOM

*As God's chosen people, holy and dearly loved, clothe yourselves with
compassion, kindness, humility, gentleness and patience.*

—Colossians 3:12

When something bad happens, when something falls apart, always, always
say something. Start with simple questions: How are you? What can I do?

In my experience, when things fall apart, you can never go wrong with
flowers and food, even when someone insists that there's nothing you can
do. I'd never come out and ask you to bring me a meal, but in one difficult
season, we ate my mother-in-law's potato thyme soup and Jessie's coconut
milk ice cream and September's chicken casserole for days on end, and we
were thankful every time we opened the fridge and didn't have to think,
our hearts and minds so full and troubled.

Flowers are always a good idea: new life in a vase. During a season of
great loss for us, friends sent a gardenia in a beautiful glazed celery-colored
pot. My track record with keeping plants alive is awful, but I tried my best,
and one morning, maybe two weeks later, I came around the corner and
there it was: one perfect bloom. I almost cried, with relief that I hadn't
killed it yet, and also with gratitude. From thousands of miles away, these
friends and their kindness reminded me that new life always follows death.

PRACTICAL EXPRESSIONS of love and sympathy
are always a good idea. Is there anyone in your life who needs to
be loved in a tangible way right now?

GOD'S LOVE MADE TANGIBLE

"The most important one," answered Jesus, "is this: 'Hear, O Israel: The Lord our God, the Lord is one. Love the Lord your God with all your heart and with all your soul and with all your mind and with all your strength.' The second is this: 'Love your neighbor as yourself.' There is no commandment greater than these."

—Mark 12:29–31

During college, I worked at a summer camp. At one end-of-term swim meet, the camper in my lane was getting tired. "You're doing great, Jessie," I yelled. "You can make it. Keep going." She panicked and swallowed a big gulp of water, so I jumped in. If she touched me, she would be disqualified, but she just needed someone close enough to keep her from getting scared again. I swam beside her, and I told her, "You're tough, Jessie, and you can make it. I'm right here, but you can make it." When we got to the end, she was tired, floppy, and teary, but she looked up at her mom and waved.

After the meet, Jessie's mom found me. "As a mom," she said, "all I wanted to do was run down the bleachers and jump in with my clothes on to finish that race with my daughter, and I'm so glad you did. Thank you for caring about my child the way I would have if I was right there."

That's what friendship looks like. Friendship is acting out God's love for people in tangible ways.

> **WHO HAS** acted out God's love in your life? Is there anyone close to you who's struggling, for whom you could jump in and show God's love in a tangible way?

ALWAYS SAY SOMETHING

Let your conversation be always full of grace, seasoned with
salt, so that you may know how to answer everyone.

—Colossians 4:6

When something bad happens, people say the wrong things so often. They say weird, hurtful things when they're trying to be nice. But it's much worse when people say nothing. When I lost my job, embarrassed and hurt and tender, I remember exactly who walked the other direction when they saw me at church and who walked toward me. The same was true with my miscarriages. I can tell you to this day what people said and, much more hurtfully, who said nothing at all.

Some people didn't know what to say, and they said just that: "I heard what happened, and I don't know what to say." That is a very good response. Some people said really helpful, really loving things. The point is this: always say something.

I know we're busy, and we forget sometimes. More than anything, we don't want to say the wrong thing. It's impolite, we've been told, to bring up nasty topics like loss and sadness. But if we don't bring it up, what are we left with? We talk about the easy things, the happy things, the weather, and then we leave one another totally alone with the diagnosis or the divorce papers.

SPEAK TO those who are suffering; don't leave them alone in their pain. Practice the sacred art of being present in pain, even when it feels scary or awkward.

STILL STANDING

As we have opportunity, let us do good to all people, especially to those who belong to the family of believers.

—Galatians 6:10

A man I've known all my life recently lost his job—his job at the church where my husband leads worship and my dad is a pastor. I was at the drugstore buying printer cartridges and suntan lotion, without makeup and in my pajamas. He didn't see me. I thought about leaving him alone, letting him shop in peace and not have to face me unexpectedly, one more person from church, one more person to explain it to.

Instead I walked down his aisle and said hello. After we talked about our families, I told him that I'd heard about his job, and that I was so sorry. I asked how he was doing. I told him that I'd been through something similar a few years ago, and that I might understand some of the feelings he was feeling. He said it was good to hear from someone who'd been through a similar thing and was still standing. We talked about what's next for him.

I didn't say anything profound. But I said something. I said something as a way of being thankful to the people who said something to me when I needed it, because I remember how much it mattered to me.

WHEN YOU'RE handed a chance to encourage someone, do it. Pray for a moment about who in your life might need your words or presence today.

May
9

A GIFT TO BE ASKED

You are no longer foreigners and strangers, but fellow citizens
with God's people and also members of his household.

—Ephesians 2:19

When you're mourning, when something terrible has happened, it's on your mind and right at the top of your heart all the time. It's genuinely shocking that the sun is still shining and people are still chattering away on *Good Morning America*. Your world has changed, utterly, and it feels incomprehensible that the bus still comes and people on the highway just drive along as if nothing's happened. When you're in that place, it's a gift to be asked how you're doing, and most of the time the answer comes tumbling out, like water over a broken dam, because someone finally asked, finally offered to carry what feels like an unbearable load with you.

We hadn't known our friends Darren and Brandy for very long when they asked about the church we left and the jobs we left. I started with the short version, not wanting to bore them, wanting to move on quickly to a lighter topic. Then Brandy said, "We actually want to hear the whole story. We want to understand who you are because of that season." I'd never bring that season up, but it's part of our history, and it meant something to me that they wanted to understand it.

A HEAVY load of grief can be shared by talking about it. Next time you encounter someone who's mourning, listen with great sensitivity, knowing that listening itself is a sacred act.

OUR PAST BRINGS US TO OUR FUTURE

"I will repay you for the years the locusts have eaten."

—Joel 2:25

I believe in a very deep way that our past is what brings us to our future. I understand the temptation to draw an angry X through a whole season or a whole town or a whole relationship, to crumple it up and throw it away, to get it as far away as possible from a new life, a new future. In my worst moments, I want to slam the door on the hard parts of our life in Grand Rapids. Deadbolt it, forget it, move forward, happier without it. But I don't want to lose six years of my own history behind a slammed door.

These days I'm walking over and retrieving those years from the trash, erasing the X, unlocking the door. It's the only way that darkness turns to light. I'm mining through, searching for light, and the more I look, the more I find all sorts of things Grand Rapids gave me. I see moments of heartbreak that led to honesty about myself I wouldn't have been able to get to any other way. I am thankful for what I learned, what I became, what God gave me and what God took away during that season.

WHAT HAVE the hard, dark seasons of your life yielded in light and insight and growth and gifts? Have you sifted through those times, looking for those gifts? Ask God to bring light out of that darkness.

WHY WE WRITE

Shout for joy to the LORD, all the earth.

—Psalm 100:1

A writer friend came over yesterday. She's written a novel. She brought over a fat, beautiful binder full of story, and I can't wait to read it. We talked about publication and agents and sharing your work, about marketing and the internet and a million other things. And we talked about why we write.

You know those conversations when you think you're helping someone, sharing from your vast well of knowledge, only to realize that this person is actually instructing you, reminding you of something fundamental that you've forgotten?

My friend sat across the table from me, and it seemed like she could have combusted into flames, burning with sheer, clean passion about this story. After she left, I realized that some days I forget why we write, and she reminded me.

I write because other writers' words changed my life a million and one ways, and I want to be a part of that. I began writing because there were things I wanted to say with so much urgency and soul I would have climbed a tower and shouted them, would have written them in skywriting, would have spelled them out in grains of rice if I had to.

HAVE YOU ever had a conversation like that, when someone you're helping ends up reminding you of something basic and important that you've forgotten?

A BIG BOY & A BABY BOY

His mother treasured all these things in her heart. And Jesus grew
in wisdom and stature, and in favor with God and man.

—Luke 2:51–52

With your first baby, or at least with our first baby, you're so excited for them to get big! Big! Big! You want them to do things, to become their big, grown-up selves, to show you that they're geniuses, precocious in every way. But I want to keep Mac tiny. I want him to be my baby forever. I totally might be one of those moms who carries a four-year-old in a BabyBjörn, legs dangling past my knees. I'll keep him in footie sleepers until he's twelve, cut his meat until he has a driver's license. Stay a baby, darling.

I feel like our boys are the perfect ages right now—a big boy and a baby boy. I don't need Mac to get big; I already have a lovely, stinky, adventurous, chatty big boy. That position's been filled, and what I need is for Mac to stay my baby—my tiny, snuggly, smiling baby boy.

But this is perhaps the heart of parenting: despite my aching, desperate baby-love, it's my job to help him into being a big boy. It's my job, my honor, to walk him, quite literally, from baby to toddler to boy to man.

IF YOU have children, what has it been like for you to watch them grow from one stage to another? What stages are you looking forward to most? What are you looking forward to in the stages yet to come?

WHAT I NEED TO LIVE WELL

He will cover you with his feathers, and under his wings you will find refuge.

—Psalm 91:4

I'm in a season that's kind of bonkers. I have a busy calendar, but more than that, I have a lot to think through, get right, get written, create, and communicate. And I'm going into it a little bit fried—quick to tears, waking up in the night, ragged and rough-edged. So this morning I asked myself what I need to live well through this season. What needs to be added to the calendar? What needs to be shifted? What choices will help me? What will only make things harder?

I made a plan for this next month. Then I closed my computer, and I got a massage, complete with candles and ylang ylang essential oils for relaxation.

My impulse is always toward work, pushing, guilt, rushing. But what restores me, what allows me to interact well with my family, what allows me to get good writing done, is almost always the opposite. And I'm finding that when I practice things like rest, grace, peace, prayer, self-care and slowness, the work gets done just the same. Well, just the same except less crying and less apologizing to my family. I'll take it.

SO OFTEN, our inclinations run counter to what we truly need. When your stress level starts to rise, what are your impulses? What have you found that helps you the most?

FUTURE FACES

He said to them, "Let the little children come to me, and do not hinder
them, for the kingdom of God belongs to such as these."
—Mark 10:14

There's a photo of me on the wall in my parents' house, one of my senior pictures. I picked two I liked, and my mom picked one I thought was weird— my expression was veiled, like I knew a secret, and I didn't look like myself, I didn't think. I liked the ones that were broad smiles, straightforward, happy-looking. But my mom insisted on this other one because she said she had a sense, when she looked at it, of the woman I'd become in the future. She was right. That photo looks strangely like me now, twice the age as when it was taken, and the ones I liked are time capsules of a moment that came and passed.

I see flashes of Henry's future face all the time in him, partially because he looks so much like me and like my dad. And because he's on the tight-rope walk of little boy and big boy. Yesterday at his kindergarten screening I saw both of them—the little boy and the big—in alternating moments. He was shy and proud; he was uncertain and full of swagger. He was little and he was big, right in the same day, in the same moments.

HAVE YOU seen flashes of their future faces in your own children? How does that feel to you? Take a few moments to pray for their future.

THE BOY INSIDE THE BABY

Then Jacob called for his sons and said: "Gather around so I can tell
you what will happen to you in days to come."...All these are the
twelve tribes of Israel, and this is what their father said to them when
he blessed them, giving each the blessing appropriate to him.

—Genesis 49:1, 28

It's our job to let our children grow up, to let them become big and smart and grown-up, but it's so tempting to keep them little forever, or at least to try. These six months have been the blink of an eye, the season I'd longed for, some of the sweetest months of my life. There's nothing like a first baby, but the second time around has a loveliness all its own, because you know what's coming—you know that this baby, this tiny, odd wild animal will grow into a person with words and ideas and personality.

It's like Michelangelo chipping the block of stone to free the sculpture inside: the grown-up boy is in there, furled tightly like a bud on a branch, unfolding ever so slowly and then sometimes all at once. Now that I know Henry the five-year-old, I can see evidence of this boy all the way back, in his earliest moments: strong, imaginative, full of energy. And so I peer into Mac's little face: Who will you be? What clues are you leaving us even now about the boy inside all that baby?

HOW HAVE you seen the unfolding of a child's personality, either your own son or daughter or another child close to you? What clues did they give about who they were becoming?

May
16

THE SACRED WORK OF MOTHERING

A kindhearted woman gains honor.

—Proverbs 11:16

There are a thousand things I learned from my mother. I learned that your world will never be small if you love to read, because you can be anyone, anywhere, at any period in history. My mom taught me that age is something to celebrate and not something to fear, and when Henry was born, she taught me how to rock a newborn to sleep.

Almost every woman mothers, in one way or another. I used to think it was an all-at-once thing, that you go to the hospital a woman and come out a mother, like going through a car wash with a dirty car and coming out with a clean one.

Now that I am a mother, it is clear to me that I have been mothered by a whole tribe of women, some who had children of their own, and some who didn't. I thank God for each one of them, and thank them for mothering me when I needed it, and for giving me such a rich variety of images for what it means to be a mother.

When any of us mother—when we listen, nurture, nourish, protect—we're doing sacred work.

WHAT DID you learn from your mother? Were you mothered by other woman as well? What kind of images did they give you for what it means to be a mother?

A LITTLE HELP

*Command them to do good, to be rich in good deeds,
and to be generous and willing to share.*

—1 Timothy 6:18

I need older, more experienced moms to help me. I am so deeply happy to be back in the same town as my mother and my mother-in-law, but for the first two years of Henry's life, I loitered in the baby section at Target, trying to make eye contact with strangers. I'd start with something obvious, like "Oh, do you use those bottles? Are those good bottles?" If they answered with even remote friendliness, I'd push my luck: "What do you think about sleep schedules, just while I have you here. And you know, what do you think about public versus private education and which brand of car seat do you prefer and will I ever feel normal again?"

If you're a mom, and you've been through this drill before, those of us who are still in the day to day of very hands-on parenting really need your help. If you see someone like me in the baby aisle at Target or at church or in your neighborhood, we really are every bit as desperate as we look, and we could use some help. And a nap. And a shower. But mostly, just a little help.

DO YOU remember being desperate for help—as a new mother, or perhaps in some other overwhelming situation? Who came alongside you in that season? Is there anyone you know who needs help in this season?

GRACE FOR MOMS

Let us therefore make every effort to do what leads to peace and to mutual edification.

—**Romans 14:19**

Let's think about grace—grace from a God who loves us and values us and picks us up every time we fall, with just exactly the same love and tenderness you feel when you pick up your kids after they've fallen. Let's think about grace from a God who loves our sons and daughters even more than we do. And let's think about the grace we show one another when we finally drop the comparisons and the catalog images and really walk with one another, on the good days and the bad days. Let's think about honesty and helping and telling our stories. Let's give each other a break and a little help and some soft places to land.

If you're a mom, what you do is nurture and protect and give grace. You do it all the time, and it's very important, because it reminds us, in daily, tangible ways how God nurtures and protects and gives grace. And maybe today the one who really needs that nurturing and protection and grace is you.

IF YOU'RE a mom, are there other moms in your life who have shown you grace? Are there ways that you can show grace to moms that you know?

ON COMPARING

*Do not let any unwholesome talk come out of your mouths, but only what is helpful
for building others up according to their needs, that it may benefit those who listen.*

—Ephesians 4:29

One of the most important things I've learned about mothering was from my friend Nancy. She told me that when you compare yourself to another person, you always lose, and at the same time the other person always loses, too. Each of us has been created by the hands of a holy God, and our stories and the twists and turns of our lives, the things that are hard for us, and the things that come naturally, are as unique to us as our own fingerprints. She told me that one way to ensure a miserable life is to constantly measure your own life by the lives of the people around you.

We even do this with pregnancy sometimes. Everyone wants to talk about how much weight you gained, in comparison to how much weight they gained. In what other possible scenario is this an appropriate topic of conversation? I think that the people who ask are really just looking for an opportunity to brag about how little weight they gained. You just tell every pregnant woman you see that she's glowing, even if she's the size of a Volkswagen, and leave it at that. Especially in a season so precious and hormone-crazed, let's encourage one another toward grace and compassion.

> **DO YOU** ever find yourself comparing your life to someone else's? Take some time to thank God for the way that he created you, and for the ways that your life history has shaped you.

OLD STORIES

Now the Lord is the Spirit, and where the Spirit of the Lord is, there is freedom. And we all, who with unveiled faces contemplate the Lord's glory, are being transformed into his image with ever-increasing glory, which comes from the Lord, who is the Spirit.

—2 Corinthians 3:17–18

Someone described me recently as "a confident, outgoing mom and a successful writer." I looked around for who they could possibly be talking about.

No matter what happens to me and how I change, in many ways I'm still telling a very old story of who I am. I think I might not be the only one.

A friend's mom came to town this weekend. She's great and difficult, both, and my friend was debriefing the visit with us the next day. Someone asked, "How does your husband deal with some of your mom's rough edges?" And she said, "Well, what's helpful is that he doesn't automatically turn into his twelve-year-old self when my mom's around. But I still do."

So true, right? There are people and situations that take us back to old stories, and even though we're moms now, not children, or even though we're business owners now, not adolescents, we find ourselves acting out stories that haven't been true for a long time, or stories that were never true to begin with.

> **WHEN WAS** the last time you found yourself acting out an old story that is no longer true (or maybe never was)? Use that experience to help you reflect on what is true about you today.

CHANGING THE STORY

Let the redeemed of the LORD tell their story—those he redeemed from the hand of the foe, those he gathered from the lands, from east and west, from north and south.

—Psalm 107:2–3

When I was growing up, I was smart and I was overweight. I was the unattractive person in an attractive family, but my mind was quick—it was easy for me to remember things, and it was easy for me to be funny. So that's what I became—everyone's chubby, funny friend. I was easy to be around, agreeable, capable. I knew how to make other people feel comfortable, how to draw them out, how to tell self-deprecating stories about myself.

What that story really says is, *Just be friendly and pleasant. Make a joke. Don't worry about really achieving anything, or doing anything hard, or being great in any way. You are a sidekick, a wing-man, a supporting character in someone else's story. You are a punch line.*

That old story isn't helping me anymore, so I'm writing a new story. I work hard, and I've developed my skills as a writer and speaker. I might have more to contribute than I thought, and being funny and pleasant might not be the highest things to aspire to any longer.

Even as I write these words, I can feel myself sitting taller, squaring my shoulders, growing up.

I'm changing the story.

WHAT IS the story that you're living by? Is it still true and helpful in your life today?

THE KEY

Whoever refreshes others will be refreshed.

—Proverbs 11:25

My friend Annette and I met our freshman year in college. She was funny and fun, a strong, intuitive, wise person whose words carried serious weight with me, just as they do now.

We always said that sometime we wanted to live in the same town, and one day, against all odds, Annette and her husband, Andrew, and their ninety-five pound dog, Sydney, moved to our town.

While they looked for a house, they lived with us. For two months, the four of us and the dog tripped over each other and laughed and told stories and talked about how hard it is to move. The day they moved into their new house, they left before we were up, and when I went downstairs there was a card from them. When I opened the card, a key slid out, and I started to cry, because this special, crazy season was over, and they were giving back our key. But it wasn't our house key. It was their new house key. The card said, "You are as much a part of our home as we have been a part of yours."

The closer you get to someone, the more power that friendship has to make your life bigger and richer.

FRIENDSHIP IS one of those gifts from God that just gets better and better the more it is enjoyed. Picture the faces of your friends, and thank God for everything they bring to your life.

THE CLOSER YOU GET

*Jonathan said to David, "Go in peace, for we have sworn friendship with
each other in the name of the LORD, saying, 'The LORD is witness between you
and me, and between your descendants and my descendants forever.'"*

—1 Samuel 20:42

I didn't always know how to open myself deeply. Moving to Grand Rapids,
a town that was tricky for me for all sorts of reasons, the fear and the
loneliness snapped my heart shut like a drum. Then Annette and Andrew
moved across the country and into our neighborhood and day by day,
phone call by phone call, breakfast by breakfast, Annette taught me that
the closer you get, the closer you get. When you allow someone past all the
doors you were taught to keep closed, what you find is a kind of friendship I didn't even have a category for. I've spent most of my life holding my
breath and hoping that when people get close enough they won't leave, and
fearing that it's a matter of time before they figure me out and go.

And every time I told Annette the truth, or asked for something difficult, or opened a scary conversation, when I thought she would back away,
she walked forward. And by walking forward, she changed me, and now,
everywhere I go, everywhere life takes me, I'll be looking for this, for this
kind of friendship that my dear friend Annette taught me.

WHAT ARE your fears, expectations, and hopes about
friendship? How have they changed over the years? Have you
been changed by certain friendships? How so?

GET THERE

Do not forsake your friend or a friend of your family.

—Proverbs 27:10

If you're lucky enough to have a group of close friends that you connect with deeply, who are in your same season of life, all right in your very own town, I hope that you soak it up, that you lie around in each other's back-yards every Saturday afternoon or stay up late on one another's porches three nights a week. But if you're like me and those faces are far away, get a weekend on the calendar and get there.

Share your life with the people you love, even if it means saving up for a ticket and going without a few things for a while to make it work. There are enough long lonely days of the same old thing, and if you let enough years pass and you let the routine steamroll your life, you'll wake up one day, isolated and weary, and wonder what happened to all those old friends. You'll wonder why all you share is Christmas cards, and why life feels lonely and bone-dry. We were made to live connected and close, as close as my college girlfriends and I were for a few days in California, holding one another's babies, taking turns stirring whatever's on the stove.

THERE IS no substitute for time spent together, face-to-face in the same place. How are you taking time to enjoy and nurture your relationships with friends nearby? When do you see those friends who live far away?

Spicy Peanut Noodles

I can't get enough of these, and I have a jar of this sriracha-spiked peanut sauce in my refrigerator basically all the time. Feel free to nudge it in the salad direction: shredded carrots and cabbage, cucumbers cut into sticks, slivers of red pepper. Adding a handful of roasted shredded chicken makes it a meal.

· ·

1 cup crunchy peanut butter

1 tablespoon sriracha

juice of one lime

1 teaspoon soy sauce

1 teaspoon brown sugar

½ cup hot water

1 pound spaghetti, cooked

½ cup crushed peanuts

3 tablespoons black sesame seeds

½ cup chopped cilantro

4 scallions, thinly sliced

· ·

» Combine peanut butter, sriracha, lime juice, soy sauce, and brown sugar. Stir in hot water to thin the sauce.

» Toss the sauce with the cooked spaghetti. Garnish with crushed peanuts, black sesame seeds, cilantro, and scallions. Serve immediately or chill in the the refrigerator until ready to serve.

THE HOME TEAM

Many claim to have unfailing love, but a faithful person who can find?

—**P r o v e r b s 2 0 : 6**

Lately, I've been working on my commitment to the home team. Everybody has a home team: it's the people you call when you get a flat tire or when something terrible happens. It's the people who, near or far, know everything that's wrong with you and love you anyway.

There are two reasons you need to know who your home team is. First, you need to know who they are because they need you. These are the people you visit in the hospital no matter what. These are the ones who tell you their secrets, who get themselves a glass of water without asking when they're at your house. These are the people who cry when you cry. These are your people, your middle-of-the-night, no-matter-what people.

The second reason you need to know who your home team is, is because then you know who your home team is not. Everyone else is everyone else. Each of us have a finite amount of time and energy. You can give yours to your home team. Or you can spend it haphazardly on an odd collection of people who need something from you because you don't want to say no to them.

WHO IS on your home team? How much of your time and energy is going to them, versus a random assortment of other people?

A LIMITED AMOUNT

I, wisdom, dwell together with prudence; I possess knowledge and discretion.

—Proverbs 8:12

It's so easy to give everything we have to the first people who ask, or the people who ask the most often, or the people who are always in crisis. I like solving problems, saving the day, swooping in with the right dress or the right words or the right solution. Because of this, I've been known to offer the use of my wedding dress to people I meet on airplanes, to throw parties in honor of people I barely know, and to accept full emotional and psychological responsibility for people I only know from Facebook. These are not my best choices, but I'm working on it.

There is in fact a limited amount of time, caring, and energy. I'm generally the last to admit this. I prefer to believe that I am the warrior queen of unlimited relational energy, and that a full calendar is no match for my capacity and skills. Right about then, I get the flu. Or my son does. Or I start crying in the car and can't figure out why. It's usually because I've given more than I should to people who aren't a part of my daily world. They're not the ones who need it.

IT FEELS good to say yes, to act on every generous impulse. It's less fun to be mindful of our human limitations. What does it look like when you overspend your time, caring, or energy? Ask God to help you become a wise steward of these resources he's given you.

OVER & OVER

Let the wise listen and add to their learning, and let the discerning get guidance.

—Proverbs 1:5

In my first job out of college, one of the people I worked with drove me crazy. He pushed my buttons and hurt my feelings and twisted my words, and I couldn't get past it. After months and months, my genius boss Greg said, "You're not crazy. You're not making this stuff up. He's a difficult person to work with." I exhaled, vindicated, feeling like a deeply discerning person. But then Greg said, "You're not wrong about this guy, but why does it bother you so much? Why does his way of being make you so crazy?"

Then he added: "It's okay if you don't know now. You'll have plenty of chances to figure it out, because when someone or something taps into your deep emotion like that, God will keep sending that same kind of person or situation into your life over and over until you choose to do the work of understanding it and growing past it."

It's absolutely true. You can learn it the first time, or you'll find that same situation staring you in the face over and over again. There it is, an opportunity to grow, to transcend and transform, to break that terrible pattern.

WHEN SOMETHING provokes in us a reaction that's out of proportion, that's often a sign there's a lesson for us to learn and a way for us to grow. Is there a person or situation in your life right now that might represent an opportunity to grow?

BEAUTY AFTER BROKENNESS

*Dear friends, now we are children of God, and what we will be
has not yet been made known. But we know that when Christ
appears, we shall be like him, for we shall see him as he is.*

—1 John 3:2

I'm more certain than ever that prayer is at the heart of transformation. And also that God's will has a lot more to do with inviting us to become more than we previously have been than about getting us to one very specific destination.

I'm beginning slowly to recognize my own fears—why some changes are so scary for me, how the crazy-meter ratchets up little by little. I notice these things now and pay attention. When we pay attention and when we grow, we become freer, more flexible, more faithful, more able to ask for help. We become less fearful, more comfortable with the idea of life as a beautiful mess.

You want me to say that when you grow, finally, all the changes will stop, but they don't. There will always be another one, another opportunity to grow, to shed your skin, to rise like a phoenix from the ashes, to break out of your cocoon like a perfect new butterfly.

The clichés and the references to mythology and classic literature fit, because we're all trying to emerge new from the pain, beautiful after the brokenness, to live out that central image of Christianity: life after death.

AS LONG as we are growing, we have cycles of change ahead of us—with the possibility of becoming more than we were before.

ACCUMULATING SHADOWS

Just as you share in our sufferings, so also you share in our comfort.

—2 Corinthians 1:7

If you stay anywhere long enough, it will start to accumulate some shadows. And those shadows make it no less beautiful. It makes it something like home. It anchors you there in ways that a steady diet of pleasantness never will. I remember sitting on the steps of the blue house in South Haven when a friend told me her marriage was ending. One year, when a friend and her kids arrived, while our kids yelped and hugged, my friend cried with me on the porch, caught off guard by the memory of announcing her pregnancy the year before, only to have it end in miscarriage weeks later.

One summer I sat with a friend while she sobbed about a breakup, and on that same porch, I had one of the hardest conversations of my life with another friend. We looked out at the street, not at each other, sitting shoulder to shoulder as I told her that I thought her drinking had gone too far, and that something big had to change. Life unfolding, rich and broken and beautiful and heartbreaking, in that town, under those trees, along that stretch of beach, on that porch.

IT'S EASY to long for nothing but good news and carefree days, but a full life includes the broken and dark and difficult parts, too. Thank God for walking with you in the seasons of heartbreak.

TENDER STORIES

May the favor of the Lord our God rest on us; establish the work of our hands for us—yes, establish the work of our hands.

—Psalm 90:17

One of the true hazards in writing is that you yearn to write deeply honest things that rise up from lessons learned the hard way...and then you have to learn those lessons the hard way. I had written a chapter on jealousy, and after I looked at it for a while, it seemed sort of flat and cartoon-y. I prayed for a new way to write that chapter, an incisive and honest way to talk about being jealous. And not a week later, wouldn't you know it, at dinner with some friends, I found out something about a mutual friend of ours that absolutely annihilated me with jealousy. It was a thousand straws that broke a thousand camels' backs, and I was tumbling around and around with these vicious, terrible jealous feelings, like I was in the spin cycle with a box of rocks. That's the last time I pray for a good chapter on anything, except being gorgeous or winning the lottery or something. You pray for wonderful, honest, gritty, tender stories to write, but then you have to live through them.

IS THERE anything in your life that you've been talking about, but not yet living on a deep level? What step could you take today toward practicing, not just talking?

UNDER THE GLASSY SURFACE

"You will seek me and find me when you seek me with all your heart."

—Jeremiah 29:13

What writing teaches me is that God is waiting to be found everywhere, in the darkest corners of our lives, the dead ends and bad neighborhoods we wake up in, and in the simplest, lightest, most singular and luminous moments. He's hiding, like a child, in quite obvious and visible places, because he wants to be found. The miracle is that he dwells in both. I knew he dwelt in the latter, the bright and beautiful, because I had been finding him there for years, in the small moments of beauty and hope that poke through the darkness of our days.

But lately I have been finding him not just under the darkness, but in it, right within the blackness and deadness of these days. I have found a strange beauty in the darkness, one I've never seen, a slower, subtler beauty, like how an old woman's skin is more telling and rich than a teenage girl's, how a storm can make you feel more deep emotion than a sunny day ever did. When I write, I find a whole new universe I never saw before, like being underwater for the first time, having never before seen what's under the glassy surface.

SPEND A few moments thinking about God's presence. Are there times when you didn't feel it, but you now know he was there?

June

1

WEDDING PRESENT

Show me your face, let me hear your voice; for your voice is sweet, and your face is lovely.
—Song of Songs 2:14

A few times a year, I officiate a wedding. I usually meet with the bride and groom about a week before, and there are a few pieces of advice I always give. The first is that from this point on, nothing can get added to the wedding to-do list. Things can only be taken off the list—either because they're completed or abandoned. But nothing gets added—no last-minute project, no stroke of genius DIY you saw on Pinterest. If it's not already on the list, no matter how charming, adding it will only make you crazy.

And then I tell them that while *they* can add nothing to the list, I can, in fact, add two very important things to their list. First: a no-wedding-talk date. Second: rest, whatever that means—sleep, an unscheduled hour, a walk, a bath. They always look at me like I'm nuts. I can see them thinking, "We're up to our ears in seating charts and programs to assemble and family drama to mitigate, and you want us to go on a date and then take a nap?"

Actually, yes. Because what will make their wedding day *perfect* is not the flowers or the favors, but a bride and groom who are happy, connected, present.

WHETHER YOU'RE headed to your own wedding or to a neighborhood barbecue, coffee with a friend or dinner with your family, the most important thing to bring is a present heart.

PEOPLE CAN CHANGE

Do not withhold good from those to whom it is due, when it is in your
power to act. Do not say to your neighbor, "Come back tomorrow
and I'll give it to you"—when you already have it with you.

—Proverbs 3:27–28

I have long considered that there are two kinds of people: people who can run marathons and people who can't. And I was in the latter category. But when something makes you cry, it means something. Against my preferences, watching people cross marathon finish lines makes me cry. I finally said out loud, "Sometime I'm going to do that." I decided that in two years, I'd be ready. Then I got an e-mail from my friend Nate. Registration for the upcoming Chicago Marathon was open, he said. Was I still up for it?

I wrote a reply: No, not this year. *Next year.* As soon as I wrote it, I knew that would always be my answer: *next year, next year, next year.* I deleted those words and began again. *Yes,* I replied. *I'm signing up.* And I did.

I tend to believe the worst about myself—I could never do that, or I'll always be like this. But then I remember that day, that season. People can change. I can change. All it takes sometimes is paying attention to your tears, and ignoring that voice that tries to hypnotize us with, *next year, next year, next year.*

> **IS THERE** anything that inexplicably makes you cry? What small step could you take toward meeting a personal goal today?

SOMEDAY

All hard work brings a profit, but mere talk leads only to poverty.

—**P r o v e r b s   1 4 : 2 3**

Last Monday, I registered to run the Chicago Marathon with Team World Vision. I've been talking about this for a long time, and there are a million reasons that make now the right time. Because I want to get over my fear. Because I believe that discipline and fearlessness in one area can spill over into all sorts of other areas, and I could use a whole lot more of both in this season. Because it's been a hard winter and spring, and sometimes you have to do something a little bit radical to move yourself on to a new place. And because the cold air and the sound of my feet on the ground sometimes pound away the sadness a little bit, and I like that feeling.

Another reason: because I'm trying to remove the word "someday" from my vocabulary. I've always said I'll run a marathon someday, and then I make a plan—first this, then this, then after that, marathon. But my life looks so different than I thought it would this year. There's nothing standing in the way of me running the marathon this fall, instead of the next or the next or, honestly, never.

"SOMEDAY" CAN be a seductive word. It carries intent and promise, that certain things will eventually be part of our lives. But it also lets us off the hook. Is there anything in your life that's living in the distant cloud of "someday"? What's keeping you from moving and working toward it now?

RUNNING & TALKING

You discern my going out and my lying down; you are familiar with all my ways. Before a word is on my tongue you, LORD, know it completely.

—Psalm 139:3–4

When I began training for the Chicago Marathon, the runners kind of freaked me out. Every time someone mentioned a ten- or twenty-mile run with glee and anticipation, my stomach dropped. Then they'd say something like, *If you can get to the starting line, you can get to the finish line.* That didn't seem remotely true and didn't help at all.

But I went back week after week. I began to understand what drove the acronyms and slogans and the almost violent positivity: you need that kind of enthusiasm to get you up that early, to prod you along those miles.

Every Saturday, the Team World Vision runners showed up under the tender, brightening sky, nervous and sleepy. We ran and talked and ran and talked. It's amazing what you'll say out loud at mile 15, when no one's looking you in the eye. You talk about chafing and rashes and digestive abnormalities, and then someone tells the story of how she got sober, or what it was like when his mother died. It's all out there, with nothing but the drumbeat of your feet and the rhythm of your ragged breath and the green of the trees on the path.

HAVE YOU ever run a marathon, or fulfilled some other physical goal that pushed you beyond what you had thought you could do? What did you learn from that process?

A NEW RESPECT FOR MY BODY

I do not run like someone running aimlessly; I do not fight like a boxer beating the air.

—1 Corinthians 9:26

I've always had the sense that something fundamental between my body and my soul was disconnected, like a very important wire got cut at some point, like my body is off on its own, doing its own thing, lazy and undependable. But when I signed up to run the Chicago Marathon, I put on my running shoes—shoes that had been to the coffee shop and the farmers market but had never been running—and shuffled around our neighborhood.

Training began in April, and our first group run was a three-mile timed run. Three miles was the upper edge of my limit. But over the months, my body got stronger and the miles got easier. At one point a friend said, "Whoa, Shauna, you have runner's calves." It may have been the best day of my life. Each week of the summer the miles got longer—ten miles, sixteen miles, twenty miles. Each week I was surprised at what my body could do. In the same way that giving birth had connected me to my body in a new and meaningful way, training for the marathon gave me a new respect for my body, for how strong and powerful it was.

HOW DO you feel about your body? Do you feel connected to it? Do you feel respect for it? How do you nurture it? How do you challenge it?

Summer Salad

I've been making this twice a week this summer, partially because I can buy every bit of it at the farmer's market, save the feta, salt, and pepper. For years I've grilled or boiled the corn, but these days I love salads with raw corn, sweet and crunchy.

6 ears of corn, cut from ears, raw

2 cucumbers, diced

4 peppers, red, yellow, or orange, diced

1 pint grape tomatoes, halved

1 bunch fresh dill, chopped

1 bunch fresh basil, chopped

8 ounces feta, crumbled

salt & pepper to taste

» Combine all ingredients and adjust the herbs and salt and pepper to taste. This gets even better after a couple hours, so I sometimes do the chopping while everyone's eating breakfast, and then by dinner it's perfect—full of flavor and crunch, sharp from the feta, sweet from the corn, clean from the cucumber, bright from the herbs. This tastes just exactly like summer to me.

CLEAN, COOL WATER

"Come, you who are blessed by my Father; take your inheritance, the kingdom prepared for you since the creation of the world. For I was hungry and you gave me something to eat, I was thirsty and you gave me something to drink."

—Matthew 25:34–35

When I ran the Chicago Marathon, my friends and I all signed up to run with Team World Vision. Our family has sponsored a child through World Vision for years, and the money raised by Team World Vision runners buys wells and water purification systems for villages in Africa.

Sometimes as I ran, I prayed for the people who would benefit from clean water as a result of the money we were raising. I'm generally a terrible fund-raiser, and in most situations I'd just end up writing a check so I didn't have to go through the awkwardness of asking people for money. I had no trouble, though, asking for money on behalf of Team World Vision. I wrote letters and made phone calls, and as I ran, I prayed for mothers and fathers and children half a world away whose lives could change as a result of access to clean water. On the training runs, our coaches reminded us to stay hydrated and encouraged us to pray every time we opened our water bottles, to let the clean, cool water become a symbol of the reason we were running.

SO MANY people around the world lack a source of clean water altogether and are vulnerable to water-borne illnesses. How could you help with this global need?

CATCHING ON

Dear friends, let us love one another, for love comes from God.

—1 John 4:7

In all of my scrambling to do the right thing and be the right person, I miss some of the most important things I think God might be asking me to do. For the last several years, I have been too busy for interruptions. I work and work on behalf of a good cause, at the expense of all the things I would see if I slowed down enough to look around my life. I wanted to be productive and useful and focused, and I turned into someone who was frazzled and scattered, and who could not bear the emotional weight of her own life, let alone someone else's.

This week, listening to God and doing what it seemed like he was asking looked a lot like doing nothing, really. I changed plans and bought gifts and said prayers and made a little bed on the couch for my friend who needed a soft place for the night. There is nothing particularly noble or difficult about anything I did. I did the average things that needed to be done in the lives of the people around me. And I think I'm catching on to something that God wanted from me all along.

HAVE YOU ever been so caught up in a good cause that you lost sight of the people around you? Take a little time today to lay aside your agenda and listen for what God is asking of you.

THIS TINY MOMENT

If we love one another, God lives in us and his love is made complete in us.

—1 John 4:12

Today my friend Julie let me bring her dinner. Her husband, Doug, had two very scary seizures in the last two days, and a zillion tests and scans and appointments with neurologists. They had just come home from the hospital, and they were sitting on the front porch when I drove up, and Lilly, their three-year-old, was riding her big-girl bike on the sidewalk in her pink underpants. It was ninety-four degrees today, and they were exhausted.

Being with them made me think about the idea that everything is okay. That idea is cruel in its untruth. The bottom just falls out sometimes, and nobody is exempt. I can't take away the seizures or tell Lilly that it's never going to happen again, although I would if I could. But I can be there, and I can feed them, and I can listen to their stories, of funny things the doctors said, and the strange and infuriating things family members invariably say in tense situations. I can sit in silence in the heat and stillness of a sticky June night, knowing that everything is not okay, but that this tiny moment is.

ALTHOUGH WE can't make everything okay, we can show up and show love in the middle of whatever's going on. How have the people in your life been there for you when you needed them? Is there anyone who's going through a difficult time that you need to reach out to?

GOD'S PRESENCE

*Every good and perfect gift is from above, coming down from the Father
of the heavenly lights, who does not change like shifting shadows.*

—James 1:17

My friend Nancy is a nature person. To know her is to know that the created world—mountains, wildflowers, sunshine—is the tie that binds her to God, that demonstrates his presence to her in the deepest ways. For my dad, it's the water. The sounds and smells and rituals of life on the water bind him to God in ways that nothing else does. For my husband, Aaron, it's music. And for me, it's the table.

What makes me feel alive and connected to God's voice and spirit in this world is creating opportunities for the people I love to rest and connect and be fed at my table. I believe it's the way I was made, and I believe it matters. For many years, I didn't let it matter, for a whole constellation of reasons, but part of becoming yourself, in a deeply spiritual way, is finding the words to tell the truth about what it is you really love.

GOD IS endlessly creative in how he shares his presence with each of us. And the specific way he chooses to connect with you matters. What is that tie that binds you to God?

WARM & HEALING

You were once darkness, but now you are light in the Lord. Live as
children of light (for the fruit of the light consists in all goodness,
righteousness and truth) and find out what pleases the Lord.

—Ephesians 5:8–10

Some years ago, at the end of a green and windy June, we had one of those nights that I'm still thinking about. It was a scheduling nightmare, a plan that any sane person would have abandoned. But one of the cracked-up and crazy parts of me is the part that absolutely will not call off party plans. That Sunday night at the lake, our dinner guests were tired, coming bedraggled and late from all corners. Most of them had never met. No matter, I said.

We were tired, staring at unfamiliar faces, trying to remember names and make conversation. And then, just like it always does, food and wine and time around the table braided us together, and we started telling stories and jokes, laughter bubbling through.

That night was right in the middle of the hardest season Aaron and I had yet experienced, a long stretch of uncertainty and fear. It was an oasis, a port in the storm, a moment of levity and connection in the middle of a season that felt distinctly lonely and tangled. In a season of darkness, it was a burning flame, warm and healing.

THE DARKER the season, the smaller the act required to bring healing. What are the small acts of connection and tenderness that you've experienced in this season?

June

11

THE MIRACLES IN FRONT OF US

"At the beginning of creation God 'made them male and female.' 'For this
reason a man will leave his father and mother and be united to his wife, and
the two will become one flesh.' So they are no longer two, but one flesh."

—Mark 10:6–8

Of all the things I get to do, officiating weddings for people I love is my absolute favorite. When you officiate a wedding, you're right there in the moment of *before* and *after*, of single and married, of independent and "till death do us part." I believe in the way God knits two people together when they stand before him on their wedding day. Something sacred happens in that moment, something that will, with grace and intention and faith and hard work, build upon itself and grow in power and beauty and durability with each passing year.

It's easy, when your own world feels dark and fragmented, to become self-focused, only able to see the frustration and pain of your own life. However, life hands us opportunities at every turn to wake up from our own bad dreams and realize that really lovely things are happening all the time. Sometimes a wedding has put me back in the right direction, reminding me that it's not all about me, and that love matters more than almost anything.

HAS THERE ever been a time when you almost missed something extraordinary, caught up in your own anxiety or pain? How did you push yourself back into the present, out of your own head?

FEEDING BABIES & TELLING STORIES

A person finds joy in giving an apt reply—and how good is a timely word!
—**Proverbs 15:23**

When Henry was a baby, he and I flew to visit friends in California. There were four college girlfriends with three baby boys under eight months old in a two-bedroom house for three days.

We couldn't get all of us and the car seats in one car, so we walked everywhere with our strollers, to get ice cream and coffee and the best Chinese takeout I've ever had. One afternoon Kirsten roasted a chicken and some kale—crispy, almost nutty—and we sat on a blanket in the backyard in the sun, letting the boys roll around, telling the same college stories we've told and heard five hundred times. We rotated from the kitchen to the sunny backyard, to the front porch to the fluffy rug in the living room, feeding babies and telling stories.

We laid on the blanket under the lemon tree drinking Sancerre while the babies napped, and I realized why this kind of time together matters: because there are things you can't know, and questions you can't ask, and memories you can't recover via e-mail and voicemail. It was about being there to really see what's exactly the same and what's totally different about each one of us.

SOME WORDS are only spoken face-to-face. That's one reason time with friends from far away is so precious.

SCRAPS OF WISDOM

I myself am convinced, my brothers and sisters, that you yourselves are full of goodness, filled with knowledge and competent to instruct one another.

—Romans 15:14

When Henry and I spent a weekend in California with my college girl-friends and their babies, the conversations were so rich. In the same way that we helped each other figure out how to get the babies to sleep, and all threw in our opinions about a good marinade for skirt steak, we offered one another our stories and bits of advice, the scraps of wisdom and experience we've gathered up around ourselves along the way. We're not therapists or child development experts, but we're giving everything we can to our families, and really, the challenges are pretty similar. The solutions are, too: we found that almost every one of the rough spots we discussed under the trees could use an extra round of listening, a liberal dose of forgiveness, and a solid effort at empathy.

We talked, of course, a lot about parenting. A large part of parenting comes down to observing your actual little person, and shuffling through acres of advice to select the piece that meets your little one's need just perfectly. It all comes down to close observation, willingness to take advice, ability to try something new when all the old things have stopped working.

THERE IS much wisdom to be found in discussion with good-hearted friends. Who are the people in your life that guide you along the way?

June

14

THE NEWBORN FOG

"I will refresh the weary and satisfy the faint."

—Jeremiah 31:25

It's possible for motherhood, especially new motherhood, to be so entirely isolating. You live in the rarified world of your house with a tiny darling who doesn't talk, and you stumble through the days, one blending into the next, in yoga pants smeared with diaper cream, nursing and rocking, nursing and rocking. Your world changes utterly, but your friends' lives don't, necessarily. They love your new little one, but they either have older children and remember this season well, and are a little glad they're finished with it, or they don't have their own children and can't imagine it. In any case, you're the only one in the newborn fog. But for a weekend Henry and I spent in California with my college girlfriends and their babies, we weren't alone at all.

Because we had the time, because we could let conversations wind and unwind, because we could start them at dawn and pick them up again in the afternoon and add a few more thoughts in the evening, we circled down to the places you never get to when you just see one another at weddings, giving out funny sound bites over bites of cake.

THERE'S NOTHING like a gathering of close friends to refresh us and strengthen us. Who are the people who restore you most? Take a minute to thank God for them.

June

15

ON LOSING THE PLOT

When hard pressed, I cried to the Lord; he brought me into a spacious place.

—Psalm 118:5

I've lost the plot recently. I'm too busy, the to-do list is too long, and instead of putting on the brakes when I needed to, I pushed that idea away and committed to more and more things. Of course, it all looks so much worse when you're tired. I'm tired. I'm cry-when-I-stub-my-toe, entertain-sleep-fantasies kind of tired. That magnifies everything.

The one day this week that I have a sitter so I can plow through some long-overdue work, I scheduled to have the carpets cleaned. See? Evidence of having lost the plot. My husband laughed out loud and told me to cancel that immediately.

I'm trying again today, trying to give my energy to what's most important, not just what's right in front of me. And I'm reminding myself of the biggest thing: God made a gorgeous rich world, stuffed with glowing green trees and child cheeks and good friends. When I spin out into my own anxieties and frantic days, I miss out. It's all there, waiting to be seen, discovered, heard, entered into. And I'm determined not to miss it today.

DO YOU ever lose the plot in your life? What helps you to recover? Ask God what he wants you to see today.

THE OLDER-SISTER, TINKERBELL VOICE

The teaching of the wise is a fountain of life.

—Proverbs 13:14

My friend Kirsten is two years older than I am, but when we met she seemed impossibly older, in a good way, like an exotic, world-wise older sister with whom I would never catch up. She's the Technicolor version of me: blonder, louder, curvier, more creative, more fearless, more expressive. She's me, and then some. She's the me I would be if I could.

Even now, separated by a decade, marriages, babies, two thousand miles, she's the older-sister, Tinkerbell voice in my head. I find myself asking fairly often what Kirsten would do in a particular situation, because when I think about things the way she thinks about them, whatever I'm facing becomes a whole lot clearer. She has a particular resolve, a sense of self and groundedness that I don't always have. She's better at making the choices that work for her, regardless of how common or uncommon they are.

So many times in the years we've known each other, Kirsten has shown me what it means to make a life, to craft a way of living and being that works and makes life workable and sweet, and for every time, I'm thankful.

IF YOU find a friend who's wiser than you are and a few steps ahead of you on the path, it's a great gift to learn from her. Send a text or make a call today, thanking that friend. And take a minute to thank God for the mentors and guides he's placed along your path.

June
17

PATRON SAINT OF CHANGING YOUR LIFE

He is wooing you from the jaws of distress to a spacious place free from restriction, to the comfort of your table laden with choice food.

—Job 36:16

After my friend Kirsten and her husband bought a big fancy house with a big heavy mortgage, she said she felt like a grown-up—trapped in a job she didn't love to pay a mortgage for a home she didn't love.

They moved to Alameda, a beachy island across the bay, leaving the fancy house in the city still for sale. She said they were moving to save their lives and their marriage, and that the loss they took on the house was worth every penny, because it let them breathe again, live again.

Kirsten is my patron saint of changing your life, of not waiting for someone else to rearrange it for you, of not driving a good idea into the ground when it's clear it isn't working, of paying close attention to what you want and need and making it happen.

I thought of Kirsten when I finally said out loud, "This is what I want: I want to live near my family in a little house with lots of windows." Not rocket science, but for a girl who sometimes can't make a grocery list because I get so tangled up about what I want in life, a very big deal.

WHO HAS shown you how to handle change courageously, thoughtfully, proactively? How have you followed their example? Is there any area of your life in which you need to consider making a change?

Jennifer's Catbirds/Carnitas

Jennifer is a native Californian, which means she has strong feelings about things like carnitas. I asked for her recipe after a Cinco de Mayo party where her carnitas stole the show. We'd just had a conversation about the evils of auto-correct, and then she sent me her carnitas recipe, which auto-corrected to Catbirds. The name stuck, and in our little corner of the world, these will forever be "Jennifer's Catbirds."

1 (3½- to 4-pound) boneless pork butt, fat cap trimmed to ⅛-inch thick, cut into 2-inch chunks

1 teaspoon ground cumin

1 small onion, peeled and halved

2 bay leaves

1 teaspoon dried oregano

2 tablespoons juice from 1 lime

2 cups water or beer

1 medium orange, halved

1 tablespoon sweetened condensed milk

½ can Coca-Cola

tortillas

GARNISHES

1 jalapeño, minced

lime wedges

1 cup cilantro

1 cup minced white or red onion, pickled or fresh

1 cup thinly sliced radishes, pickled or fresh

sour cream

» Adjust oven rack to lower-middle position and preheat oven to 300 degrees. Combine pork, salt, pepper, cumin, onion, bay leaves, oregano, lime juice, and water or beer in large

Dutch oven (liquid should just barely cover meat). Juice orange into medium bowl and remove any seeds (you should have about ⅓ cup juice). Add juice and spent orange halves to pot. Add sweetened condensed milk and cola. Bring mixture to simmer over medium-high heat, stirring occasionally. Cover pot and transfer to oven. Cook until meat is soft and falls apart when prodded with fork, about 2 hours, flipping pieces of meat once about halfway through cooking.

» Remove pot from oven and turn oven to broil. Using slotted spoon, transfer pork to bowl; remove orange halves, onion, and bay leaves from cooking liquid and discard (do not skim fat from liquid). Place pot over high heat (use caution, as handles will be very hot) and simmer liquid, stirring frequently, until thick and syrupy (heat-safe spatula should leave wide trail when dragged through glaze), 8 to 12 minutes. You should have about 1 cup reduced liquid.

» Using 2 forks, pull each piece of pork in half. Fold in reduced liquid; season with salt and pepper to taste. Spread pork in even layer on wire rack set inside rimmed baking sheet or on broiler pan (meat should cover almost entire surface of rack or broiler pan). Place baking sheet on lower-middle rack and broil until top of meat is well browned (but not charred) and edges are slightly crisp, 5 to 8 minutes. Using wide metal spatula, flip pieces of meat and continue to broil until top is well browned and edges are slightly crisp, 5 to 8 minutes longer. Serve immediately with warm tortillas and garnishes.

June
18

RUNNING

Let us consider how we may spur one another on toward
love and good deeds... encouraging one another.

—Hebrews 10:24–25

Running taps into all my fears about myself, that I'm not strong, that I can't make it, that somewhere between my mind and my body, something important is broken. Every few years I run once, out of guilt and self-hatred, and that one time is so terrible that it buys me a few more years of not running.

Then my friend Kirsten became a runner—a devoted, healthy, strong, long-term, long-distance runner. It threw me for a bit of a loop. I thought, *If she can do it, maybe I can do it.*

So I started running. When it was hard, which was all the time, I reminded myself of the things she'd told me: give it time, respect the three-mile run, just lace up your shoes and don't think about it so much.

When the actual day came to run the marathon, she flew out from San Francisco to run with me, and when she walked into our hotel room, I burst into tears, nervous and relieved that my partner had arrived. It sounds cliché to say I couldn't have done it without her. This time, though, that cliché is absolutely true.

SOMETIMES WE can guide each other along toward courage and health. Who's done that for you? Who could you be a guide for in this season?

ONE STEP

The LORD makes firm the steps of the one who delights in him; though he may stumble, he will not fall, for the LORD upholds him with his hand.

—Psalm 37:23–24

Sometimes I meet women who are so passionate they're about to jump out of their skin. They want to get their hands dirty and dive neck deep into something that keeps them up at night. They don't know what to do. They don't know how to move forward, so they're vibrating with pent-up passion turning rapidly to frustration.

So I tell them the story of my mom. When my mom was my age, she was a stay-at-home mom. She wasn't yet an oil painter or a potter or an AIDS activist or an expert on peacekeeping. My mom began in her forties. She is thoroughly alive in her sixties. If you're just now discovering your passions and gifts in your thirties, or forties, or seventies, there is still time. The path doesn't have to be a straight line, and often it only makes sense when you look back at it. It doesn't have to be full-time, or all-or-nothing, or all-at-once. I tell them what my mom tells me—that you just have to take one step, and that when you do, the next one will appear.

There's still time, I tell them and I tell myself. *There's still time.*

DO YOU have passion or energy or frustration that you don't know what to do with, or gifts that you suspect lie buried, untapped? What is just one step that you can take?

HONESTY'S INVITATION

LORD, who may dwell in your sacred tent? Who may live on your holy
mountain? The one...who speaks the truth from their heart.

—Psalm 15:1–2

When my mom turned sixty, my best friends and hers gathered around my dinner table for food and wine and laughter and storytelling. I've known her best friends for years, but as the night went on, I realized I didn't know how they all came to be friends.

One after another, these women told the stories of how they first became connected with my mom. The constant in all those stories is that her honesty invited them to be honest, too. Her writing and speaking and truth-telling—so deeply against the grain for most pastors' wives—made these women feel like they could tell the truth, too. Some of them sought her out in the darkest seasons of their lives because she had written so honestly about the darkest seasons of her own life.

We sat around that table for hours—our plates and glasses filled and refilled. We told stories and read poems and passages from the Bible and lines from songs, toasting and celebrating all the ways my mom has made our lives better, has inspired us and set us free, and has been an example for us of how life can be if we dare.

HONESTY GIVES others the freedom to be honest as well, opening up the possibility of deeper connection and friendship.

LAYING DOWN MY ANXIETY

Therefore I tell you, do not worry about your life, what you will eat or drink; or about your body, what you will wear. Is not life more than food, and the body more than clothes?

—Matthew 6:25

There is one tiny thing I don't like about summer: I'm not wild about swimsuits. It's been years since I've had a summer where I wasn't pregnant or nursing or post-baby-puffy. Even before that, I was never a swimwear model candidate. On my best days, I can look decent in jeans, but swimsuits don't do me any favors, and as luck would have it, I spend a good portion of the summer up at the lake, wearing a swimsuit from morning till night. I love being at the lake, of course, but at the beginning of every summer, I have to do a little internal business, organizing my thoughts and feelings and phobias, getting myself ready to let everyone I know see me in a piece of clothing that could fit into a sandwich bag.

But as my friend Sara always reminds me, no one's actually thinking about me as often as I think they are. Probably my friends are not actually counting the days till summer to see if I've finally turned into a supermodel. Probably they're thinking about their own lives or current events or any number of things that have nothing to do with how I look.

GOD HAS given us this season to enjoy. What fear or anxiety is keeping you from full life? What would it look like to lay it down?

SUMMER AT THE LAKE

I praise you because I am fearfully and wonderfully made;
your works are wonderful, I know that full well.

—Psalm 139:14

So here we are again, my favorite time of year, summer at the lake, and the idea of someone—anyone!—seeing me in my swimsuit makes me feel a little anxious. I want to find any and every excuse to stay covered, stay inside, stay invisible.

But if I do that, I'll miss the best parts of summer. I'll miss the beach. I'll miss the breathtaking plunges off the back of the boat into really, really cold water. I'll miss paddle boarding and boogie boarding. I'll miss watching Mac float around, kicking his legs with a huge smile on his little face, and I'll miss racing Henry in the lake from there to there a thousand times in a row.

So this is what I'm going to do: I'm going to swim. I'm going to paddle-board. I'm going to make sand castles and make-believe and make memories with my kids. I'm going to cannonball into the icy lake water. I'm going to live in the body God made me, not because it's perfect but because it's mine. And I'm going to be thankful for health and for the ability to run and move and dance and swim.

EMBRACE THE joys of summer by dancing, swimming, sailing, wriggling your toes in the sand, or even just feeling the sun on your face!

HERE I COME

My frame was not hidden from you when I was made in the secret place, when I was woven together in the depths of the earth.

—Psalm 139:15

I'm not going to give in to the cultural pressure that says women's bodies are only beautiful when they're very, very small. I'm going to take up every inch of space I need. I'm not going to hide. I'm not going to bow out of things I love to do because I'm afraid people won't love me when they see me in a swimsuit. I'm going to practice believing that I am more than my body, that I am more than my hips, that I am more than my stretch-marked stomach. I'm going to allow my shoulders to feel the sun, and even (gasp!) my thighs, instead of making sure I'm always, always safely covered and out of your view.

I'm not going to bow to the voice inside my head that says I should be ashamed of myself for being so unruly and wild. I'm not going to develop a relationship with my cover-up that borders on obsessive. This summer, I'm not going to hide.

This is my promise to you, and also my invitation.

Repeat after me: *swimsuit, ready or not, here I come.*

OUR BODIES are amazing gifts from a loving God. What would it take for you to live well in your body this season?

ON SHAME

The LORD is my strength and my shield; my heart trusts in him, and he
helps me. My heart leaps for joy, and with my song I praise him.

—Psalm 28:7

Shame whispers to us that everyone is as obsessed with our failings as we are. It insists that there is, in fact, a watchdog group devoted completely to my weight or her wrinkles or his shrinking bank account. Shame tricks us into believing there's a cable channel that runs video footage of us in our underpants twenty-four hours a day, and that all the people we respect have seen it. Shame tells us that we're wrong for having the audacity to be happy when we're so clearly terrible. Shame wants us to be deeply apologetic for just daring to exist.

But I've been watching that footage on a loop for too long. I've been my own watchdog group for decades. I want to do something risky. I want to dare to exist and, more than that, to live audaciously, in all my imperfect, lumpy, scarred glory, because the alternative is letting shame win.

This is the promise I'm making: this summer, I'm not going to be ashamed of my body. Or at the very least, I'm not going to let a lifetime of shame about my body get in the way of living in a rich, wild, grateful, wide-open way.

HOW DOES shame haunt you? What would it look like to let God's love be your shield against the voice of shame? How might your life change? How might you change?

A NEW WAY OF LIVING IN MY BODY

*Jesus called his disciples to him and said, "I have compassion for these people;
they have already been with me three days and have nothing to eat. I do not
want to send them away hungry, or they may collapse on the way."*

—Matthew 15:32

It didn't occur to me when I was younger that there was a way to live in my
body, my too-big body, without shame and abuse. It seemed like it was my
responsibility to punish it, and that if I were kind to it, that would have
been sanctioning its disobedience. I believed that if I released the hatred
and the pressure by an inch, it would expand, like cupcake batter puffing
up and spilling over onto the pan.

What I wanted more than anything was to not have a body. This body
that I dragged around had betrayed me so deeply, over and over, by having
the audacity to be fat. I hated it, in the particular and venomous way you
hate someone you used to love, someone who was supposed to be on your
side and who was fighting against you.

After two decades of frustration and shame, these days I am less than
hateful toward my body, and in shining moments, even quite kind to it. I
work hard to see it less as this distant distinct shell, and more like a nice
person that I might like to be friends with.

HOW HAVE your feelings about your body changed over
the years? Do you ever think of it as a friend? Do you have
compassion toward it? What would that look like for you?

A SURPRISING TRANSFORMATION

The righteous will flourish like a palm tree, they will grow like a cedar of
Lebanon.... They will still bear fruit in old age, they will stay fresh and green.
—Psalm 92:12, 14

One night in July, our dear friends Jim and Jodi were married. The bride
was preceded down the aisle by her son, daughters, and grandchildren,
and the groom was surrounded by his sailing buddies, among them my
brother. In the vows they wrote, Jim talked about his life before Jodi, and
how deeply he valued his independence. For years, he's worked and traveled and skied and sailed on his own schedule, at his own whim. And
then came Jodi, this gorgeous woman whose deepest commitment is to her
children and grandchildren, and the life she invited him into was more
about Santa than ski season and more about naptime than staying out
all night. Watching Jim become a partner and companion, a father and
grandfather, has been a moving and surprising transformation, and he's
more surprised than anyone.

That night didn't feel like a beginning, the way some weddings do. It
felt like we were stopping to notice and celebrate this glorious thing that
had been inching its way into existence day by day, growing like a slender
tough stalk, until one day you realize it's become a strong tall tree, provid-
ing shade and protection to everyone under its branches.

HAVE YOU seen moving and surprising transformations in the
lives of the people you love? What was that like?

BROTHER PRAYERS

I have not stopped giving thanks for you, remembering you in my prayers.

—Ephesians 1:16

One year for Todd's birthday at the lake, my parents hosted dinner, but I cooked. I made turkey burgers and Mexican-grilled corn and watermelon feta salad. I made blueberry crisp, oats and pecans scattered all over the counter. I worked silently, let phone calls go to voice mail, ignored my to-do list. For the first time in a long time, I wasn't multitasking. I wasn't watching the baby while getting Henry a bowl of cereal, or trying to write a few more sentences before Mac woke up from his nap. I wasn't rushing anywhere, wasn't packing or unpacking a cooler or a tote bag or a suitcase or a diaper bag. I was only there, and I was the only one there.

All the chopping and measuring and stirring felt like a sacred act, and I found myself praying for my brother as I cooked, thinking about his life, his year to come. I prayed for every part of his life—for his health and safety, for his friendships, for his dreams and fears. I prayed for what the year might hold, and I thanked God for him, for the gift that it is to be his sister.

IF YOU have a sibling, take a few minutes and thank God for that relationship, for their life, and for the memories you share.

PRAYER

I prayed for this child, and the LORD has granted me what I asked of him.

—1 Samuel 1:27

As a part of my brother Todd's birthday gift, my mom put together a slide show of his sailing trip around the world, so after dinner we looked through hundreds of images of remote anchorages and unfamiliar landscapes, sunsets over the water and green mountains rising out of rough navy seas. His sailing trip began and ended in South Haven. They left early on the morning of Henry's first birthday and arrived back in this same harbor the day after Mother's Day almost two years later, the very best Mother's Day gift my mom could have asked for.

People always asked my mom if she was scared, having him so far away on such a small boat, and she always answered the same way. She told them that one of the chief aspects of mothering is prayer, and that she had learned very early with a son like Todd—a son who loves to sail and snowboard and ride dirt bikes and drive race cars and build motorcycles—that prayer was the only thing that would keep her sane.

HAS THERE ever been a season in your life when prayer was the only thing that kept you sane? In what ways was God's presence comforting to you?

GOD HEARS US

*One day Jesus was praying in a certain place. When he finished,
one of his disciples said to him, "Lord, teach us to pray."*

—Luke 11:1

After years of dreaming about it and months of talking about it, my brother, Todd, and our dear friend Joe officially decided to sail around the world, to leave their jobs and homes, to sell guitars and motorcycles and fancy bachelor TVs and take a once-in-a-lifetime trip. They bought a boat last June and worked on it all summer in the harbor in South Haven.

Early one morning, we stood on the dock while Todd and Joe silently stowed the last few items, did the last few chores. We drank coffee in the dark and took turns snuggling Henry in his footie pajamas. We stood in a circle and prayed for safety and wisdom and kind seas.

Our family rule is that we never pray for adventure, especially when it's about a boat. On one family vacation twenty years ago, a guest asked for adventure as she prayed before breakfast, and then we sailed straight into a tropical depression, complete with swirling winds, lightning, and an unrelenting downpour. We never saw the sun again that trip, and now we never, ever pray for adventure.

GOD LISTENS and hears us when we pray. Have you ever felt that you got more than you bargained for when he gave you exactly what you asked for? What do you avoid asking for?

Sara's Lasagna

This is one of those recipes that's played out like a game of telephone—I think it's Sara's, and Abby thinks it's mine, and who knows where Sara got it, and we all make it differently. This is dead-of-winter-in-the-Midwest comfort food at its yummiest.

• •

1 pound zesty sausage

1 pound sweet sausage

1 onion, sliced

2 red peppers, sliced

1 (28-ounce) can diced tomatoes

1 (6-ounce) can tomato paste

6 cloves garlic, minced

2 teaspoons ground oregano

1 teaspoon dried basil

1 pound no-boil lasagna noodles

1 (10-ounce) bag baby spinach

8 ounces ricotta

8 ounces shredded mozzarella

8 ounces Parmesan, shredded

• •

» Brown the sausage, then drain. In the same pan, sauté the onion and peppers until soft, and set aside. Over medium-low heat, combine the sausage, onions, peppers, tomatoes, tomato paste, garlic, oregano, and basil.

» Spread one thin layer of sauce in a 13 x 9-inch pan. Add three lasagna noodles, a layer of spinach (use half), cheese (half the ricotta, one third each of the Parmesan and mozzarella), and sauce. Repeat this layer again. Add another layer of noodles, a layer of sauce, and the remaining Parmesan and mozzarella.

» Bake at 375 degrees for 40 to 50 minutes. Let rest for 10 minutes, then serve.

FOR A BRIDE

How delightful is your love, my sister, my bride!
—Song of Songs 4:10

When people tell you that your wedding day is the best day of your life, it sort of sounds like they're saying that it's all downhill after the wedding. So many pastors make it a point to tell you, right during the ceremony, that it's all fun and games while you're wearing the dress and holding the flowers, but that serious business starts when the dancing stops. That's true, in some ways. Marriage is a serious business, and there's a lot to marriage that you can't see from where you're standing in the front of a church, bridesmaids surrounding you.

But on that day, you cannot imagine the beautiful, life-altering, soul-shaping things ahead of you. I know you believe that you could not possibly love him more than you do right now. I understand that. I felt that. I was wrong. What you feel on your wedding day is like dipping your toe in an ocean, and with every passing year, you swim farther and farther from the shore, unable, at a certain point, to see anything but water. This is just the beginning, and you can't imagine the love that will bloom between you over time.

IF YOU'RE married, how has the love between you and your husband grown and changed since the day of your wedding? What would you say to a bride on her wedding day?

BENDING AGAIN TOWARD PARTNERSHIP

The LORD blessed the latter part of Job's life more than the former part.

—Job 42:12

There is something sweet and shining about a young bride and groom, and their first home and dishes and set of towels. But there is a different beauty and force when two people who have been down that road far enough to hit some bumps decide to bend themselves once again toward partnership. Where there was naïveté, here there is sobriety. Where a young bride leaves her family, an older bride brings hers with her. Where a young groom hopes all goes well, an older groom knows what to do when it doesn't.

When our friends Jim and Jodi got married, that night felt sacred and beautiful and imbued with something heavy. It was a hard-won celebration, a willingness to fall again, to teach and be taught, to enter through a door both had believed was closed forever. We danced and ate cake and toasted them with champagne and told crazy old sailing stories. We laughed and let the kids stay up way too late and watched the bobbing mast lights on the sailboats in the harbor, hypnotized by the beauty and hope of that night.

GIFTS THAT come later than expected sometimes have a power and sweetness all their own. Have you ever seen this in your own life, or in the lives of people you love?

A GIFT WORTH SEEING

You have stolen my heart, my sister, my bride; you have stolen my heart
with one glance of your eyes, with one jewel of your necklace.

—Song of Songs 4:9

Sometimes when life gets really busy, I can get so caught up in the chaos that I risk losing sight of the reason for it all. For instance, a to-do list for a rehearsal dinner at our house hid the story of my sister-in-law, Amy, whose wedding we were celebrating the next day. That night, over chicken korma and tandoori, two families told stories and laughed and prayed together, anticipating the next day's ceremony. After a decade of broken, painful relationships, Amy stood looking out over our city, surrounded by both families, as she married Austin, a man who is all of the things she hoped for. She was a glowing bride, flushed with beauty and even more so with love. The day of her wedding to Austin began a new thing in her, a beautiful, lively, hopeful, generous way of living, a woman in full bloom. That's the luminous, beautiful thing hiding underneath the blur of the menu and the seating and the candles. What looked, on the calendar and the to-do list, like a dinner was actually one of God's best gifts, worth celebrating, worth seeing.

IT'S EASY sometimes to get so caught up in the logistics of an event that we lose sight of what we're there to celebrate. Has that ever happened to you? When was the last time you really absorbed the beauty of a wedding or other milestone?

DO YOUR THING

"The LORD your God is with you, the Mighty Warrior who saves.
He will take great delight in you; in his love he will no longer
rebuke you, but will rejoice over you with singing."

—Zephaniah 3:17

I worked at a summer camp for years and years, and when I picture taking care of one another, I think of a game we used to play at camp. We
had those in-ground trampolines, and the girls would line the edges with
their hands up, spotting the girl who was jumping. When it was your turn,
you'd bounce and dance and do crazy spins, whatever you wanted. The rest
of us would sing, *"Hey Sam, do your thing, do your thing. Hey Sam, do your thing, do your*
thing." And when Sam was done, she'd call the name of the next girl, who
would jump into the center and start her silly jumps and dance moves, and
we'd sing to her: *"Hey Taylor, do your thing, do your thing."*

That's how it's supposed to be: you get the courage to do your thing because the people you love and trust are telling you, *"Do your thing! Do that thing you*
were made to do." They've got their hands up; they're protecting you. You're safe
because of them. And they just keep reminding you to *do your thing*.

WHO IN your life is reminding you to do your thing? Have
you invested in the kind of relationships where you do that for
one another?

OPENING THE WINDOW

Speaking the truth in love, we will grow to become in every respect
the mature body of him who is the head, that is, Christ. From him the
whole body, joined and held together by every supporting ligament,
grows and builds itself up in love, as each part does its work.

—Ephesians 4:15–16

One night in Fiji, Todd and Joe and Aaron and I talked about the things we want to do in our lives. That was a season when it was kind of all open, waiting to be re-created, each on the cusp of something, but we didn't know what. So we talked about how God made each of us, what we're good at, what we're not, what we might do, what we never will.

Sometimes we get so tangled up in our own perceptions of ourselves that we lose perspective, seeing only our failures and bad habits. In difficult seasons, it's almost impossible to remember that feeling of being great at something or being proud of yourself.

We reminded one another that night, and we dreamed on behalf of one another. Left to our own devices, we sometimes choose the most locked up, dark versions of the story, but a good friend turns on the lights, opens the window, and reminds us that there are a whole lot of ways to tell the same story.

WE CAN'T grow and become who God created us to be in isolation; it happens in love and within the body of Christ. Who are the people who encourage you to dream good dreams?

THE LAGOON

You will shine among them like stars in the sky as you hold firmly to the word of life.

—Philippians 2:15–16

That night in Fiji the conversation felt as fresh as the wind blowing in off the lagoon. Travel is important because it takes us far enough away from our everyday lives to see those lives with new clarity. When you're on the other side of the world, when you're under the silent sea, watching a bright, silent world of fish and coral, when you're staring up at a sky so bright and dense with stars it makes you gasp, you begin to see the fullness of your life, the possibility that prevails.

You don't have to go to the other side of the world, but you do have to get out of those same four walls you're always staring at. Drive to the city, or to the country, or to a lake whose shores are totally unfamiliar to you. Listen for new rhythms and sounds, and watch your life refract and shift against a new backdrop. You'll see things you didn't know were there, and recognize selves long hidden. Sometimes a new sense of possibility is found practically in your own backyard, viewed for the first time from a new vantage point.

> **TRAVEL BREATHES** new life into our sense of what is possible, and allows us to see our lives from a new perspective. When was the last time a new location opened up something new in you?

A NEW SEASON

Weeping may stay for the night, but rejoicing comes in the morning.
—Psalm 30:5

There have been seasons when I've been dimly aware of the goodness of the world, but that goodness hasn't seemed nearly as real as my frustration, anxiety, or sadness. My mind knew everything was fine, but my dreams were filled with broken images, and I burst into tears at the drop of a hat. Things feel different now, like the goodness is palpable, and the minor annoyances are just that, minor.

Being in a lovely place doesn't automatically mean happiness—we lived in this same blue house two summers ago, after Aaron left his job at our church in Grand Rapids. While the sunsets were beautiful and the wind on the water was warm and fresh, I cried in the shower and alone in the car that summer. My memories of last summer are filled with heartbreak. Every morning here I walk past the condo where I had the miscarriage, the balcony I sat on while I watched the boats on the river, feeling numb and hollowed out.

This summer feels worlds away from the last two, and maybe some of the brightness in my spirit comes from having moved through those seasons into a new one. I feel hope again, and possibility.

WHEN WAS the last time that you felt a change of season in our heart and dreams? What kind of season are you in right now? How might you honor this season, whatever it may be?

LITTLE & BIG

Even small children are known by their actions.

—Proverbs 20:11

Henry was sick over the weekend, and he wanted to sit on my lap and have my arms wrapped around him as tightly as I could. I didn't complain for a second. Then last night he said, "I've been thinking about the bad choices I made today. I'm really sorry, Mom. I'm going to make better choices tomorrow." What more can one expect from any adult than that? What a big man!

He wears a little Timex, even though he can't tell time, and most days he wears a clip-on tie. His favorite jeans these days are, in his words, his "rock 'n' roller skinnies." Seriously. Five might be the perfect age for a human—smart and sweet, the perfect mash-up of little and big.

Aaron and I remind each other that kids aren't vanity projects, and they're not extensions of our own images. This is especially helpful when Henry goes to school in rainbow-striped pajama bottoms, cowboy boots, and a Chicago Bears sweatshirt that doesn't quite fit over his belly. He's a person, not a paper doll. We're his parents, not his marketing team. And being his parents is one of our favorite things.

IF YOU have children, have you ever been tempted to treat them like an extension of your own image? How so? In what ways have you deliberately given your children the freedom to be their own distinct persons?

July
8

TEN GIRLS

While he was still a long way off, his father saw him and was filled with compassion for him; he ran to his son, threw his arms around him and kissed him.

—Luke 15:20

Years ago, I began leading a small group of ten girls. They were a blur of bright tank tops, flat-ironed hair, and Birkenstock clogs, and I always felt like I was in the middle of a tornado or a high-speed chase.

I didn't actually intend to be their small group leader. I worked on the student staff, and we were short on volunteer leaders for a retreat. I said I could take a group, just for the weekend. Somehow, it was communicated to the girls that I would be their leader forever and ever, and when they found out, they pounced on me and hugged me and jumped up and down, and I didn't have the heart to say that I had really only agreed to love them for the weekend.

We started meeting every week. They called at all hours of the night and day, and stopped over at my house and my office constantly, and apparently never had anywhere else to be after their visit. They sometimes got so excited to see me that when they hugged me, they knocked me down, even though it was never more than five days since I'd seen them last.

HAVE YOU ever been bowled over by genuine love and enthusiasm from someone that was totally unexpected? What was that like for you? Did it change you or have a long-term effect on your life?

BECAUSE THEY WERE MINE

Jesus said, "Simon son of John, do you love me?" He answered, "Yes,
Lord, you know that I love you." Jesus said, "Take care of my sheep."

—John 21:16

When I led a small group of ten teenage girls, there were tiny moments of brilliance that first year. One of them would tell me something really true and important about her life, or ask me something about life with God that really mattered to her. But I planned to make it through one year and then find a new leader for them. I worked long hours, and nights and weekends. I was engaged and planning a wedding. They needed so much more than I was prepared to give them—more time, more honesty, more support, more help.

But I began to love them, not because they were the finest, most upstanding kids in our student ministry, because they weren't. They had their moments of upstanding-ness, and they had moments of absolute insanity. I loved them because they were mine, because we were us, because of the funny, sweet, and strange things they did and said. They became a central part of my world, my thoughts, my prayers. My schedule became more and more wrapped around their term papers, proms, and problems, and my home became more and more the safest landing spot for this strange, whirling little gypsy wagon of girls.

WE LIVE out the love of God when we care for those he brings into our lives. Have you ever been surprised by who you came to love, because they became yours in some way?

July
10

GYM SOCKS & AUTHENTICITY

In him you too are being built together to become a
dwelling in which God lives by his Spirit.

—Ephesians 2:22

It seems that women typically experience shame about two things: their bodies and their homes. I was hit with both one day when a friend stopped over unannounced. When I'm writing at home, it's as though I am a home-bound invalid. No makeup, hair in a ratty bun just above my forehead. Crooked glasses, Aaron's gym socks. I wasn't just a little ragged around the edges; I was terrifying. Not only that, but my whole house smelled because I hadn't done the dishes for days.

Just the week before, I'd told this friend that while I'm writing about food, I'm finding that a lot of it is about shame, about the ways we feel inferior, and because of those feelings, we hide. Of course, it's all fun and games to talk about, and then the next thing you know, you're in your husband's gym socks and your kitchen stinks. You've got a chance to practice what you're preaching, and you're breaking out in hives. But I took a deep breath, and she sat there listening to me across my dirty coffee table, and we talked about community and family and authenticity. It's easy to talk about, and really hard sometimes to practice.

OPPORTUNITIES TO build friendship and community don't always come at the most convenient times, but we have to grab them when we get the chance.

BEING THERE

Children's children are a crown to the aged, and parents are the pride of their children.

—Proverbs 17:6

I want my children to know my parents, and not just from emails or short weekend visits. I want my dad to teach them to snorkel someday the same way he taught me, swimming just in front of me with his arm stretched out to the side, letting me hang on that arm and pulling me along with him.

I want to hear every single little thing that my brother has to tell me. Todd is a man of very few words, but every once in a while on vacation he starts talking, while we're taking the golf cart to the club, or putting away the boat at the end of the day. I can badger him via email and cell phone all year long about his life or his family or his job and end up knowing very little, but on vacation, sometimes he gets on a roll, and I want to be there when he does, even if it means we sit on the dock till the sun sets and we're freezing, or even if I have to play basketball with him at the court in town.

WHEN WE break from our busy routines, we can have conversations and share experiences with our family that would never happen otherwise. When was the last time you made space for those moments?

July
12

STORING UP MEMORIES

"Do not store up for yourselves treasures on earth, where moths and vermin
destroy, and where thieves break in and steal. But store up for yourselves treasures
in heaven, where moths and vermin do not destroy, and where thieves do not
break in and steal. For where your treasure is, there your heart will be also."

—Matthew 6:19–21

Vacations are more than vacations. Vacations are the act of grabbing minutes and hours and days with both hands, stealing against the inevitability
of time. I want to sock away memories like gold coins because I'm going to
need them someday to get me through the years. There will be a day when
our family as we know it will no longer exist, and I want to know in that
moment that I wasn't at the office or doing the dishes when I could have
been walking on the dock with my dad, when I could have been drinking
tea and eating ginger cookies on the porch with my mom. I don't want to
be building my bank account or my abs or my dream house when I could
be dancing with Aaron at the beach bar on New Year's Eve, when I could
be making crackers and cheese for dinner because we were on the boat till
way after the shops closed, sunburnt and sandy and windblown, and happier there and together than anywhere else with anyone else.

TIME SPENT making good memories with people you love
is never wasted. What might you have to give up in order to make
these kind of experiences a priority?

210

WHEN MEMORIES ARE ALL WE HAVE

I will sing the Lord's praise, for he has been good to me.

—Psalm 13:6

My mom and dad and brother have grown through the years into my closest friends, the people who tell me the most searing truth, who catch me when I fall, who give me soft places to rest and present to me a bright future when the only one I can see from my vantage point is dim and breaking before my eyes. Families can go either way, and I take no credit for the way we've gone. I accept it like a gift or a winning lottery ticket, and I hold that ticket in my hand tightly, and I take every chance I can get to be with them, for an afternoon, for a weekend, for a vacation, and every moment feels like being given one more winning ticket.

We've invested our vacations with as many memories as we can make, crammed them full of love and conversations and stories and long walks and meals and boat rides, because there will be a day when memories are all we have, and I want to know that we have more than we need to last us the rest of our lives.

TAKE A few moments and thank God for your family, or for the friends that feel like family, and for all they bring to your life.

LEAVING MY JOB

But you, Sovereign Lord, help me for your name's sake; out of the goodness of your love, deliver me. For I am poor and needy, and my heart is wounded within me.

—Psalm 109:21–22

I left my job at the church. Looking back, I see more clearly what had gone bad without my realizing it, what I added to an already difficult situation. I tried and tried to make something work that had stopped working a long time before.

People leave jobs all the time. It stings, and you get over it and move on and find a new place to work. Jobs are things you do, they're not badges of who you are, they're not as important as your family or your soul.

I know those things, but when I left my job, I lost that sense that I was okay, that I would be okay again. I was sad, scared, and ashamed. One of my deepest secret beliefs is that I am not a good person, not talented or helpful in any way, and someday everyone will find out. This felt like confirmation of those feelings.

Without intending to, I had shoved way too much of myself into my job, more than a job can possibly bear, and I set myself up to fall a terrible distance, if something ever happened to that job. And then, of course, it did.

OUR JOBS are a big part of our lives, and it's easy to invest too much of ourselves in them. Have you ever left a job in such a way that you lost all confidence about the future? What helped you get through that season?

NOTHING LEFT TO LOSE

The Spirit God gave us does not make us timid, but
gives us power, love and self-discipline.

— 2 Timothy 1:7

About two months after I left my job, I spoke at a conference. My bio in the program had been printed when I was still working at the church, and now I felt like a liar, like I had no right to speak at this conference anymore. I was unemployed and pregnant and I was going to have to stand up in front of almost a thousand people, and I had nothing to say to them.

I walked out onto the stage and said, "I'm going to tell you right now that you are not going to like what I have to say. But I'm pregnant, which means I'm as big as a house, I eat like a linebacker, and I throw up in public. At this point, I have nothing left to lose. So I'm just going to tell you what I think."

I had spent almost a decade creating services in churches, and I told the truth as I see it about that work, about its value and its challenges. It wasn't clever or polished. There were no slides or video clips or touching anecdotes, but it was the best talk I had ever given.

WHAT KIND of experiences have you had where you felt like you had nothing left to lose? Were you surprised by how they turned out? What did you learn from them?

EGGS & BASKETS

Do not put your trust in princes, in human beings, who cannot save.

—Psalm 146:3

When I worked at the church, I put all my eggs in the job basket, until it became impossibly heavy, and it broke. When I gave back my computer and my keys, I gave back my identity, my confidence, my legitimacy.

At a speaking engagement several weeks later, I felt like I had no right to be there, but I stood onstage and told the audience things my friends and I had learned while we worked at churches, the lessons we learned the hard way, and the things I wish I had known when I began.

After my talk, I felt like I was in free fall. I didn't have a title or a business card anymore. But to my surprise, I found that I had my own experiences, mistakes, and successes, and those are things you don't give back when you turn in your keys and your laptop. I took up my own space and told my own stories, stories that I earned along the way. I felt, possibly for the very first time, like I was holding my own eggs in my very own basket. I hate how I got there, but it feels like an important place to be.

HAVE YOU ever put all your eggs into the job basket? Or into anything else that could not hold them? What was that like for you? What baskets do you have eggs in right now? Are you pleased with where they are?

TRUSTING THE WIND

"The wind blows wherever it pleases. You hear its sound, but you cannot tell where
it comes from or where it is going. So it is with everyone born of the Spirit."

—John 3:8

I grew up on the water, spending my summers on a tiny lakeshore town in Michigan. We ran the beaches, soaked up the sun, picked blueberries. But if there was wind, we sailed. We dropped everything. We'd race down the marina—*wind! There's wind!*

For a sailor, the wind is everything. If you want to be in control of what's happening, you don't sail. If you want certainty, you get a power boat and you stick to engines instead of wind.

I feel that tension in myself sometimes: to trust the wind or to control with my own engine. I *want* to be a sailor. But in my fearful moments, I feel the impulse to fire up an engine, to pick a spot and head there fast, to burn some fuel instead of waiting around for the wind to do its powerful but invisible work.

I'm learning that the wind is where it's at. When you trust the wind, when you wait for life to lead and unfold in its own timing, the feeling is exciting and calm in the very same moment, one of the best feelings in the world.

WHAT IS your inclination: to trust the wind and let life unfold, or to fire up an engine and make something happen? Is there an area in your life where you need to wait for the wind?

July
18

ON PRAYER & MY FRIEND MARGARET

*On him we have set our hope that he will continue to
deliver us, as you help us by your prayers.*

—2 Corinthians 1:10–11

I've learned that when my friend Margaret is praying for something, that *something* is happening. When she prays at our table, she always begins: "Hey God, it's us." She doesn't just pray at the table, of course—she prays when she walks and when she nurses Eloise. She wakes up in the night to pray and whispers prayers as she falls asleep.

Many years ago, she felt deep unease about a friend's upcoming wedding. She prayed and prayed, and when she sensed she had to say something, she risked their friendship. The friendship broke. But then the engagement broke, too, and after a while the friendship was repaired, because even though Margaret knows things deeply, she holds them gently.

She prayed for me when I was desperate to conceive and carry a healthy pregnancy. She gave me a ring to remind me that she was praying, and when I see it in my jewelry box, I almost always weep, remembering the way my friend prayed for me, with confidence and hope I didn't have.

Margaret is teaching me to pray. I'm thankful to have her around my table regularly so that her intimate, passionate, faith-deepening way of living and praying rubs off on me and gives me something to aspire to.

WHO IS teaching or has taught you how to pray? What have you learned from them? Who are you teaching in turn?

HOME

A man leaves his father and mother and is united to his wife, and they become one flesh.

—Genesis 2:24

One of the things I said to Aaron in our wedding vows was, "When I am with you, wherever we are, I am home." It was a beautiful and romantic thing to say, and I really felt it. Then just a few months after our first anniversary, a friend asked us to think about moving to Grand Rapids, Michigan, three hours away, for Aaron to be a worship leader in his church.

We drove up to Grand Rapids to talk to our friend, and when we got back into the car, I cried most of the way back to Chicago. I could feel the inevitability of it, and I had already begun to mourn.

When I said to him on our wedding day that when I was with him, I was home, I did not mean, "Let's move to Michigan and see if I'm right, okay?" I meant, "I love you so very much, and let's stay in Chicago where my parents and my friends are, how about that?" But I said, before God and seven bridesmaids, that Aaron is my home, my partner, my number one, and so I moved to Michigan. I was quite naïve, and promised to live, no matter what, with and for and deeply connected to this other person. Thank God.

SOMETIMES THE promises and commitments we've made are invitations to grow and live in new ways. Where have you seen God's hand draw you to new growth?

FIXER-UPPERS

"My grace is sufficient for you, for my power is made perfect in weakness."
—2 Corinthians 12:9

When we moved to Grand Rapids, we bought an English Tudor house built in 1920. It had arched doorways and hardwood floors and funny little corners and built-in cabinets. I thought of myself as an old-house person, someone who appreciates character over perfection. We moved in and started fixing it up, painting, and putting in new outlets and fixtures.

Then I went over to a friend's house—a new house. I was overcome with jealousy, not because her house was fancy or big, but because the toilets didn't run, and none of the windows were painted shut, and none of the doorknobs got stuck.

When I got home, all I could see were the fixer-upper things that were not yet fixed up. Uneven floors. Cracked tiles. Squeaky drawers. Clanking radiators. Bats. Mice. The funny smell in the basement.

On my worst days, I start to believe that God is a new-house God. That everything has to work just right. That I need to be completely fixed up. But a lot of the people God uses to do amazing things don't have it all together. A lot of the best stories in the Bible, where God does sacred, magical things through people, have characters with shady pasts. Serious fixer-uppers.

GOD ISN'T looking for perfection. He loves us so deeply just as we are. Sit for a moment, and let your mind and heart rest in his great love, unswayed by all your broken parts.

OLD HOUSE

*He who began a good work in you will carry it on to
completion until the day of Christ Jesus.*

—Philippians 1:6

Some of my struggle to love our old house in Grand Rapids, unfortunately, was about what other people thought. I'm fairly certain that our house was the bad house in the neighborhood, that our neighbors were whispering to each other disapprovingly. One day when a woman drove by very slowly, like she was giving us the once-over, I had to stop myself from screaming out the window, "We're doing the best we can! We've only been here like five minutes!"

But I didn't know that lady. The person having a problem with the house, clearly, was me. And it wasn't about the house. It was about me. I couldn't handle any more things that were not quite right in my life, because I felt like that's all I had. I'm a lot like that old house, cracked and mismatched and patched over.

On my very best days, I practiced letting it be an old not-fixed-up house, while I practiced being a not-fixed-up person. I walked around my house, looking at all the things that I should fix someday, and I imagined God noticing all the things about me that should get fixed up one day, and loving me anyway and being okay with the mess for the time being.

GOD'S LOVE for us isn't threatened by our broken pieces. We are each a work in progress, and he's the one completing the work, with all kinds of love and patience.

AS IS

As a father has compassion on his children, so the LORD has compassion on those who fear him; for he knows how we are formed, he remembers that we are dust.

—Psalm 103:13–14

I practice believing that, bottom line, God loves me as is, even if I never do get my act together. When we lived in that old house, I would put my hand on the plaster wall, nubbly and textured, and think thankful thoughts about the walls. I would put my hand on the floor, and think thankful thoughts about the floor, even though it was scratched and ridged and you could see where one of my black heels lost its little cap and the metal part left tiny round divots in the floor, over and over, like confetti stamped into the wood. I imagine that God does that to me, puts his hand on my head, on my heart, on my savage insecurities, and as he does it, he thinks thankful thoughts about me.

In my best moments, when I calm down and listen very closely, God says, "I didn't ask you to become new and improved today. That wasn't the goal. You were broken down and strange yesterday, and you still are today, and the only one freaked out about it is you."

GOD IS slowly transforming us. In the meantime, along the way, take a few breaths and express your thankfulness for his patience.

NOURISHMENT

Better a dry crust with peace and quiet than a house full of feasting, with strife.

—Proverbs 17:1

We have a friend who really wants things to be fun. So much so, in fact, that I finally grumbled to my husband mid-fun at one of our friend's events, "It's not fun if you have to manhandle us!" I think it bothered me so much because, like all things that make us crazy, it reminded me way too much of myself. I've overthought, overplanned, and manhandled so many parties and meals over the years.

In entertaining, as in every area of life, there are experts and rock stars, people who load us up with expectations and set impossibly high standards so that most of us give up and the rest of us feel terrible about ourselves when we inevitably fall short.

But entertaining isn't a competition. It's an act of love, if you let it be. You can twist it into anything you want—a way to show off your house, to compete with your friends, to earn love and approval. Or you can decide that every time you open your door, it's an act of love. You can decide that every time people gather around your table, your goal is nourishment, not neurotic proving. You can decide.

NOURISHING THE people around our table means ignoring the clamorous voices of own insecurities and tending instead to the needs of the people we have invited in.

Curried Cauliflower

This is one of our go-to weeknight dinner staples—healthy, easy, full of flavor. We eat it with chicken and quinoa, or steak and brown rice...anything!

••

1 head of cauliflower, chopped

¼ cup olive oil

3 teaspoons curry powder

3 teaspoons cumin

1 teaspoon cayenne

salt and pepper to taste

handful of raisins

handful of chopped almonds

small handful of chopped cilantro

••

» Preheat oven to 400 degrees.

» Slice the cauliflower into bite-size pieces, then drizzle with olive oil. Sprinkle curry powder, cumin, cayenne, salt, and pepper over cauliflower, and toss well. Roast at 400 degrees on a rimmed baking sheet for 20 minutes, or until edges are brown, tossing once. When you toss halfway through, add raisins and almonds. After you remove it from the oven, sprinkle with cilantro, then serve immediately.

CONSCIOUS DECISIONS

To humans belong the plans of the heart, but from the
LORD comes the proper answer of the tongue.

—Proverbs 16:1

Recently I saw a friend I hadn't seen in years. "I heard you're engaged!" I cried as I hugged her, exuberantly. "Congratulations!"

"I'm not engaged," she said. "I was, and I'm not anymore." Oh, heavens. I started to apologize, but she put her hand on my arm and interrupted me.

"It's all right," she said. "Breaking the engagement was the first conscious decision of my life."

What an extraordinary statement. And as I spent time with her, I could see the truth of her words, the bloom of her eyes and skin and spirit. She had made a fundamental, defining choice, and it brought life and hope to her world.

Her words rang in my ears because I wanted to make a conscious decision of my own, and her words gave a name to something I'd been aching for a long time. Many of the key decisions in my life just seemed like the most natural progression. I want to live *consciously*, like my friend does. I want to be brave enough to make changes, awake enough to move past what's planned and expected.

WHAT WAS the first conscious decision you ever made? In this season, are there any conscious decisions that you need to consider making?

YOU'LL GET THROUGH

Praise be to the God and Father of our Lord Jesus Christ, the Father of compassion and the God of all comfort, who comforts us in all our troubles, so that we can comfort those in any trouble with the comfort we ourselves receive from God.

—2 Corinthians 1:3–4

I saw an old friend last week, and as we caught up, she told me about her job, a temporary one, and her living situation, a temporary one. She lost her job earlier this year, and that loss hasn't yet worked its way out of her life. She's one of the most joyful, exuberant people I know, but I could tell she was exhausted and scared, and that this season has been a heartbreaking one.

Oh, I get it, I told her. I get where you are right now. I know what it's like to long for a new year, to feel like everything's on hold and you don't recognize your own life even though it's right in front of you. I know what it's like when the things that always used to make you happy don't do the trick anymore, because they can't break through the sadness and fear that are covering over everything in your life.

I was there, I said, and I'm not there anymore, and I'm so thankful. You'll get through this, and you'll find yourself in an entirely new place. You'll find your old self again. You'll laugh easily and sleep well. It will happen. *I promise.*

WE GIVE to each other the goodness we've received from God: comfort, encouragement, the firsthand knowledge of seasons of healing that follow seasons of pain.

"YOU TOO?"

It was good of you to share in my troubles.

—**Philippians 4:14**

One evening I was at my favorite bookstore, feeling fragile and overwhelmed. I was looking through the cards that have quotes on the front, those big, inspirational, "seize the day"-type quotes, from people like Eleanor Roosevelt and Albert Einstein. If you read them on a good day, you're like, "I will, Eleanor Roosevelt, I will change the world one tiny moment at a time!" But on a bad, cranky day, you think, "Well, that's why you people are famous, because you do wonderful, inspirational things, and all I do is try to get through the day without crying or losing my mind." I just felt worn out and hollow. This whole big wall of cards was making me feel more broken down and scraped away inside, so far from inspiration and hope. Then I saw one in the corner, in black and white, that said, "You too? I thought I was the only one."

I started to cry. Really cry, the kind of tears that have been waiting to come out for a long time. That night I didn't need big, great, beautiful words from important people. I just needed to know that I wasn't alone. "You too? I thought I was the only one."

WE NEED each other. We need to know we're not alone. Who in your life might need to hear from you today, to know that she is not alone?

LONGING

Rejoice with those who rejoice; mourn with those who mourn.

—**R o m a n s 1 2 : 1 5**

Most of us are longing for something. Longing is part of living in the not-yet-heaven. I know people who are longing to marry, longing to be healed from disease, longing for their children to come home, longing for the financial pressure to release. I get that longing is part of how we live.

But some days I have felt angry and boxed in, like the system was rigged against me and everywhere I turned, someone else's body was blooming with new life, while mine still, again, was not. I knew it wasn't personal. But it feels personal on some days. When you're afraid no one will ever love you, a friend who falls in love feels cruel. When your back is breaking under worry and fear about money, someone else's good fortune breaks your back just a little more.

That's why it's hard, I think, to live out that beautiful line from the Bible and rejoice with those who rejoice and mourn with those who mourn. When you've got reason to rejoice, you forget what it's like to mourn, even if you swear you never will. And when you're mourning, the fact that someone close to you is rejoicing seems like a personal affront.

WHO CAN you join in rejoicing today? Who can you join in mourning?

July
28

SEASONS

What strength do I have, that I should still hope? What
prospects, that I should be patient?

—Job 6:11

It seems cruel that major life events tend to happen in seasons. During college application season, I remember my shame and embarrassment about not being accepted to my dream school. It was even more tender because one of my best friends had been accepted to that same school. We had been walking together, and I hit a dead end while she kept walking.

There's also the wedding season. Weddings are especially hard if you've recently broken up with someone, or if it's been a long time since you've kissed someone and really meant it.

The next wave is the baby wave. Announcing your pregnancy is a highly fraught process, knowing that it will make someone else cry, possibly in front of you, but more likely in the car later, or after they hang up the phone. I've been on both sides of those tears. For a while several of us commiserated, calling one another after we wiped our tears, but that little band became smaller each month. While I was thrilled for those who became pregnant, the few of us still left wondered who would leave next for the land of bellies and baby gear.

DO YOU know anyone who is hurting in the midst of one of these seasons? Is there a way you might reach out to her and provide some comfort?

TELL YOUR STORY

Then Peter stood up with the Eleven, raised his voice and addressed the crowd.
... "God has raised this Jesus to life, and we are all witnesses of it."

—Acts 2:14, 32

In one of my favorite Tyler James songs, he says "my life's not a story about me." My life is not a story about me. And your life's not a story about you. My life is a story about who God is and what he does in a human heart. My story is about the people on my street, the things I read, the way we raise our child, the things I've done and the things that have been done to me. A story is never about one person. It has a full cast of characters, connected by blood or love or jealousy.

Tell your story. Don't allow the story of God, the sacred, transforming story of what God does in a human heart, to become flat and lifeless. It always goes back to the beginning, no matter how far we've wandered off course. When Christ walked among us, he entrusted the gospel to plain old regular people who were absolutely not religious professionals. If you have been transformed by the grace of God, then you have within you all you need to write your manifesto, your poem, your song, your battle cry, your love letter to a beautiful and broken world.

IN WHAT ways have you kept silent about your story, believing it doesn't matter?

SHARING SORROWS

Comfort, comfort my people, says your God.

—Isaiah 40:1

There are some moments these days, since the miscarriage, when I feel like a failure because my body wasn't able to do what so many other women's bodies can. I see them with their kids, a year apart, one after another. That will never be true for me and for our family. I'll always remember, even if we do have more children someday, the loss we experienced last summer. But what has healed me more than anything else are the stories of other women who have experienced similar things. I've needed grace, and I've needed women who share their sorrows with me, and allow me to share my own.

My friend Nancy lives in California now, and when she heard that I lost the baby, she sent me a card. It said, "Rest, heal, you will be a mother again." And when I read it, I put my head down and sobbed, in sadness, but also in gratitude, for a woman who knows me well enough, even after all these years, to know what words will stitch me back together when my heart is broken.

WHEN HAVE you been able to share your sorrows with other women, and have them share their sorrows with you? Is there anyone in your life right now who needs some words of comfort that you know how to give?

WE CAN DO THIS TOGETHER

There is a time for everything, and a season for every activity
under the heavens...a time to tear and a time to mend.

—Ecclesiastes 3:1, 7

I once told Aaron that if I found out I wasn't pregnant that month, I'd break something glass, just to feel it shatter in my hands. And then I found out I wasn't pregnant. Again. I didn't break anything, but I posted something on my blog about how I was feeling.

Later that week I had lunch with my friend Emily. I hoped she hadn't read my post. She was one of my seventeen pregnant friends, and I wanted it to be a sweet, happy lunch. And it was. We talked about all the lovely baby stuff, and then she gave me a gift.

She said she had read my post, and that this is the point in friendship when sometimes two friends walk away from each other for a while, because the pain and awkwardness and tenderness are too great. She said she thought we could do better than that.

She handed me two pairs of safety goggles.

She said, "When you feel like shattering something, I'll be right there with you. We'll put on our safety goggles. I'll help you break something, and then I'll help you clean it up. You've been celebrating with me, and I'll be here to grieve with you. We can do this together."

HAVE YOU ever had a friend share generously in your pain or joy, even though they were in a very different sort of season?

HOPE & HEARTBREAK

"About this time next year," Elisha said, "you will hold a son in your arms." "No, my lord!" she objected. "Please, man of God, don't mislead your servant!"

—2 Kings 4:16

Aaron and I stopped "trying" to have a baby, because it was making me crazy and breaking my heart. I needed to get off that hamster wheel for a while, because I felt dizzy and all scraped away on the inside.

For no good reason, one dark morning, I took a pregnancy test. The pregnancy-test people have a racket going because of people like me, crazed and desperate enough to take a test about every six minutes for absolutely no reason, just in case we've gotten pregnant somehow since the last test, or just in case the last twenty-four tests were wrong. For a while, taking a pregnancy test was about as routine as brushing my teeth.

I found that each time a test was negative, it stopped the dreaming and hoping for a while. Taking the tests was a way of puncturing the balloons of hope, because if I didn't, they would lift and lift without any evidence, and their falling back down every month was too painful. The hoping was breaking my heart.

DO YOU struggle with hope, for a baby or for some other long-desired happening? Take a little time to intentionally be with God alongside your hope and your pain, and rest in him awhile.

FEAR

*Hear my cry for mercy as I call to you for help, as I lift
up my hands toward your Most Holy Place.*

—Psalm 28:2

When I found out I was pregnant with Henry, I felt delight. But this time, one split second after the deep happiness, what I felt was fear. I prayed, but mostly in a manic way, almost chanting out loud, *please, please, please.* After the miscarriages, I'm one of those patients who drives doctors and nurses crazy, because I know too much about the dark side of this. I know what *we'll see* means, and what *hmm* means, during an ultrasound. Worst of all, I know what silence signals. Silence is always, always bad.

My cousin Melody was pregnant as well, after one healthy child and three miscarriages. One night, when we were all gathered around our table, another friend asked me if I was feeling nervous, and I redirected the question to Mel, who was almost thirty weeks along. "Well, I'm nervous, of course, but I'm sure it will get better. Mel, when did it get better for you?"

She didn't bat an eye. "I wish I could tell you something different, but I'm scared every single day. We know too much. We know what can happen."

WHAT IS it that you fear? Does that fear come from the unknown, or from knowing too much? Come honestly to God with your fear and let him bear it with you.

PRAYER FROM OUR FRIENDS

*The Spirit helps us in our weakness. We do not know what we ought to pray
for, but the Spirit himself intercedes for us through wordless groans.*

—Romans 8:26

One morning, early in the pregnancy, there was blood. The door of my
heart swung shut and locked like the door to a safe, impenetrable. An
ultrasound showed a hemorrhage. There was a 50 percent chance that the
hemorrhage would diminish. That left a 50 percent chance that the hemorrhage would grow, and the baby would not survive.

For me, fifty-fifty may as well have been zero-zero. I began to mourn.

My husband and parents reminded me that fifty-fifty is good, but I
couldn't get there. I asked for help and prayer from a couple of close friends.
I was so thankful for people who prayed with faith and expectancy and
courage when all I felt was fear and dread. My own prayers were ragged,
desperate, their fabric torn with anger and shot through with bullets of
accusation and bad memories.

Then at my follow-up appointment, the best possible news. The hemorrhage had diminished. Everything was fine. Alongside fear and gratitude, I
felt the first precious rush of hope.

WHATEVER IS tender or painful in your life, you don't have
to carry it alone. Who can you ask to pray with you and for you?

ON RECEIVING LOVE

God demonstrates his own love for us in this: While
we were still sinners, Christ died for us.

—**Romans 5:8**

When I was pregnant with Mac, I threw up several times a day until the morning I delivered. Being sick forced me to confront the part of me that believes people only love me and keep me around because of what I can do for them. Some people are included because they're beautiful, or rich, or really smart, or professionally successful. I get to stick around because I get stuff done. I'm a workhorse. And all of a sudden, I couldn't work. I couldn't earn my keep, on practical and metaphysical levels.

I've long wanted to be better at accepting help, at admitting weakness, at trusting that people love me just because they do. It would have been lovely to learn those things when I wanted to, the way I wanted to. But we never grow until the pain level gets high enough.

Being so sick for so long was a painful education, but one I needed, one that forced me to embrace the risky but deeply beautiful belief that love isn't something you earn, but something you receive, like a balm, like a benediction, even when you're at your very worst.

IS THERE a part of you that believes love has to be earned? Who are the people in your life that you know love you just because they do? God loves you that way, too.

Baked French Toast

One of my dearest friends makes this especially for holidays, and one Easter when we were both pregnant, after everyone else left the table, we settled in with forks and gobbled up every last bite of this amazingness. It's a perfect brunch or holiday breakfast, and it's great for guests—you can have it in the fridge the night before, just hanging out and getting yummier as it sits. I like to serve it with the Green Chile Strata, because they're both make-ahead, but so different—everyone's happy.

1 loaf cinnamon swirl bread, cubed

1 (8-ounce) package cream cheese, cubed

8 eggs

2 ½ cups milk

6 tablespoons butter

¼ cup maple syrup

» Butter a 13 x 9-inch baking pan, and then cover the bottom of the pan with half the bread cubes. Scatter the cream cheese cubes over them, then top with the remaining bread cubes. In a blender, combine eggs, milk, butter, and maple syrup. Pour over the bread and cream cheese mixture. Cover and refrigerate a few hours or overnight. Bake uncovered at 350 degrees for 30 to 40 minutes, or until a knife inserted in the middle comes out clean. Let stand about 10 minutes before cutting. Serve with warm maple syrup.

BETTER LATE THAN NEVER

Hope deferred makes the heart sick, but a longing fulfilled is a tree of life.

—Proverbs 13:12

We intended to dedicate Henry as a baby. Really, we did. But when Henry turned five, it was still on my to-do list. I was complaining about it, and my cousin Melody jumped in. Her daughter Marley is Henry's age, and they hadn't yet done a dedication.

Melody and I each miscarried three babies in the years between the births of our big kids and our babies. On some wordless, tender level, we kept thinking if we waited, we'd have new babies to dedicate. For five years we kept thinking *pretty soon, any time now*, right? Surely? If you haven't lived it, you can't understand the toll those months of *pretty soon, any time* took on our hearts.

We set a date and decided to keep it simple: a mini burger bar, Brannon's spicy Caesar salad, Uncle Tim's potato salad, and strawberry cardamom shortcakes for dessert. Melody and I and our kids and husbands sat near the fireplace, surrounded by our family and a few friends. Our kids wriggled and babbled while we all read together the words of dedication, and then my father-in-law prayed a blessing for our kids.

Better late than never, indeed.

> **HAVE THERE** been big things, tender things, in your life that came at a different time than when you hoped they would, or thought they should? Invite God into that longing and sorrow for a while.

AS ONE

Many waters cannot quench love; rivers cannot sweep it away.

—Song of Songs 8:7

Aaron and I were married on a hot August night on Michigan Avenue in Chicago, near the lake and Buckingham Fountain and the Art Institute. I walked down the aisle to a Beatles song, and we danced and ate crab cakes and chocolate cake. We watched the fireworks over Navy Pier blend in with the glitter of the city sky. It was both sweet and a little bit wild, like the best parties are.

I had thought that Aaron and I became a family the day we were married. What I have found, though, is that the web starts as just one fine filament on that day, and spins and spins around us day by day. And on some days, the strands spin around us double-time, spinning us like a top and binding us like rubber cement.

Family is not made by ceremonies or certificates, and not by parties and celebrations. Family gets made when you decide to hold hands and sit shoulder to shoulder when it seems like the sky is falling. Family gets made when the future obscures itself like a solar eclipse and in the intervening darkness, you decide that no matter what happens in the night, you'll face it as one.

WE ARE bound together by all our shared experiences, and especially by sticking together during the tough times. Take a moment to thank God for the people who have been knitted into your life through time and experience.

WHAT TRAVEL TEACHES

No stranger had to spend the night in the street, for
my door was always open to the traveler.

—Job 31:32

One of the best parts of my childhood was traveling with my dad. He spent most of his work time at our church, preaching and leading the staff, but sometimes he traveled to other churches, meeting with pastors to talk about faith and leadership and the great privilege that it is for ordinary people to be a part of God's story being written on earth. When I was in elementary school, he took me all over the country. In junior high and high school, I went with him to France, Spain, and Germany, to India and Australia.

My dad worked long hours on those trips. While he worked, I explored and ate. People are sometimes horrified when they hear that I wandered so many big cities all alone as a young teenager, but I found that people all over the world were charming and helpful, and that there might not be as much to fear as we think. I hope our children find the world to be as big and wonderful as I do because of the travel I was able to do at a relatively young age.

WHAT HAS traveling taught you? How has your view of the world been shaped by the people you've met while traveling—or by people who have traveled to where you live?

ON BEING WITH

Brothers and sisters, when we were orphaned by being separated from you for a short time
(in person, not in thought), out of our intense longing we made every effort to see you.

—1 Thessalonians 2:17

Last night we had good friends over, because I won't see them for a while with all the traveling I'll be doing this fall. After all our kids were in bed, we ate Boursin cheese and dark chocolate almonds and strawberries. We drank wine and laughed and caught up, and the sweetness of last night is making my heart ache a little, missing them in advance.

I love what I do, and I'm so deeply thankful to travel for work to so many beautiful parts of the world, but at the same time, I don't want to miss even a moment in this, my everyday life, the blood and bones of day to day.

Maybe this is how it's supposed to be. My friend Steve says that you're a lucky person when you love to go to work in the morning, and you equally love to come home at the end of the day. So I've resolved to be here, present to what life hands me here. And when it is time to be somewhere else, I will be there, present to what life hands me there.

DO YOU find yourself feeling torn between different aspects of your life, between work and home or between travel and the day to day? What helps you to be truly present in each place? Take a moment today to thank God for all of these things you love.

RIDING THE WAVES

He builds his lofty palace in the heavens and sets its foundation on the earth; he calls for the waters of the sea and pours them out over the face of the land—the Lord is his name.

—Amos 9:6

I learned about waves when I was little, swimming in Lake Michigan in navy blue water under a clear sky, and what I learned was this: if you try to stand and face the wave, it will smash you to bits, but if you trust the water and let it carry you, there's nothing sweeter. And a couple of decades later, that's what I'm learning to be true about life, too.

The world is changing all the time. Someone is falling in love right now, and someone is being born. A dream is coming true in some city or small town, and at the same moment, another dream is crumbling. A marriage is ending somewhere, and it's somebody's wedding day, maybe right in the same town.

If you dig in and fight the changes, they will smash you to bits. They'll hold you under, drag you across the rough sand, scare and confuse you. But if you can, in the wildest of seasons, just for a moment, trust in the goodness of God, who made it all and holds it all together, you'll find yourself drawn along to a whole new place, and there's truly nothing sweeter. Unclench your fists, unlock your knees and the door to your heart, take a deep breath, and begin to swim. Begin to let the waves do their work in you.

IN ALL our lives, there are waves. They threaten to take us under, but we're always protected by a God who loves us so deeply.

THE TRACK STAR

Your eyes saw my unformed body; all the days ordained for me
were written in your book before one of them came to be.

—Psalm 139:16

My dad grew up with Joel Jager, in Kalamazoo, Michigan, in the same church, the same school. When my dad moved to Chicago, he and Joel were roommates. Joel's been an audio engineer at the church for over thirty years, and he's like an uncle to me.

This year, Joel's son, Evan, is a senior in high school. He's a runner, and he has won every conference meet, regional meet, and sectional meet he's run. He won state, set a course record, and was ninth in the nation last year. Evan is a phenomenon, that rare combination of natural talent, determination, discipline, and sportsmanship. Joel is proud of that kid, and he loves to watch Evan run.

Joel has never run a day in his life. Joel had polio as a small child and walks with a pronounced limp. When he overexerts himself, he pays for it with a lot of pain for several days afterward. When I was little, I felt very sad and angry about Uncle Joel's legs. And now my dear uncle-friend Joel has a son who is a track star. How's that for sacred hands working behind the scenes, weaving poetry into our lives? It makes me believe in God anew.

WHERE DO you see God working behind the scenes, weaving poetry and redemption into your life?

A WORD ON THE INTERNET

"Do not judge, or you too will be judged."

—Matthew 7:1

A word on the internet: I love you, dear internet. I love that I can learn things and stay connected to people and buy things with one click. But now every time I buy something, I get a follow-up email asking me to "rate my experience." Um, I ordered diapers and then they came. Seriously? A review?

I'm certainly not the first one to point out the ugliness of a culture that wants to rate every experience just immediately after it happened. It seems very cool and democratic to give every person with an internet connection an equal vote on a restaurant or a movie or a book, but over time I think this leads to a culture of unchecked and unaccountable criticism. In the same way that we're in danger of posting what we're doing on Facebook instead of actually doing that thing we're doing, I think we're in danger of thinking that constantly evaluating and rating things is an innocuous practice. And I don't think it is. I think that mindset is corrosive and dangerous over time.

When we become too accustomed to rating and evaluating every single thing, right as it's happening, we start to lose our ability to enjoy things for their imperfections, and we don't allow space for unexpected joys.

HOW MUCH of your time and energy do you find yourself spending evaluating and critiquing your experiences? How does that affect your enjoyment of everyday life?

IRL

If I speak in the tongues of men or of angels, but do not have
love, I am only a resounding gong or a clanging cymbal.

—1 Corinthians 13:1

I know plenty of people who give the very best of themselves to what they're putting on the internet, and their church, their friends, or their family gets the scraps. I know that there is never enough time, never enough energy, never enough of everything to go around.

There's only one way I'm going to make the math work in my life: IRL (In Real Life) above all else. If I can't be present and available every second to the great powerful vortex that is the internet, that's going to have to be okay. You can trust that I'm reading board books to Mac or sounding out Spiderman books with Henry. I'm with my husband or my friends, people who know me well and keep me sane. When things get crazy, I've learned to dig even more deeply into IRL.

The best of me is not in my books and not on my blog. The best of me is what I give to my husband, our boys, our families, our dear friends. In a season that sometimes feels stretched to breaking, I won't allow them to suffer. My first priority is and will always be IRL.

IT'S EASY to let the internet suck up a lot of our time. How does the time and energy you invest IRL stack up against the time and energy you spend online? Does that accurately reflect your values and loves?

INTERNET REGRETS

Love is patient, love is kind. It does not envy, it does not boast,
it is not proud. It does not dishonor others, it is not self-seeking,
it is not easily angered, it keeps no record of wrongs.

—I Corinthians 13:4–5

When I've regretting saying something on the internet, it's never been about love. I've never regretting loving or encouraging or celebrating something. I have often regretted slamming or dismissing or criticizing something, because when I do that online, it's outside of relationship, outside of shared understanding, outside of context.

I know what generates loads of blog hits. I know that controversy is currency. But I think it's worth asking about who you're taking down, in the hopes that your snark and wit will go viral. I think it's worth asking about what happens over time to your insides when you decide to be a hater, when you decide to be the police of the internet, crusading for something or other.

There are enough haters. There always will be. And right at the same time, there will always be enough beauty, enough hope, enough good, if we decide to be people who are always on the lookout for it. I want to use my voice to bring light and hope and beauty. I want to search for what's good, and shout about that.

HAVE YOU ever said anything online that you regretted later? What guidelines do you live by online?

ON CONVERSATION

If you have any encouragement from being united with Christ, if any comfort from his love, if any common sharing in the Spirit, if any tenderness and compassion, then make my joy complete by being like-minded, having the same love, being one in spirit and of one mind.

—Philippians 2:1–2

In the last few years, I've been hurt by careless and unkind words about me and my books online. But way before that, I was a pastor's kid, and I heard people say terrible things about my parents and their friends, people who had given everything they had to do what they believed God was calling them to do. Sometimes reporters were unkind.

I burned through my willingness to argue the rights and wrongs about how to do church when I was about eleven. I got sick of pastors taking shots at one another publicly when I was about thirteen.

And then the internet came along, and anyone with a laptop can insert themselves into a conversation that isn't about them, and pretty soon we're all flinging uninformed opinions around the internet, name-calling and drawing lines in sand, telling ourselves that this is an important conversation.

But is it a conversation? Or is it an easy way to air opinions you never have to back up about real people with real lives and feelings and families?

HOW MIGHT you be able to show tenderness and compassion toward people who have differing opinions, in your real life and in your online world?

THE CONTEXT OF RELATIONSHIP

If it is possible, as far as it depends on you, live at peace with everyone.

—Romans 12:18

I'm surprised how often people ask me to weigh in on this or that small scandal in faith-related happenings or the church world or Christian publishing, when this pastor says that thing about that other pastor, when this author writes negatively about that church or other author. The fact that people are asking these questions doesn't surprise me—but the fact that they're asking *me* does surprise me, because I *never* bite, and unless something unforeseeable and dramatic changes in the future, I never will.

It's not because I don't have strong opinions—I do, and anyone who knows me well knows that there's no shortage of those strong opinions...but that's the point: I share those strong opinions in the context of relationship, because I think that's the healthiest place for them.

Around our table we have all sorts of conversations and disagreements and differences of opinion. But we can hear each other's voices, and we know one another's stories. We can create a loving, kind framework to hold all the differing voices. It's near impossible to do that online. And so I've made it a policy that I don't.

> **IT'S OFTEN** difficult to create the conditions for kind and loving communication online. How do you choose to handle conversations about differences of opinion?

PHYSICAL & SPIRITUAL

*Mount Sinai was covered with smoke, because the LORD descended
on it in fire. The smoke billowed up from it like smoke from a
furnace, and the whole mountain trembled violently.*

—Exodus 19:18

Even though so much of modern life and theology insists that what matters is my mind, my soul, my inner self, my heart, there is still this nagging part of me that knows on some deep level that the things we see and touch and hear and taste are spiritual, too. The dichotomy between spiritual and physical doesn't make sense to me, and it didn't make sense to the Exodus writers either. The olives and the wine and the ideas and the stones and the mountain and the soul all matter deeply and signify something important, instead of the ideas and the souls being truly important, and the rest just being props on loan from the theater department.

Exodus brought to the surface and brought to life this little part inside me that whispered, "I thought so! I hoped so!" I think the best stories always do that, always resound somewhere below our stomachs with a sense of rightness, a sense of congruence with the way we were made and the way we understand ourselves.

HOW DO the physical and intangible aspects of spirituality intermingle in your experience? Reflect on how entering into them both thoughtfully and deliberately might enrich your spiritual life.

Wild Rice Salad

When I ran a marathon, this was one of the things I craved constantly, and it's a great option for a crowd—filling, flavorful, versatile, and only gets better if you leave it in the fridge all night. You can add in anything that sounds good to you, but I like to keep the flavors on the Mediterranean side of things. If you're serving this as a side to meat, or serving it to vegetarians, feel free to omit the sausages.

I start the water boiling first thing, then shake together the vinaigrette. While the rice is cooking, I slice all the add-ins, and pan fry the sausages, if using.

RICE
2 cups wild rice
4 cups water

» Bring water to a boil, then add rice. When it resumes a boil again, turn the heat down to simmer. After 45 to 55 minutes, remove from heat and fluff with a fork.

VINAIGRETTE
1 tablespoon Dijon mustard
1/4 cup balsamic vinegar
1/4 teaspoon salt
1/8 teaspoon pepper
1/2 cup olive oil

» Shake together in a jelly jar, taste, and adjust accordingly.

» Toss the cooled rice with vinaigrette, reserving a little for the end. Then add in handfuls of:

grape tomatoes, halved
Kalamata olives, halved
Bocconcini (small balls of fresh mozzarella), halved
artichoke hearts, quartered
roasted red peppers, cut into short strips
spicy Italian sausages, pan-fried and cut into coins

» Drizzle with remaining vinaigrette, and add salt and pepper. Serve cold or at room temperature.

EXODUS

*Moses cried out to the LORD, "What am I to do with these
people? They are almost ready to stone me."*

—Exodus 17:4

I was surprised to find myself very connected to the story of Exodus. It's a great story, a big, sweeping story about the sea and the desert and the sky, but it's also a story of incredibly fine detail, like a Fabergé egg, like a large painting with teeny tiny brushstrokes. As much as it's a very important story, about big themes and pervasive truths about the nature of God and his people, a finely wrought web of ideas and ideals, it's also about blood and bones and midwives and frogs and fires and bread.

Exodus, and the Bible as a whole for that matter, usually comes sanitized and shrink-wrapped, like chicken breasts at the grocery store in their flat, tidy little plastic packages. But when I read it this time, it seemed more like a bunch of chickens in somebody's backyard, kicking up dust, squawking and screeching and pecking each other, with red and black and white feathers glinting in the hot sun. It's less like a commentary, with footnotes and indexes, and more like a crime novel or a gothic tale of love and belief and betrayal, a story about family and fear and animals and anger.

WHEN WAS the last time a book or passage from the Bible came vividly alive to you? What was that like for you?

DIFFERENT & NOT SO DIFFERENT

Make sacred garments for your brother Aaron to give him dignity and honor.
…Have them use gold, and blue, purple and scarlet yarn, and fine linen.

—Exodus 28:2, 5

On the days that we studied Exodus, I felt myself walk through the rest of the day differently. I ate my hummus and bread and olives at lunch feeling like I was a part of something old and elemental, like eating good, fresh food made by someone's hands was something important. It made me think about the yarn of my scarf, how someone made it with their hands, and how threads and garments and colors mattered so much when they built the ark of the covenant.

Even though a million things are different than they were then, like e-mail and Gore-Tex and Zone Bars and dishwashers, some things are not so different, like bugs and yeast and the impulse to worship. There's still a big story, disguised as regular life, and the big story is about love, death, and God, about bread, wine, and olives, about forgiveness, hunger, and freedom. Exodus was the Wild West, lawless and risky, and it's the cities we live in, bursting with life and meaning, and someday, when the future brings a world we can't even imagine now, Exodus will be there, in the songs and sounds of a people who still wander and yearn for home.

WHAT PARTS of the Bible resonate deeply with your daily life? How do you see your own daily life differently because of that?

WHAT MY FRIEND NEEDED

*In humility value others above yourselves, not looking to your own
interests but each of you to the interests of the others.*

—Philippians 2:3–4

Kristi had offered their home for a Friday night baby shower. That Friday morning, though, I heard from Kristi. Her healthy, active mom had gone to the ER and come home with a diagnosis of advanced liver cancer. Kristi was seven months pregnant, but they got permission from their doctor to leave that night to be with her mother in Calgary.

When I put myself in her place, I thought the last thing she needed was the pressure to leave the house perfect for entertaining. I told her we'd host, that I didn't want her to have to do one more thing.

You didn't tell them to move houses, did you? I told you. I want to do this. Kristi's eyes filled with tears. *It's all done. We're ready. I need to know that something will stay the way it was.*

Then I understood. What *I* may have needed didn't matter. What my friend needed was totally different. She needed to know that something was going as planned while everything else felt so deeply out of control. We don't learn to love each other well in the easy moments. Love is born when we misunderstand one another and make it right.

OFTEN, WHAT a friend needs in a given situation is different from what you might need. Ask God to help you listen well, so that you hear your friends clearly and understand their hearts deeply, so that you can love them well.

August
20

PUSH

Plans fail for lack of counsel, but with many advisers they succeed.

—Proverbs 15:22

I depend quite heavily on my personal board of directors—a little group that acts as compass and guide. I like to feel connected and surrounded by a little tribe that weighs in on the way I'm living in each season.

For many years, what I needed from those most important voices in my life was a push—*You can do this! Your voice matters! You have something to say! Don't be afraid!* My husband, my best friends, my mentors, my family have been such constant and necessary cheerleaders—*Do this! Try it! Write it! Say it!*

I would never have become a writer without those voices. Some people have that *deep-in-the-belly, against-all-odds, though-none-go-with-me* confidence and ambition about their calling or their dream. I am not one of them.

But Aaron wouldn't let me stop. He pushed me and encouraged me. He's my number one biggest supporter and cheerleader. He totally affirms my writing, traveling, and working. My parents, extended family, and close friends have pushed me in the best possible way, too. I'm so thankful for that.

In different seasons, these people have given me all the different kinds of support that I've needed. And I am so thankful.

DO YOU have a personal board of directors, people you rely on for guidance and perspective? Is there anything you need a push toward—to get out there, risk something, try something, start something? Who could, lovingly and wisely, give you that push?

PERMISSION

Better one handful with tranquility than two handfuls
with toil and chasing after the wind.

—Ecclesiastes 4:6

Recently, I've needed permission to slow down, to say no, to admit my fragility and exhaustion.

When I said, *"Babe, I'm too tired, I can't catch up. Something's wrong,"* Aaron gave me the first avalanche of permission in this season.

When my friend and mentor Nancy invited me to an event in California and I sent a wild, rambling, e-mail about how overwhelmed I felt, she replied: *STOP. Say no. Remake your life in a way that works for you, and remake it now.*

When I said to my dad, *I think I need next year to be really different. I'm kind of too tired. I'm kind of scared,* he replied, *I'm so glad to hear this. I've been worried about you, and I love that you're going to slow things down.*

When I told our small group, *I can't do it. Maybe this would work for a stronger person, but I'm done trying to pretend I can run like this,* Matt said, *We don't care what you do or don't do. We're actually not impressed by you. We love you, and that's a different thing.*

What a gift. Those four voices gave me the permission I needed to remake my life.

ARE YOU feeling exhausted and overwhelmed? Do you need to let something go, to walk away, to put down something that you've been carrying for way too long? Do you need permission or affirmation for those choices? Who can give that to you?

RAVENOUS

"Blessed are you who hunger now, for you will be satisfied."
—Luke 6:21

I think I may have a larger appetite than most people. I want more food, more time, more people, more places, more parties, more everything. *More* is a big theme in my life. Other themes in the same vein: hungry, insatiable, and gluttonous.

I'm ravenous in all sorts of ways. I'd like to host a dinner party about every other day. Life is delicious, and I want to gobble it up in big bites, eating, drinking, reading, talking, traveling—everything. I want everything. I'm hungry for everything, all the time. Bookstores make me ravenous, as do city streets and airports and glossy fashion magazines. So much to see, taste, touch, try, do. I can feel myself come to life, eyes open, taking everything in, fingers running over textures, ears pricked for sounds.

Our deepest darknesses are always the other side of the coin of our brightest selves. Exuberance and celebration are wonderful things, and I'm thankful for the ways that they play out in my life. But there's a darkness under that shimmer, and it keeps me exhausted and running, year after year, always thinking that maybe this time, maybe this time, I can fit it all in, and nothing will fall through my fingers.

HAVE YOU been running too hard, consuming too much? What keeps you running and consuming, and what will it take for you to slow down and rest?

August
23

DISCIPLINE THAT HEALS ME

Blessed is the land...whose princes eat at a proper time—
for strength and not for drunkenness.

—Ecclesiastes 10:17

I want to be the kind of person who makes peace with her body. I want to live with peace and confidence, without deprivation and shame. I don't want to live by rules and regulations, but I also don't want to be ruled by my appetites.

I resist and kick at discipline every chance I get, and then when I break down and do something hard, I find that it builds something in me, that it makes me stronger, not just in that area but in all sorts of areas. So for years I was a dieter, a shame-laden hider, fearful and vibrating with self-loathing. Then I was an eater, finally letting myself make peace with my appetites, wary and defensive about any attempt to limit or control.

And now these days, I'm something else, something new. I try to feed myself with care and attentiveness, without shame, without punishment. In some seasons, I choose discipline, not because I'm out of control, not as a punishment, but because it heals me, helps me, and builds and resets something good inside me.

WHAT HAS been your experience with your appetites? With shame and deprivation? With discipline and attention? What could you do today to feed yourself with care and attentiveness, with an eye toward healing?

FEASTING & FASTING

*I urge you, brothers and sisters, in view of God's mercy, to offer your bodies as a
living sacrifice, holy and pleasing to God—this is your true and proper worship.*

—**Romans 12:1**

The word that helps me these days is *fasting*, although I'll plead permission
to use it loosely. I have fasted strictly, as a spiritual discipline, consuming
only broth and juice for a certain amount of time. But I'm using the word
fasting these days as an opposite term to *feasting*—yin and yang, up and down,
permission and discipline, necessary slides back and forth along the continuum of how we feed ourselves.

Maybe certain people can develop a food perspective that they main-
tain seamlessly twelve months a year. Good for them. Maybe that's something I'll be able to do when I'm all grown-up and filled with moderation
and wisdom. Probably not, though. I think I just might be one of those
people who will always need some guardrails along the way.

I love the feasting part of life. I don't want Thanksgiving without stuffing or Christmas without cookies and champagne. I don't want to give up
our family tradition of deep-frying everything we can think of on New
Year's Eve. But I'm learning that feasting can only exist healthfully—physically, spiritually, and emotionally—in a life that also includes fasting.

DO YOU approach food in the same way year-round? Or
do your habits change in various seasons? Are you run by your
appetites, or able to shift in each season?

IRON SHARPENS IRON

As iron sharpens iron, so one person sharpens another.

—**Proverbs 27:17**

What makes iron sharp—what shapes it—are two things: heat and force. You start with heat, because heat is what makes metal malleable. Force is what moves it once you've added the heat. The two work together.

As iron sharpens iron, so one person sharpens another. God uses the people in our lives to tell us the truth about ourselves, to shape us, and to help us be more like Christ. For a friendship to be a transforming friendship, you need the same things as when you're working with metal. Heat and force.

The heat is trust: the sense of being known, accepted, and loved. It's that feeling of warmth when someone knows your story, your family, your strengths and weaknesses, when you know they love you no matter what. Heat is a sense of togetherness, of grace and safety.

And force is truth. It's when someone who cares about you takes the time and the risk to say something difficult, to push you to be better, to call out more from you. Heat is trust and force is truth, and transformation through friendship doesn't happen without both of those things being present.

WHO ARE the friends that you share trust with? Do you tell each other the truth? How have these friendships transformed you?

BEGIN WITH TRUST

*One who has unreliable friends soon comes to ruin, but
there is a friend who sticks closer than a brother.*

—Proverbs 18:24

Heat is what makes metal flexible, able to be shaped and moved. The same is true in relationships: you always start by building trust, little by little, story by story, meal by meal. You always start by building trust. After there's heat, you apply force. To just heat it up makes no change in the long run. To truly transform a piece of metal, you don't just need heat, you have to add force. And heat without force is ineffective. You would never heat a piece of metal unless you wanted to transform it. Just heating it would be useless.

And the same is true in friendship: you begin with trust, but you're transformed by truth-telling. All the trust in the world will not transform you, if there's no truth-telling.

And the opposite is true, of course, both in the shop and in our lives: Banging on cold metal is useless, and loud, and it wears you out. Don't bother swooping in with the truth if you haven't taken the time to build up some trust. Force without heat is both painful and ineffective—both in metalworking, and in life.

HOW HAVE you seen trust and truth-telling at work in your own friendships? Who are you currently building trust with?

August
27

THE VALUE OF TRUTH-TELLING

Whoever rebukes a person will in the end gain favor
rather than one who has a flattering tongue.

—Proverbs 28:23

God can do extraordinary things through friendships that have an equal measure of heat and force, of trust and truth, but most people lean more to one side or more to the other.

Correcting someone, even though it's hard, will gain more favor over time than flattering someone. When there are people in your life who won't ever correct or challenge, who insist that you're perfect just the way you are, that doesn't feel right, does it? If there's no truth, over time, there's no trust. If someone doesn't protect you, doesn't want you to change or get better, doesn't love you enough to overcome the awkwardness of truth-telling, all that love-y, safe, warm trust doesn't feel safe anymore.

The most significant growth in my life in the last few years has come because someone I love told me the truth just when I needed to hear it. Sometimes that truth was encouraging—I'd been going down a dark and self-critical path and they reminded me of God's love for me. And sometimes it's been truth that challenges—when someone looks you in the eye and says, *Because I love you, I want to tell you this, even if it's a little hard to hear.*

WHICH WAY do you tend to lean—toward heat or force, trust or truth? Is there anyone you love who needs to hear the truth from you right now?

TRUTH WITHOUT TRUST

If I speak in the tongues of men or of angels, but do not have
love, I am only a resounding gong or a clanging cymbal.

—1 Corinthians 13:1

In relationships, heat is the trust, and force is the truth, and for transformation, the goal is equal parts heat and force. So what happens when
there's an absence of trust and an overflow of truth?

On the internet there's a whole lot of truth and strong belief and feedback—and absolutely no trust or relationship. You can say what you think,
as nasty and opinionated as you want to be, and you don't even have to tell
people your real name, let alone learn their name or story or background.
You get to yell (in all caps) what you think about absolutely everything—*I
didn't like that restaurant. Your candidate is terrible. Those people are wrong.* The internet
is one big screaming, opinionating example of truth without trust.

How often have you found yourself truly moved to change, to choose
a better path or make something right, because someone on the internet
screamed about it?

I'm not saying the internet is inherently bad. I'm saying it allows us
to communicate our strong beliefs and opinions outside of relationship,
and that's a lot like swinging a hammer at a piece of ice cold metal, hoping
it will transform.

WHAT HAS been your experience of truth outpacing trust?
Did you learn anything useful from it?

ON GOSSIP

*With the tongue we praise our Lord and Father, and with it we curse human
beings, who have been made in God's likeness. Out of the same mouth
come praise and cursing. My brothers and sisters, this should not be.*

—James 3:9–10

The goal is that our closest relationships are marked by equal parts heat and
force so that God can use trust and truth to shape us. Most of us tend toward
one side or the other—more heat, or more force. More trust or more truth.
But there's another category: those who have all the heat in the world to your
face, and all the force in the world behind your back. Gossip is so dangerous, because it makes you feel like you told the truth. And you did. Just not
to the person involved. It scratches that itch, that impulse to tell the truth,
but it has no power to transform, and it destroys trust.

When you speak negatively about someone, you begin to think more
negatively about that person, and so does the person you were talking to.
Gossip infects everyone involved—it creates false little alliances, false trust:
you and I get it, he doesn't. We're on the inside, giggling just a little about
that guy over there. Words are power. You can use them to sharpen, to in-
spire, to call to Christlikeness, or you can use them to make yourself feel
safe and included.

HOW HAS gossip affected you? How are you using the power
of words? How could you use them in a braver, more loving way?

SUMMER ALL YEAR LONG

Harvest the wine, summer fruit and olive oil, and put them in your storage jars.

—Jeremiah 40:10

When I was growing up, Sunday afternoons were family time—private, casual, silly. After church, my dad was tired but happy, loose, easygoing. My brother and I got to watch the Bears game while we did our homework in the study instead of doing it at the kitchen table like we usually did. My mom made sushi for lunch, and for dinner, blueberry crisp.

My mom baked her blueberry crisp in a round, blue earthenware baking dish, deep enough for there to be several inches of warm, bursting berries under the sweetness of the crisp topping. The dish had a fitted lid and handles on each side, and she would bring it down to the study with potholders and with the lid on, so that even if we had seconds, it was still warm.

She topped each bowl of crisp with a scoop of Breyers vanilla bean ice cream, flecked with dark specks of vanilla, and the ice cream melted into the crisp layer and the hot berries in thick, creamy rivers. It was a treat to taste the summer flavors of the lake back at home in the suburbs during the winter.

WHAT FOOD-RELATED traditions or memories does your family enjoy? Are there any that you'd like to start?

SOMEONE STRONGER THAN I WAS

Your Father knows what you need before you ask him.

— M a t t h e w 6 : 8

When Mac was ten days old, he developed a high fever and was admitted to the PICU. The first night, because Henry was also sick, I ended up staying at the hospital alone with Mac.

That night was bleak—I felt insubstantial, like my bones and blood were gone and I was vapor. I felt profoundly, deeply alone. I could have asked for company, and my friends and family would have come. But I didn't know what I needed, let alone how to say it.

The next morning, Aaron was at the pediatrician with Henry, my mom was trying to get home from out of town, and my dad had a day full of meetings. My dad stopped over before his first meeting. It was clear to him that I was hanging by a filament, dazed and worn-out. "I think I'll stay," he said calmly. He called his assistant and told her his meetings needed to be rescheduled.

That act registers to me as one of his finest parenting moments. I don't know what was written on my face that morning, but I needed to not be alone, in the most desperate of ways. I needed someone to be stronger than I was that day.

WHAT DO you remember as your dad's finest parenting moments? Who else has stepped into that role and been strong for you when you needed it? If you are married, how have you seen your husband do that for your kids?

ON ASKING FOR HELP

I rejoiced greatly in the Lord that at last you renewed your concern for me.
Indeed, you were concerned, but you had no opportunity to show it.

—**Philippians 4:10**

When I was writing *Bittersweet*, I sent an e-mail to friends and family that said in part, "*Bittersweet* has a been a really difficult project for me. And it's due in a month. I'm looking for a way to feel a little less isolated. I don't know what that looks like. I just know that one of the best ways to feel stronger than you are is to invite the people you walk with into your life and days."

By the end of the day, my inbox was bursting with messages. People prayed for me. They sent me scripture, poetry, cards, thoughtful texts, loads of great advice, and even gifts. They checked in with me, did careful reading, and gave great feedback.

People really do want to care for us and help us, but most of us are afraid to ask. I don't often give my friends opportunities to enter into the messier moments of my life in real time and help me. But I did this time, and this is how I want to live: connected and not too proud to receive, honest and strong because the people around me are strong, and because they believe in me more than I believe in myself on some days.

WHAT DOES it feel like for you to ask for help? To receive help? How has this affected your relationships in the past? Keep an eye out for times when you truly could use some help from the people you love and trust.

WORDS PUT US BACK TOGETHER

*One who has unreliable friends soon comes to ruin, but
there is a friend who sticks closer than a brother.*

—**Proverbs 18:24**

After my last week at my job in Grand Rapids, I made homemade macaroni and cheese and roasted vegetables for our house church, and after dinner, they asked me how I was doing. I was brimming over with anger and confusion and fear, wild with emotion. I was barely comprehensible, running from one fear to the next. I felt embarrassed about not being able to move forward more quickly, and about being a wreck, and about the tears that were all over my face.

At one point, Joe interrupted me. "You can feel however you want to feel right now. Except one thing. I keep hearing you say that you're embarrassed. I want you to stop saying that. You can feel angry, betrayed, whatever. But I don't think you have anything to be embarrassed about. And I'll never be embarrassed to be your friend."

I felt like I had been ground to dust, and those words started to put me back together. During a time when I had nothing to give but venom and tears, this small circle of people were the words and fragrance and presence of God in unmistakable ways.

IS THERE anyone in your life who might need to be put back together by your words today?

September

3

SCARY AROUND THE EDGES

*"A new command I give you: Love one another. As I have
loved you, so you must love one another."*

—John 13:34

Friendship is an opportunity to act on God's behalf in people's lives, reminding each other who God is. When we do the hard, intimate work of friendship, we bring a little more of the divine into daily life. We get to remind one another about the bigger, more beautiful picture that we can't always see from where we are.

True friendship is a sacred, important thing, and it happens when we enter into that deeper level of who we are, when we cross over into the broken, fragile parts of ourselves. We have to give something up in order to get friendship like that. We have to give up our need to be perceived as perfect. We have to give up our ability to control what people think of us. We have to overcome the fear that when they see the depths of who we are, they'll leave. But what we give up is nothing compared to what this kind of friendship gives us. Friendship is about risk. Love is about risk. If we can control it and manage it and manufacture it, then it's something else, but if it's really love, really friendship, it's a little scary around the edges.

IT'S WORTH the risk of being vulnerable, being authentic, to have a chance to become real friends. When was the last time you took a risk with a friend? How did it change or enrich your connection?

267

A TRIBE

Follow God's example, therefore, as dearly loved children and
walk in the way of love, just as Christ loved us and gave himself
up for us as a fragrant offering and sacrifice to God.

—Ephesians 5:1–2

The Cooking Club began when we moved back to Chicago. There are six of us. We meet once a month, and whoever's hosting picks the theme and cooks the main course, and the rest of us fill in around that—appetizers, sides, desserts.

Those five faces around the table keep me sane, keep me safe, protect me from the pressures of daily life. It isn't because we do all the same things, live all the same ways, believe all the same things. We are single and married, liberal and conservative, runners and adamant nonathletes, mothers and not.

On the hardest days, when something scares us, we send a quick group e-mail, even as our hands are shaking, while the pain is slicing. We fill everyone in, ask for prayer, let everyone know how they can help and at the end of the e-mail, someone always says, *Thanks for being my people.*

This isn't about recipes. This is about a family, a tribe, a little band of people who walk through it all together, up close and in the mess.

DO YOU have a tribe that supports you and shares life together, good and bad? If so, take a moment to thank God for them. If not, is there a step you could take toward gathering that kind of tribe?

A TABLE BETWEEN US

When evening came, Jesus was reclining at the table with the Twelve.

—**Matthew 26:20**

I'm worn out and the house is ragged, but my mind and heart are full from last night's Cooking Club celebration for Brannon's baby. It was a lovely, wild night—babies everywhere, dishes sprawled all over the kitchen, platters of brisket and plates of macaroons fighting for space among wine glasses and forks.

As I got the house ready, I thought that it might be nice to sit in the living room. I moved furniture, made a place for presents, and set up a buffet on the round table.

When everything was ready, I tried to move everyone to the living room, and it just didn't work. I kept urging them toward the buffet, toward the couches and chairs in the living room. Finally I admitted defeat, and we pulled a love seat up to the dining room table for extra seating and settled in happily. That's where we belong, it seems—around the table.

When Josilyn moved to Haiti, she wrote us a letter to say good-bye. Her letter included this line: *I can't imagine life without a table between us.* Yes. The table is the life raft, the center point, the home base of who we are together.

WHERE IS the place in your home you connect best with others?

MY HOME

Above all, love each other deeply, because love covers over a multitude of sins. Offer
hospitality to one another without grumbling. Each of you should use whatever gift you
have received to serve others, as faithful stewards of God's grace in its various forms.

—1 Peter 4:8–10

I always wanted a home filled with people. Our home growing up was quite private. My dad worked long hours at our church, and my mom is an introvert, and those two dynamics created a home that was quiet, private, safe. It was exactly right for my family, but at the same time, I longed for a little loud. I wanted a full table, glasses clinking, laughter bubbling up over the music. I wanted cars parked all the way down the street, and people who came in without knocking, so familiar with our home that they mixed their own drinks and knew where to put the dishes after drying them.

When I moved into my own house, that's exactly what I did. The day I closed on it, I invited a bunch of friends over. It was completely empty because I hadn't yet moved in any furniture, so we sat in a circle on plastic deck chairs, eating chips and salsa served on one of those little tables you roll up and take to the beach. I filled that little town house with people I loved every chance I got—with welcome-to-town parties and going-away parties, gatherings for award shows and dinner parties.

DOES YOUR home meet your needs? Does it help you to use your gifts to serve others? What small changes might allow your home to better reflect and support who you are?

September

7

HEAT, KNIFE, SIZZLE

That each of them may eat and drink, and find satisfaction
in all their toil—this is the gift of God.

—Ecclesiastes 3:13

My friends and I didn't learn to cook, necessarily. In an effort to widen our options, to set us free to be whatever we wanted to be, many of our mothers shooed us out of the kitchen—that place of lingering oppression and captivity for many of them. They encouraged us to study and travel and participate in sports and the arts, the things women didn't get to do when they were young.

But many of us, men and women alike, at a certain point, are wandering back to the kitchen and fumbling and learning and trying to feed ourselves and the people we love, because we sense that it's important and that we may have missed something fundamental along the way. Especially for those of us who make our livings largely in front of computer screens, there's something extraordinary about getting up from the keyboard and using our hands for something besides typing—for chopping and dicing and coaxing scents and flavors from the raw materials in front of us. There's something entirely satisfying in a modern, increasingly virtual world about something so elemental—heat, knife, sizzle.

FOOD AND drink were some of the earliest gifts God gave us, and they are still satisfying today. Are you creating meaningful opportunities to nourish the people you love?

CONTENTMENT

LORD, you alone are my portion and my cup; you make my lot secure. The boundary lines have fallen for me in pleasant places; surely I have a delightful inheritance.

—Psalm 16:5–6

This is my favorite part of Psalm 16. These verses are a vision of contentment, and they can help us in two ways: as an assessment and as an aspiration. Sometimes you might look at those verses and think, *My cup and my portion? Please! Not nearly enough! Are you crazy? These boundary lines? I am not feeling pleasant at all about them.*

If that's how you feel when you read those verses, it's a sign that a lack of contentment is working its way into your life. You've bought into the idea that you know more than God knows about what will bring you true contentment. Your honest response to these verses is a warning indicator. It helps you know how much inner work, with God's help, needs to be done. It's painful, but it's helpful.

If you feel your heart resounding with these words, you're living with contentedness. You're letting God's vision for your life define your expectations for it. You're letting his parameters be your parameters. When you begin to love the boundary lines God has placed on your life, you begin to experience true joy, true freedom, and true contentment.

WHAT IS your gut-level response to these verses? Be honest with God about it, and if you don't love the boundary lines he's given you, ask him to help you see the beauty in them.

LEARNING WITH OUR HANDS

Wisdom will enter your heart, and knowledge will be pleasant to your soul.

—**Proverbs 2:10**

One winter I went to a week-long culinary boot camp at The Chopping Block, a recreational cooking school in the city. What I learned there is that we learn by doing. We learn with our hands and our noses. We learn by tasting the stock, feeling the hum of the knife back and forth, listening for the sounds of hot oil. We roll an omelet out of a pan wrong five times in a row, and then the sixth time, the whole group cheers because one of us made one perfect omelet.

Almost everything I know in the world, I learned from novels, memoirs, and stories. I could practically draw you a map of Milan, Rome, or Venice, even though I've never been to any of them. I've read about how to make the perfect Old Fashioned, tend a rose garden, butterfly a pork loin.

But then you find yourself standing at a bar or kneeling in the dirt or holding a very sharp chef's knife, and you realize all at once that it doesn't matter what you've read or seen or think you know. You learn it, really learn it, with your hands. With your fingers and your knife, your nose and your ears, your tongue and your muscle memory, learning as you go.

WHAT'S ONE thing you've researched and read about but haven't yet experienced? What's a concrete step you can take today?

SCARY HEADLINES

*I urge...that petitions, prayers, intercession and thanksgiving be
made for all people—for kings and all those in authority, that we may
live peaceful and quiet lives in all godliness and holiness.*

—1 Timothy 2:1–2

I got a letter recently from our bank. Enclosed was a lovely little story, possibly written by a child, about rain and umbrellas and waiting out a storm, and essentially, it was a two-page way of saying, hey, don't freak out. Um, I wasn't, really, till my bank sent me a letter about storms and floods written either for or by a seven-year-old.

Deep breath. On the days when I'm tempted to lie down on the ground and let the anxiety I feel about our world flatten me like a steamroller, instead I pray. I speak to God, sometimes out loud, often in the car, frequently in the shower. I ask for help about things I don't understand. I ask for peace, and grace, and the ability to see outside myself. I pray for people who are at the mercy of the scary headlines—auto workers who are losing jobs, children whose parents are unable to provide for them. And I pray for the people who can solve these problems—politicians, pastors, philanthropists. I pray for a way through, a light at the end of the tunnel.

THERE ARE so many things going on in this world that we have no control over. Prayer is the alternative to anxiety that can be crushing. How do you—or how might you—pray in response to those things?

SEPTEMBER 11

I will take refuge in the shadow of your wings until the disaster has passed.

—Psalm 57:1

September 11, 2001, was a Tuesday. Aaron and I had been married two weeks and had arrived home from our honeymoon just two days before. We didn't totally understand the implications of what had happened. No one did, of course. But we knew instinctively that it was a night to spend with family, and we realized with a jolt that that's what we were. We were family.

But he wasn't yet, at that point. A wedding didn't make him my family, or a honeymoon, or grudgingly giving him a little bit of space in the bathroom. What did make him my family was the decision to stay home with him on that Tuesday night, to sit, holding hands, watching the news for hours. Our first impulse was to go home to our parents' houses. Instead we stayed in a house that didn't particularly feel like home for either one of us at that point, and it became a little bit more of a home that night. That's how family gets made.

WE BECOME family by the choices we make as we respond to each day, whatever that day brings. Who has become family in your life, because you've chosen to invest deeply?

September

12

TODAY

Let us rejoice today and be glad.

—Psalm 118:24

I know that the world is several versions of mad right now. Pessimism and grimness sometimes seem like the only responsible choices. I wake up at night and think about pesticides and international politics and fundamentalism and disease and roadside bombs and the fact that one day my parents will die. I worry about the world we're creating for my sons.

That's why I'm making a shameless appeal for celebration. I need optimism and celebration and hope in the face of violence and despair and anxiety. The other road is a dead end. Despair is a slow death, and a lifetime of anger is like a lifetime of hard drinking: it shows in your face and your eyes and your words even when you think it doesn't.

The only option, as I see it, is a delicate weaving of action and celebration, of intention and expectation. Let's act, read, protest, protect, picket, learn, advocate for, fight against, but let's be careful that in all that accomplishing and organizing, we don't bulldoze over a world that's teeming with beauty and hope and redemption all around us. Before the wars are over, before the cures are found, before the wrongs are righted, Today, humble Today, presents itself to us with all the ceremony of a glittering diamond ring: *Wear me,* it says. *Wear me out. Love me, dive into me, discover me.*

TODAY, SOMEWHERE nearby, beauty and hope are quietly glimmering, waiting to be noticed.

DO SOMETHING

Elijah said to her, "Don't be afraid. . . . Make a small loaf of bread for me from what
you have and bring it to me, and then make something for yourself and your son."

—1 Kings 17:13

When the world seems filled with terrible news, it brings me a little peace to try to help. I volunteer sometimes at our church's food pantry, and often I show up, distracted and stressed, worried that I don't really have the time away from my computer to do this, that I'll fall behind, that I'll never make any writing progress if I keep using writing time to do other stuff. And then I sit across the table from a woman holding a baby, and we talk about her family. We walk together through the pantry, picking out fruit and meat and bread. I walk her to her car and help load the groceries in the trunk. As I leave, I know that I didn't solve her problems, by any means, but that for a few weeks, her cupboards will be full, and I was a tiny part of bringing that about.

When you're worried, when you're overwhelmed, when it all seems like too much, it really helps to do something, even something small. Buy groceries for one person in your life who could really use them. Offer to babysit for new parents. Bring someone flowers. Do something.

THERE'S NEVER any shortage of bad news or of people who need help. How could you help one person in your life this week?

LABELING

Leaving her water jar, the woman went back to the town and said to the people,
"Come, see a man who told me everything I ever did. Could this be the Messiah?"

—John 4:28–29

There was a person in my life who made me crazy. She was control, control, control. Perfection, perfection, perfection. Her anxiety brought out my anxiety and exhausted me. I'm sorry to say I did what we often do with people who make us crazy. I labeled her: *control freak.* I congratulated myself for being so laid-back compared to Little Miss Hand Sanitizer.

Then one night she told me about what life was like for her as a little girl, about how she practically lived at the hospital when her mom was dying and how careful they had to be about germs. Her little-girl self had taken it upon herself never to be dirty because it could make her mom sick.

I blushed with shame, furious with myself that I had done it again: I labeled and distanced. I didn't listen. And when I finally did listen, the story made it all make sense.

Aren't we all like that in some way? Impossible. Crazy-making. Until someone sticks around long enough to hear the story of how we got here, what winding journey brought us along and made us who we are.

WHO IN your life is driving you crazy? Have you labeled them? How well do you know their story? Ask God to give you the opportunity to learn more of that person's story and understand them in a new way.

NO THROWAWAY MOMENTS

I have learned the secret of being content in any and every situation.

—Philippians 4:12

I sat with an old friend today. She and her husband have endured unimaginable loss throughout the course of their lives and another very fresh loss in these last months.

We sat in the golden, fading light of a Chicago spring. Our kids ran around the screened porch, and the grass was impossibly green, almost glowing. She told me the particulars of that most recent loss, and she was present to it, unafraid. She spoke unflinchingly, and I saw in her a vision for how I want to live. In one of her darkest seasons, twisted with uncertainty, bruised by the words of former friends, she sat with me, present and unafraid. She looked in my eyes and told me funny and sweet things about her kids, asked me about myself. She wasn't shut down, going through the motions. She was right there with me, with her kids, in all the glory and pain and mess and beauty of a spring night.

My friend knows there are no throwaway moments—not when it's easy, or hard, or boring, or you're waiting for something to happen. Throw those moments away and you will look back someday, bereft at what you missed, because it's the good stuff. It's all there is.

HOW PRESENT are you to your life right now? Are there moments you're in danger of throwing away? Why? What would it take for you to be fully present?

ALL AROUND US

Better what the eye sees than the roving of the appetite.

—Ecclesiastes 6:9

On a recent trip to Mexico, we realized our phones didn't work unless we wanted to pay a fortune in data roaming charges, and my e-mail didn't work on the desktop at the house. I checked my e-mail on my phone every morning to see if anything pressing had come up, but other than that, we did things the old-fashioned way: we left each other notes and set meeting places.

We sometimes missed each other, but there was something fantastic about saying, "I'll see you when I get back." Or, "they went for a walk, and maybe they'll be back in an hour." No constant texts, no calls back and forth from the grocery store, no check-in about whether the baby was still sleeping. No Twitter, no Facebook, no blog reading.

I felt a little jumpy, like something really major might be happening and I might miss it. But as time went on, I realized that the really major things were happening all around me. I had been missing them because my phone had become an extension of my hand, and what it said to people is that just being with them isn't enough. This view of the ocean? Not enough. Your story? Not enough.

> **OUR PHONES** and blogs and social media connect us in so many ways. Have you noticed any times in your life when they cut you off from what's going on around you? Today, make a point to put down your phone to see what you've been missing.

AN APPETITE FOR SILENCE

I have calmed and quieted myself, I am like a weaned child
with its mother; like a weaned child I am content.

—Psalm 131:2

The week in Mexico was amazing: the wide glittering sea, babies and kids, swimming and tacos and limes and laughter and people we love. But it was magical on a deeper level too, because it created in me an appetite for silence that I hadn't tasted for years, possibly. The constant chatter and conversation and mental clutter we create with Twitter and Facebook and Pinterest and blogs was, for one week, blessedly silent. It was like going on a juice fast for your brain, and as much as you're starving, you feel strong and whole and healthy and clear for the first time in a long time. After a few days, I realized how much I liked it. How much the silence sounded like music, and how much better I liked my own life in that silence.

When I think back to Mexico, I force myself to lay down my phone for a while. I practice being entirely where I am, glamorous or not, and I find that it's better to be in one place, wholly and full-heartedly, than a thousand splintery half-places, glamorous as they may be.

HAVE YOU ever gone on a technology fast—either voluntarily or accidentally? If so, what was that like? How often do you feel that you are wholly and full-heartedly in one place? Are there any changes that you'd like to make in that regard? If so, what small step could you take today?

SPLINTERS

I said, "Oh, that I had the wings of a dove! I would fly away and be at rest....
I would hurry to my place of shelter, far from the tempest and storm."

—Psalm 55:6, 8

I'm not antitechnology, but I realized during that week away that vacation isn't always about a change of venue. We travel a lot for fun and work, and we always have phones, laptops, iPads. No matter where we are, we're as connected as we are at home, sometimes more so, because we have more free time.

Like more and more people, we don't have set work hours. There are good things that go with that—flexibility, freedom, lots of time with our kids. But it means we're sort of working all the time. Aaron will get out of bed to run down to the studio to listen to a mix a producer sends him. I get e-mails about upcoming events while I'm nursing or at a museum or watching Henry's soccer practice. The best part about blending all those boundaries is also the worst part: we're always connected to everyone all the time.

In Mexico, the silence let me be completely in one place. I was totally there, without feeling like my mind was divided into a thousand small splinters, spinning out all over the world, leaving nothing but a glassy stare and twitchy fingers always reaching for my phone.

HOW DO you manage the demands of being connected all the time? Do you ever have an opportunity to unplug from any of it? Do you want to?

19

ON FOOD RESTRICTIONS

John's clothes were made of camel's hair, and he had a leather belt
around his waist. His food was locusts and wild honey.

—**M a t t h e w   3 : 4**

Many cooks and food writers have nothing but negative things to say about people who have dietary restrictions or preferences. Often it's suggested that you just make what you want to make, and everyone can find something to eat, most likely. But if feeding people around your table is about connecting with them more than about showing off your skills, isn't it important to cook in such a way that their preferences or restrictions are honored?

I've heard several chefs and home cooks say their solution is to only invite dinner guests who aren't picky, are allergy-free, and who love to eat. For me, that would mean not inviting some of my closest friends and family, and instead having some sort of open-casting call for low-maintenance eaters for my dinner parties. That sounds like a terrible plan.

Instead of being annoyed at my guests' proclivities and restrictions, I've tried to look at them as a challenge. Cooking with staples like bread and sugar is easy. Making things taste great with big-flavor items like bacon and cream is a snap. How do I honor and nourish my guests without red meat or dairy or gluten? That's where the challenge begins.

A R E   T H E R E people in your family or circle of friends with particular dietary needs? How do you feel about cooking for them, about including them in meals and gatherings?

─────── **283** ──────

WHAT WE ATE

God saw all that he had made, and it was very good.

—Genesis 1:31

Many of the most deeply spiritual moments of my life haven't happened just in my mind or soul. They happened while holding my son in the middle of the night, or watching the water break along the shore, or around my table, watching the people I love feel nourished in all sorts of ways.

The idea that faith and meaning happen in your mind or soul where no one can see them is one of the worst by-products of modern Christianity. We are physical beings. And *physical* isn't negative. If we didn't have bodies, we couldn't feel the sun on our faces or smell the earthy, mushroom-y rich smell of the ground after the rain. If we didn't have bodies, we couldn't wrap our arms around the people we love or taste a perfect tomato at the height of summer. I'm so thankful to live in this physical, messy, blood-and-guts world. I don't want to live in a world that's all dry ideas and theorems. Food is one of the ways we acknowledge our humanity, our appetites, our need for nourishment. It may seem trivial to some people, but when I'm telling a story, the part about what we ate really does matter.

GOD CREATED this physical world, and he designed the ways we experience it with our bodies. These are gifts, not to be dismissed.

MOMS & SONS

He tends his flock like a shepherd: he gathers the lambs in his arms and carries them close to his heart; he gently leads those that have young.

—Isaiah 40:11

The summer I was pregnant with Henry, my mom and I spent a week in Chicago, taking a class at a Catholic graduate school. On Tuesday morning of that week, my dad called from South Haven to tell us that my brother had been in a bad car accident. Todd called a few minutes later to tell us that he was fine, and we felt blessed and lucky and a little bit like it wasn't real, because he sounded so fine on the phone.

Later, though, we talked to Dad again, and he told us how different it would have been if the cars had been a second earlier or later in the intersection. My brother could have died that morning. This was not a near miss but a miracle.

My mom began to cry. She cried for her son, for what could have happened, for being far away from him. We both put our hands on my belly, on my son, while she talked to him through her tears. She said, "Be careful, Henry. We love you so much." We sat there for a long time, she thinking about her big, grown son, and me thinking about my tiny son, curled up inside me.

WHAT KINDS of miracles and near misses have you had in your own family? What kinds of losses? What have you learned about prayer in both kinds of situations?

Grilled Peach & Caramel Sundaes

In the summertime, I'll do anything to avoid using the oven, but I can manage the stove. Part of the reason this recipe yields a quite large amount of caramel sauce is because I can make one jar for either a full dinner party or a couple nights of guests, and store the rest in the refrigerator.

CARAMEL SAUCE

» Over medium heat, stir together:

2 cups brown sugar
1 cup half-and-half
½ cup butter

» Allow to bubble gently for 6 to 8 minutes, stirring occasionally. When it's a rich amber color, remove from heat, and stir in a pinch of salt. I usually do this before dinner, and let it sit on the stove while we eat. Then just before serving, I put the heat on low to warm it a little before adding to the sundaes.

GRILLED PEACHES

» Halve peaches and remove the stone. Brush with melted butter, and then place cut side down on a medium-hot grill. Grill for 8 to 10 minutes, or until very soft, with dark grill marks.

» To assemble: scoop vanilla ice cream into bowls, top with hot peaches, and a thick drizzle of caramel sauce. For crunch, add a sprinkle of pecans or granola.

THE ACHES OF MOTHERHOOD

Then Simeon blessed them and said to Mary, his mother:
… "A sword will pierce your own soul too."

—Luke 2:34–35

I know, cognitively, that all of parenting is an effort to give your kids the ability to live without you, beyond you. I know that Henry will make me mad, and probably date girls who wear too much makeup, or he'll have bad table manners to spite me, or play dangerous sports. He will break my heart into slivers over and over as he grows away from me, and he should grow away from me. That's the only right thing for him to do.

When I was pregnant with Henry and my brother was in a bad car accident, I felt one of the first splitting aches of motherhood. I felt that nothing in the world could hurt my son, that I am superhuman in my love for him, that if he needed me, I would fly or bend steel or wrinkle time with the force of my love. In the same moment, I knew that all mothers feel that way, and that all mothers also feel the exact inverse, the terrifying awareness that people run red lights, and that we won't be there to stand in front of our son's cars, shielding them from danger with our superhuman selves.

WHERE ARE your children in their journey to grow away from you? How has motherhood (or the longing for motherhood) caused you to ache? Who has walked with you through that?

BREAD & WINE

Because there is one loaf, we, who are many, are one body, for we all share the one loaf.

—1 Corinthians 10:17

I'm a bread person—crusty, golden baguette; hearty, grainy, seeded loaves; thin, crispy pizza crust—all of it. Flaky, buttery croissants; chewy pita; tortillas, warm and fragrant, blistered by heat. Whenever my jeans are too tight, I'm reminded that I know better than to love bread the way I do, but love is blind, and certainly beyond reason. And I am a wine person—the blood-red and liquid gold, the clink and glamour of tall-stemmed glasses, and the musty, rich, almost mushroom-y smell.

More than that, I am a bread-and-wine person. By that I mean that I'm a Christian, a person of the body and blood, a person of the bread and wine. I recognize the two as food and drink, and at the very same time, I recognize them as something much greater—mystery and tradition and symbol. Bread is bread, and wine is wine, but bread-and-wine is another thing entirely. The two together are the sacred and the material at once, heaven and earth, the divine and the daily.

BREAD AND wine bring us together in so many ways—physically, socially, emotionally, and even spiritually. Today, as you encounter the simple elements of bread and wine, pause to thank God for his sustaining love.

EVERY TIME WE ARE FED

When they landed, they saw a fire of burning coals there with fish on it,
and some bread. . . . Jesus said to them, "Come and have breakfast."

—John 21:9, 12

Food matters because it's one of the things that forces us to live in this world—this tactile, physical, messy, and beautiful world—no matter how hard we try to escape into our minds and our ideals. Food is a reminder of our humanity, our fragility, our createdness. Try to command yourself not to be hungry, using your own sheer will. It will work for a while, maybe, but at some point you'll find yourself—no matter how high-minded or iron-willed—face-to-face with your own hunger and your own humanity.

The sacraments are tangible ways to represent intangible ideas: new life becomes something we can feel and smell and see when we baptize in water. The idea of a Savior, of a sacrifice, of body and blood so many centuries ago, fills our senses and invades our present when our fingers break bread and our mouths fill with wine.

We don't experience this connection, this remembering, this intimate memory and celebration of Christ, only at the altar. We experience it, or at least we could, every time the bread and wine are present—essentially, every time we are fed.

EATING REMINDS us that in addition to food, we need spiritual sustenance every day. Today, every time you eat, let yourself be reminded of God's nourishing presence.

RECLAIMING THE TABLE

While they were eating, Jesus took bread, and when he had given thanks, he broke it and gave it to his disciples, saying, "Take and eat; this is my body." Then he took a cup, and when he had given thanks, he gave it to them, saying, "Drink from it, all of you. This is my blood of the covenant, which is poured out for many for the forgiveness of sins."

—Matthew 26:26–28

Both the church and modern life have wandered away from the table. The church has preferred to live in the mind and the heart and the soul, and almost not at all in fingers and mouths and senses. And modern life has pushed us into faux food and fast food and highly engineered food products cased in sterile packages that we eat in the car or on the subway—as though we're astronauts, as though we can't be bothered with a meal.

All through the Bible, all through the stories about God and his people, there are stories about food—about all of life changing with the bite of an apple; about trading an inheritance for a bowl of stew; about waking up to find the land littered with bread; about a wedding where water turned to wine; about the very first Last Supper, the humble bread and wine becoming indelibly linked to the very body of Christ, the center point for thousands of years of tradition and belief. It matters. It mattered then, and it matters now, possibly even more so, because it's a way of reclaiming some of the things we may have lost along the way.

WHEN WE consider how many stories in the Bible involve food, perhaps it's not something to be treated as lightly as we often do.

SACRED MEALS

They devoted themselves to the apostles' teaching and to
fellowship, to the breaking of bread and to prayer.

—Acts 2:42

When you eat, I want you to think of God, of the holiness of hands that feed us, of the provision we are given every time we eat. When you eat bread and you drink wine, I want you to think about the body and the blood every time, not just when the bread and wine show up in church, but when they show up anywhere—on a picnic table or a hardwood floor or a beach.

Some of my most sacred meals have been eaten out of travel mugs on camping trips or on benches on the street in Europe. Many of them have been at our own table or around our coffee table, leaning back against the couch. They've been high food and low food, fresh and frozen, extravagant and right out of the pizza box. It's about the table, and about all the other places we find ourselves eating. It's about a spirit or quality of living that rises up when we offer one another life itself, in the form of dinner or soup or breakfast, or bread and wine.

WHEN WE pay attention, we discover that God is with us everywhere and that every meal holds the possibility of being a sacred meal.

HUNGER & SHAME

So God created mankind in his own image, in the image of God
he created them; male and female he created them.

—Genesis 1:27

I've always been hungry. I remember being hungry as a small child, as an adolescent girl, as an adult, and just after I locate those feelings and memories of hunger, in my peripheral vision another thing buzzes up, like a flash of heat or pain: shame. Hunger, then shame. Always hungry, always ashamed.

It took becoming pregnant to finally say out loud and without embarrassment, *I'm hungry.* My first pregnancy shifted my understanding of my body and, with it, shifted my view of hunger. Even if I couldn't claim my own hunger without experiencing a shiver of shame, I could claim hunger on behalf of my baby, and that small step might as well have been a mile for all it unlocked inside me.

Several years later, I'm learning to practice gratitude for a healthy body, even if it's rounder than I'd like it to be. I'm learning to take up all the space I need, literally and figuratively, even though we live in a world that wants women to be tiny and quiet. To feed one's body, to admit one's hunger, to look one's appetite straight in the eye without fear or shame—this is controversial work in our culture.

HOW DO you feel about feeling hungry? How much space do you think God wants you to have? Ask him, and listen with an open heart for his reply.

BETTER CHOICES ON DIFFICULT DAYS

Blessed is the one who perseveres under trial.

—James 1:12

I tend to think that when everything is going well, I have the margin to do hard things, to make good choices—to read instead of watch TV, to eat well instead of eat poorly, to engage in deep conversation instead of chatter about other people.

But it's really the opposite, isn't it? It's the making of those harder, better choices right while everything's a mess that makes the mess a little more manageable. I wanted every pizza in the state of Illinois last night. But this morning I would have had to add a sense of failure to my already bruised spirits. I'm not saying I woke up feeling all better. But I do know I could have made it so much worse, that I could have added self-loathing to my tiredness, and that wouldn't have made it easier to bear.

I'm realizing this after what seems like a lifetime of saying to myself, "Well, you can't be expected to do something hard on a day like this, can you?" I did expect more from myself, and I did do something hard, and I'm thankful.

WHAT ARE the difficult choices that help you manage a challenging day? What have you discovered about this dynamic in your own life? Do you have any strategies that help you to succeed in those situations?

September

29

EATING FOR SUSTENANCE & ENJOYMENT

Let me give you some food so you may eat and have the strength to go on your way.

—1 Samuel 28:22

I learned something about hunger from my friend Sara. Sara was one of the first women I knew who ate like a man. When she was hungry, she announced it. And then she ate. A lot. We were traveling through Europe together in college, when I was in the throes of a deep and desperate hatred toward my body. I watched Sara with confusion and fascination, the way a child watches an animal he's never seen—all wide-eyed and kind of nervous. If Sara was hungry while we were on our way to a play, she'd ask us to stop. Because she was hungry. All of us stopped because she was hungry. I would have sooner lost consciousness on the sidewalk than draw attention to my hunger and, therefore, my body.

I realized that even most of the thin women I knew had learned to demur about food and hunger—*I already ate; I couldn't possibly; I'm absolutely stuffed.* But Sara loved to eat and believed it was her right, and a pleasure. She didn't overeat or undereat, cry or hide food. She just ate, for sustenance and enjoyment both, and I was fascinated.

WHAT IS your attitude toward hunger? Who has influenced it? How has it changed over the years?

STILL MYSELF

*I have seen all the things that are done under the sun; all of
them are meaningless, a chasing after the wind.*

—Ecclesiastes 1:14

I thought a lot of things would get easier once I lost weight. And some have.
But many haven't. I thought that losing weight would set in motion all the
parts of my life that seemed stuck and stalled. I thought seeing that magic,
dreamt-of number on the scale would turn me into a person who revels in
her own skin, dances in her underwear, walks into every room fearlessly
and shamelessly. I thought it would protect me from the vulnerability I had
always felt, that it would secure me, once and for all, my place in the world
of successful, happy, confident people.

What I found, though, is that if you're not chasing one fantasy, you're
chasing another. If it's not your body, it's your bank account, or your ré-
sumé or your nose or your boobs or your car or the perfect marriage or
the perfect vacation or the perfect child. For two decades, I believed that
if I could just get this one thing under control, the whole of my life would
magically bloom like a perfect, lush flower. But to my dismay, I realized
that my life was still my life, and I was still myself, just in smaller pants.

WHAT'S THE one thing you sometimes believe will change
everything for you?

BEING ON THE SIDE OF CREATORS

Then the LORD said to Moses, "See, I have chosen Bezalel . . . and I have filled him with the Spirit of God, with wisdom, with understanding, with knowledge and with all kinds of skills—to make artistic designs for work in gold, silver and bronze, to cut and set stones, to work in wood, and to engage in all kinds of crafts. Moreover, I have appointed Oholiab . . . to help him.

—Exodus 31:1–6

One of the best parts of living with another artist is that we have an ongoing conversation about what it means to live well as a creative person, and Aaron and I try to make a practice of not speaking negatively about the things that other people create. We are, of course, massively opinionated. We have strong feelings about music and writing and a thousand other things. But we're trying to be on the side of creators, not on the side of consumers and critics.

Once you've labored something into life, you know how hard it is to do—the dream and then the work and then the endless revisions. The adjustments, the bursts of inspiration and the agonizing middle stretch, where everything feels pointless. It takes guts and hard work to make things, and even more guts and hard work to share them, so we want to be people who congratulate the effort instead of nitpicking the result. I want to spend my time making things, not sitting back and pointing out what someone else should have done.

DOES IT come easily to you to applaud the efforts of other creative people, or do you tend to find yourself criticizing? Reflect on how you want to spend your energy in this area.

HARVEST

*Let us not become weary in doing good, for at the proper
time we will reap a harvest if we do not give up.*

—Galatians 6:9

Fall in Chicago is like theater: active, kinetic, rich. When Henry was a baby, Aaron and I took him for a walk in his wagon one day, and in the glow of late afternoon, we walked by a tree that had begun changing earlier than the rest. It felt like the very first moment of fall. A few days later, we went for a bike ride and got caught in a rainstorm, and the smell of dirt and the yellow of wildflowers against the gray sky were unmistakably fall.

Fall is harvest, when we're getting all the good stuff that someone took the time to plant many months ago. That's how it is when we make art. We struggle and push and plant seeds deep underground, and it doesn't look like much for a while. But then someone comes along and listens to your song or sees your painting or reads your poem, and they feel alive again, like the world is fresh and bursting, just like harvest. Plant something today that will feed someone many months or many years from now. Plant something today, because you've feasted on someone else's carefully planted seeds, seeds that bloomed into nourishment and kept you alive and wide-eyed.

OUR CREATIVITY, like all our other gifts, is meant to be invested on behalf of others.

October

3

THE TRUEST COMPASSES

Guard what has been entrusted to your care. Turn away from godless chatter.
—1 Timothy 6:20

One day I read a bunch of reviews. Some of them were great. And some were awful. So I circled the wagons. I closed my laptop, as a way of saying to myself that *I am not my work.* I do work that invites and depends on public consumption. But that's my work, not my whole self.

When you do work like mine, that line is blurry—I write about my life, my self, my home, my feelings. So when someone writes a mean review, it feels more like a personal attack than a comment on my work. But it isn't.

I work hard to invest in a small circle of friendships and family relationships that have nothing to do with the writing part of my life, and when I circle the wagons, those are the people I reach out to, people who have known me well and forever, who see the whole of my life, not just the one on the pages. Those are the voices that matter most, the truest compasses and guides. I'm learning that not all criticism should be weighed equally—and that people "out there" shouldn't have the same voice into my life as the people in my little circle of wagons.

WHOSE VOICES matter most in your life? Do you have a circle of people close to you who know you, love you, and speak truth to you? How do you make sure those are the voices guiding you?

Thai Beef Salad

I love this mix of hot and cold, and the herbs totally make it. Sometimes for a lunch party I'll serve this salad with spicy peanut noodles and chicken thighs on skewers—fresh, bright, flavorful.

2 red peppers, thinly sliced

3 bok choy or 1 cabbage, shredded (about 3 cups)

2 cucumbers, cut into sticks

1 cup grape tomatoes, halved

1 red onion, thinly sliced

1 flank steak (about 8 ounces), cooked to your preferred doneness and thinly sliced

¼ cup fresh mint, chopped

¼ cup cilantro, chopped

½ cup fresh basil, chopped

DRESSING

juice of 4 limes

1 tablespoon sesame oil

2 tablespoons soy sauce

1 tablespoon fish sauce

1 tablespoon brown sugar

1 jalapeño or red chile, thinly chopped

» Mix the dressing in a jelly jar. Combine the vegetables and toss with half the salad dressing. Arrange on a large platter. Cook the steak, allow to rest for 10 minutes, then slice thinly and place on top of vegetables. Pour remaining dressing over the top, and scatter herbs over the whole platter.

THE DEEPEST STREAM

*Deep calls to deep in the roar of your waterfalls; all your
waves and breakers have swept over me.*

— P s a l m   4 2 : 7

The years when I fought to find my place in the Christian world made me
believe in the journey and respect it, the way you respect deep water if you've
ever swam out too far and been surprised by the waves. I know what that
journey can do in people, what it did in me, and I don't take it lightly. I have
scars and memories from that season that are very sobering. They remind
me how dangerous that path is—and how beautiful. I loved those years.

Along the way, I've collected more questions than answers, but I've
fought for a few ideas that have formed a bed I can rest on, a life I can
make peace with, a dream I can cling to. I'm not a doctrinarian, because
doctrine is not the thing that God has used to change my life. I'm a reader
and a storyteller, and God chose literature and story and poetry as the
languages of my spiritual text. To me, the Bible is a manifesto, a guide, a
love letter, a story. To me, life with God is prismatic, shocking, demanding, freeing. It's the deepest stream, the blood in my veins, the stories and
words of my dreams and my middle-of-the-night prayers.

THE JOURNEY to find faith, or to make our faith our own,
is both beautiful and perilous, and we may find that God speaks
to us in astonishing ways. Take a minute to thank God for your
own journey.

COLD TANGERINES

The heavens declare the glory of God; the skies proclaim the work of his hands.

—Psalm 19:1

Right now all the leaves are falling, and there's no reason that they have to turn electric bright red before they fall, but they do and I want to live like that. I want to say, "What can I do today that brings more beauty, more energy, more hope?" Because it seems like that's what God is saying to us, over and over. "What can I do to remind you again how good this life is? You think the color of the sky is good now, wait till sunset. You think oranges are good? Try a tangerine." He's a crazy delightful mad scientist and keeps coming back from the lab with unbelievable new things, and it's a gift to be a part of it.

I don't want to get to the end and realize that my life is a collection of meetings and errands and receipts and dirty dishes. I want to eat cold tangerines and sing loud in the car and wear pink shoes. I want to sleep hard on clean white sheets and throw parties and eat ripe tomatoes. I want my every day to make God belly laugh, glad that he gave life to someone who loves the gift.

GOD HAS created an amazingly rich and beautiful life for us. How do you want to live your life in response? What can you do today to celebrate God's gifts?

VENOM

As churning cream produces butter, and as twisting the nose
produces blood, so stirring up anger produces strife.

—Proverbs 30:33

Earlier this year, a friend of mine made me really mad. Crazy mad. I felt small and scared and out of control, and like my friend was making decision after decision to hurt me. Every time I heard from her or about her, it hurt. It was like there was sharp glass on her hands and every time she got near me, she cut me, even if she swore she didn't mean to.

For a while, it brought me so much joy to be angry with her. I exhausted myself imagining the same conversation again and again, but slightly different each time, saying clever things and finding loopholes in her lame arguments. I was the captain of the debate team in my mind, and I was very busy debating her.

I kept thinking about her, and the anger and the venom were starting to feel familiar. When I thought about what happened, the muscles in my neck and back scrunched up, and I felt bad at the base of my skull. Then it got harder to breathe, and it felt like something was rotting inside me, the way something goes bad in the refrigerator.

HAVE YOU ever found joy in being angry? Do you ever stir up anger in yourself? How does it end up affecting you?

MY ANGER HURTS ME

*Get rid of all bitterness, rage and anger, brawling and
slander, along with every form of malice.*

—Ephesians 4:31

My friend Sarah asked me how I was doing one night. "Well," I said, "it's
been pretty hard lately with my friend at whom I am very angry."

"Oh," she said. "When did you talk to her?" I rolled my eyes and puffed
out my breath like I was a seventh grade girl. I didn't *talk* to her. Was she
crazy? "I, um, I actually didn't talk with her at all. I mean, it's been hard
...in my head."

Gently, kindly, she paused, waiting for me to realize what I just said.
I had been spending hours in imaginary conversations, tying myself up
in knots, harboring secret fantasies of this person falling down in public,
planning out elaborate comebacks I should have said months ago.

When I told Sarah that things had been hard in my head, I realized that
I'm the only one suffering right now. My anger doesn't hurt the person at
whom I am very angry, but it hurts me. My friend is doing great, I think, but
I stagger around in a fog of anger and clenched jaws and fists, waiting for a
showdown that will never come and an apology that will never be offered.

IT CAN seem impossible sometimes to get rid of anger. Are
you waiting for a showdown or an apology that will never come? If
so, how is that affecting you?

October

8

BECAUSE I THINK I'M RIGHT

Do not repay evil with evil or insult with insult. On the contrary, repay evil with blessing, because to this you were called so that you may inherit a blessing.

—1 Peter 3:9

When I'm trying to forgive someone, I picture myself physically lifting that person off a big hook, like in a cartoon. I never want to. I prefer to stew and focus my anger on them like a laser pointer, and wish them illnesses and bad skin. I hope that they will get fat and people will talk behind their back and their toilets will overflow and their computers will crash.

The thing that keeps me going with the anger and the rotten feelings about my friend is that I think I'm right. Really. When I think about what happened, I think she did a bad thing to a not entirely bad person named me. I want her to have to apologize. Loudly. Publicly. And give me a present, too. I want her to feel how bad I felt, how small and scared. I want her to tell me she was wrong, and promise never to do anything like that again, in writing, with a notary public present.

I think if we went to court, some strange friendship court where you can get a ruling about these things, I think I would win, still, even after all these months.

IT'S SO hard to let go of anger when we think we're right. Are you holding on to anger toward anyone right now, long after the fact, because you're right? What does that feel like?

FORGIVING TO GET MY LIFE BACK

Then Peter came to Jesus and asked, "Lord, how many times shall I forgive my brother or sister who sins against me? Up to seven times?" Jesus answered, "I tell you, not seven times, but seventy-seven times."

—Matthew 18:21–22

How do I forgive someone who doesn't think she did anything wrong? Or who doesn't care? I could maybe do it if she groveled or begged. It would be even easier if she cried a lot. Or if she told me she thought I was a genius with great fashion sense and that she wants to be like me someday. But nothing. No phone calls. No e-mails. No large, fragrant bouquets of flowers. Nothing. Why would I forgive someone who doesn't even think she needs to be forgiven?

Because I want my neck and my back muscles to stop hurting. Because I want to sleep, instead of having endless imaginary conversations. Because I want my mind back. Because I want my life back.

So I let her off the hook. I let her off once, to start, and felt pretty good about myself, until someone brought up her name at lunch, and then I got mad all over again, which threw me for a loop. I *forgave* her. Why am I still so mad at her? I felt like I bought expensive wrinkle cream and woke up more wrinkly than ever. I wanted my money back.

FORGIVENESS IS both a decision and a process. It's hard enough to choose to forgive in the first place, and then we have to do it again. And again. And again. And again.

THE GOOD WORK OF FORGIVENESS

*Bear with each other and forgive one another if any of you has a
grievance against someone. Forgive as the Lord forgave you.*

—Colossians 3:13

When I forgave my friend at whom I was very angry, I realized that I had to take her off the hook every single time, not just one big time. I had to take her off the hook in the morning, and then again at lunch, when someone gave me a new reason to be mad at her. Over and over, all day, I had to do the heavy lifting work of letting her off the hook. It was like moving a piano all the way across the living room, and then waking up the next morning and finding that it's back in the other corner, and I have to move it again. Every day I had to push that heavy piano all the way across the living room, even though I just did it the day before. It was like a full-time job, forgiving her over and over, with each new angry thought or bad conversation, but it was good work, like how good it feels to shovel snow or rake leaves in the cold air.

And I keep letting her off the hook, because when I do, I can breathe again.

IS THERE a person you have struggled to forgive? What's a specific step you can take toward forgiveness today?

October

11

A GRACE-LESS WAY TO LIVE

*Confess your sins to each other and pray for each other so that you may be
healed. The prayer of a righteous person is powerful and effective.*

—James 5:16

I have a friend who wants me to pray for the same situation in her life over
and over. She calls me, e-mails me: please pray! I get annoyed with these
messages, and I once heard myself say to Aaron, "I don't *have* to pray for
her. And I'm tired of her demanding that I do. She made a boatload of
terrible decisions, and now I *have* to pray about it?"

Uh-oh. So in my economy, we earn the right to be prayed for by making all the right decisions? Is it my job to decide who does and who doesn't
deserve to be prayed for, based on the tokens they've put into the good
decision-meter?

It gets worse, actually. She asked for my advice, many years ago, and went
against it. This situation wouldn't exist had she taken my advice. So now
my small, ugly self doesn't want to pray for her.

That's a grace-less way to live, where everything is an opportunity to
achieve or fail. It's exhausting to live like that, where everything's a performance, and you can't trust the people in your life to give you a break or
a second chance or what you really are longing for, which is grace.

> **WHEN WE** deserve grace the least, we need it the most. Is
> there someone in your life that you have a hard time giving grace
> to? Spend a few minutes practicing grace-giving to that person.

SWEETER THAN AMNESIA

For it is by grace you have been saved, through faith—and this is not from
yourselves, it is the gift of God—not by works, so that no one can boast.

—Ephesians 2:8–9

Grace isn't about having a second chance; grace is having so many chances that you could use them through all eternity and never come up empty. It's when you finally realize that the other shoe isn't going to drop, ever. It's the moment you feel as precious and handmade as every star, when you feel, finally, at home for the very first time.

Grace is when you finally stop keeping score and when you realize that God never was, that his game is a different one entirely. Grace is when the silence is so complete that you can hear your own heartbeat, and right within your ribs, God's beating heart, too.

I used to think that the ability to turn back time would be the greatest possible gift, so that I could undo all the things I wish I hadn't done. But grace is an even better gift, because it allows me to do more than just erase; it allows me to become more than I was when I did those things. It's forgiveness without forgetting, which is much sweeter than amnesia.

GRACE ALLOWS us to grow, to become more of who God created us to be. Take a few minutes to thank God for the grace he shows in our lives.

MATH & GRACE

Be kind and compassionate to one another, forgiving each
other, just as in Christ God forgave you.

—Ephesians 4:32

I don't really want to need grace. I never have been very comfortable with the idea. I don't really trust that people will show me grace. I don't show it to myself well, and when I'm doing very poorly, I don't show it to anyone else well, either.

I don't like the idea that someone can judge me and that I have to depend on their grace. I want to take that power out of their hands. I hate to think about the fact that the people who love me show me grace for all my faults. I prefer to believe instead that the math works: there are good things about me and hard things about me, but they've checked the math and because I'm funny enough, they can let go of how terrible I look most days, or if I'm interesting enough, the fact that my house is dirty isn't such a big deal. But that kind of math is specifically anti-grace. Grace isn't about netting out on the right side of things.

If arithmetic is numbers, and if algebra is numbers and letters, then grace is numbers, letters, sounds, and tears, feelings and dreams. Grace is smashing the calculator, and using all the broken buttons and pieces to make a mosaic.

GRACE IS wilder and freer than the math of earning approval. Grace is a gift. Today, settle into that gift of grace.

MOUTHFUL OF GRACE

*Finally, all of you, be like-minded, be sympathetic, love
one another, be compassionate and humble.*

—1 Peter 3:8

The nature of being a Christian—or, really, the nature of learning any-thing over a lifetime—is that sometimes you wake up and realize that some-how you're missing an essential part of your education, and that now is the time to start learning and re-learning. These things go in waves, it seems.

So these days, I'm on the lookout for grace, and I'm especially on the lookout for ways that I withhold grace from myself and from other people. At first, showing people grace makes you feel powerful, like scattering can-dy from a float in a parade—grace for you, grace for you. You become al-most giddy, thinking of people in generous ways, allowing for their faults, absorbing minor irritations. You feel great, and then you start to feel just ever so slightly superior, because you're so incredibly evolved and gracious.

But then inevitably something happens, and it usually involves you con-fronting one of your worst selves, often in public, and you realize that you're not throwing candy off a float to a nameless, dirty public, but rather that you are that nameless, dirty public, and that you are starving and on your knees, praying for a little piece of sweetness, just one mouthful of grace.

WHEN WAS the last time you received grace? When was the last time you extended it to someone else?

COME DANCE WITH ME

Be glad and rejoice with me.

—Philippians 2:18

The discipline of celebration is changing my life, and I invite you into the same practice. Come tap dance with me on the fresh graves of apathy and cynicism, the creeping belief that this is all there is, and that God is no match for the wreckage of the world we live in. What God does in the tiny corners of our day-to-day lives is stunning and gorgeous and headline-making, but we have a bad habit of saving the headlines for the grotesque and scary.

To choose to celebrate right here and right now might seem irresponsible. It might seem frivolous, like cotton candy and charm bracelets. But I believe it is a serious undertaking, one that has the potential to return us to our best selves, to deliver us back to the men and women God created us to be, people who choose to see the best, believe the best, yearn for the best. Through that longing to be our best selves, we are changed and inspired and ennobled, able to see the handwriting of a holy God where another person just sees the same old tired streets and sidewalks.

GOD IS alive, and he is transforming and redeeming his world, even when we can't see it. Where do you see the fingerprints of a loving, holy God in your life today, even in the mess and darkness?

Emily's Poppy Seed Cake

Emily first made this for me years ago, and since then I've requested it many times. I adore this sweet little cake, especially the glaze. Emily's Grammie, Mary Barnell, got the recipe from her church group, and she has been serving it at Emily's family Easter gathering for more than twenty-five years. Emily makes minicakes as shower favors sometimes, and I'm always delighted when she does.

POPPY SEED CAKE

2 cups flour

1 teaspoon salt

1 teaspoon baking powder

1 tablespoon poppy seeds

1 teaspoon vanilla extract

1 teaspoon almond extract

2 eggs

¾ cup melted butter

1 ½ cups sugar

1 cup milk

» Preheat oven to 350 degrees.

» Beat all ingredients for 2 minutes. Pour the batter into four small loaf pans or a 9 x 5-inch loaf pan. Bake for one hour. The top will crack.

ORANGE GLAZE

¼ cup orange juice

¾ cup sugar

½ teaspoon vanilla extract

½ teaspoon almond extract

» Cook orange juice and sugar together until sugar melts. Do not boil. Remove from heat. Stir in extracts.

» While cake is hot, spoon glaze over the top of the cake and let it set for at least 20 minutes before removing it from the pan.

SACRED & SURPRISING

Encourage one another and build each other up, just as in fact you are doing.

—1 Thessalonians 5:11

A couple of my girlfriends, self-professed non-cooks, asked if we could make dinner together to add a few recipes to their normal repertoires.

When people learn their way around a kitchen, it becomes a life-giving, healing place to be. A lot of our long-tangled food issues get brought out into the light when we stand in front of the cutting board or in front of the stove. Sacred and surprising things happen when we gather around a table and share food made with love and by our own hands.

It happened that night, certainly. We laughed and told stories and bumped into one another in the kitchen. When it was all ready, we sat at the table together for ages. We talked about the food—the smells and flavors—and then we talked about all the other things you talk about around a table, like how hard it is to say no, and how heartbreaking it is when a friend really isn't a friend. We talked about learning how to relax, and learning how to be gracious with ourselves.

They left with recipes and instructions, and the next morning, I ate leftover bacon-wrapped dates for breakfast. Win-win, I'd say.

WHEN WAS the last time you created space for relationship, for time together with people you care about? What plans could you put in place today to connect in a meaningful way?

RECIPES & COOKING

"I have the right to do anything," you say—but not everything is beneficial.
"I have the right to do anything"—but not everything is constructive.

—1 Corinthians 10:23

I'm not really a recipe girl. My mom always teases me about it, knowing that when I say I used a recipe, all it means is that at some point, some list of ingredients and techniques were involved as I threw things in pans, as I sliced, poured, salted, and peppered with seeming randomness. She does not particularly appreciate this cooking style, and sometimes she has to leave the kitchen because my loosey-goosey approach makes her nervous.

There are, of course, some times when recipes are more important than others. When you're baking bread, for example, if you were to decide the yeast wasn't important, you'd have something between pita and a paper plate. In cooking as in life, there are some nonnegotiables, but not nearly as many as you think. Learning to cook is all about learning those nonnegotiables and then playing around with the rest. Recipes are how we learn all the rules, and cooking is knowing how to break them to suit our tastes or preferences. Following a recipe is like playing scales, and cooking is jazz.

HAS THERE ever been a time in your life when you stepped outside of established rules and expectations? What did you discover through that process?

FOR-NO-REASON PARTIES

They feast on the abundance of your house;
you give them drink from your river of delights.

—Psalm 36:8

I'm a big believer in for-no-reason parties—those last-minute parties, where the house is less than squeaky clean, where the guest list is "whoever could come with three days' notice," and the menu is "whatever I could think of and whatever goes with feta or chutney."

There's something about seeing your house filled with people you love, something about feeding people, especially on days when it seems like you can't make a dent in any of the larger, more theoretical challenges in life.

I may not know where we'll be in five years or how exactly we'll pay the mortgage the next few months or when we'll have another child, but I do know how to make dinner, and to see the people I care about gobble it up makes me feel like something is right, even when it seems like nothing is. There's something so healing about those quiet moments at the table, when everyone's mouth—or mind or heart—is full, when you feel connected and nourished and content, even if it's just for a split second.

IN THE midst of chaos there are small things that make you feel connected and grounded. What are those small things for you today?

LIVING WITHOUT SHAME

Great is your love, reaching to the heavens; your faithfulness reaches to the skies.

—Psalm 57:10

I've been catastrophizing about my weight since I was six. I've lost the pounds and gained them, made and abandoned plans and promises, cried tears of frustration, pinched the backs of my upper arms with a hatred that scares me.

And through all that, I've made friends and fallen in love, gotten married and become a mother. I've written and traveled and stayed up late with people I love. I've walked on the beach and on glittering city streets. I've kissed my baby's cheeks and danced with my husband and laughed till I cried with my best friends, and through all that it didn't really matter that I was heavier than I wanted to be.

The extra pounds didn't matter, as I look back, but the shame that came with those extra pounds was like an infectious disease. That's what I remember. So these days, my mind and my heart are focused less on the pounds and more on what it means to live without shame, to exchange that heavy and corrosive self-loathing for courage and freedom and gratitude. Some days I do just that, and some days I don't, and that seems to be just exactly how life is.

WHAT DO you carry shame about? What gifts and happy times have you enjoyed in spite of that issue? Let gratitude well up in your heart, and offer it to God. What would it look like for you to live without that shame?

FINDING COMMUNITY

Paul left Athens and went to Corinth. There he met a Jew named Aquila... who
had recently come from Italy with his wife Priscilla.... Paul went to see them, and
because he was a tentmaker as they were, he stayed and worked with them.

—Acts 18:1–3

I've been in what seems like a thousand groups that never really came to-gether, and just a few that really did. I think a lot of groups, church-based or otherwise, fail because they can't find themselves under the weight of expectations placed upon them. Sometimes when we start small groups, we saddle them with the idea that they have to be deeply intimate and transfor-mational right at the first meeting. We force connections that aren't there, fumble through topics and conversations and routines that feel forced and hollow, and then we wonder why we don't actually want to go that often.

Sometimes it does work to set out together for intimacy, honesty, truth-telling. But more often you find those things by going through the back door—serving together, cooking together, reading together. When you do what you love with people who love the same thing, something is born into your midst and begins to connect you. When you walk with someone, listen to their story, carry their burden, play with their kids, that's community. When you find yourself learning from them and inviting them into the family places in your life, that's community, and wherever you find it, it's always a gift.

WHAT HAS your experience been with small groups? Where have you found community?

October

21

SHARING EVERYDAY LIFE

A friend loves at all times, and a brother is born for a time of adversity.

—Proverbs 17:17

It seems like Cooking Club has been meeting together forever, but it's been three years this month, and that's worth remembering—it doesn't take a decade, and it doesn't take three times a week. What it does take is sharing everyday life together, messy and real.

We've gone to funerals and birthday parties together, reported bad test results, gotten advice about sick kids, made trips to the ER, walked together through postpartum depression. We've visited each other's babies in the hospital, and we've brought over meals and sleepers and blankets. We've talked about faith and fear and fighting with our husbands, sleeping through the night and anxiety and how to ask for help when we need it. Around this table we've mourned the loss of eight pregnancies, and even as I write those words, it seems a cruel and unusual number.

What we've built is impressive—strong, complex, multifaceted. Like a curry or Boeuf Bourguignon, something you cook for hours and hours, allowing the flavors to develop over time, changing and deepening with each passing hour on the heat, rich and lovely and unexpected.

WHO DO you share everyday life with in real time, when it's messy or bitter as well as when it's lovely and sweet? How do you nurture those connections?

SOFT PLACES TO LAND

"By this everyone will know that you are my disciples, if you love one another."

—John 13:35

For me, when we gather people around our table, it's about the gathering, not the table settings. If I had to build a Rose Parade float for a centerpiece every time I have people over, I'd never have people over. I have white dishes, lots and lots of them, and they're cheap, because I never want to be broken-hearted when something breaks. Same with glassware. We have very pretty three-dollar wine glasses, and when someone inevitably knocks one over, I love being able to tell them that really, it's not a big deal. Because that's one of the highest values in our home: safety. I want to have a home where people feel like they can rest—like they can wear slippers, get themselves a glass of water, settle in for an evening.

It's about what works for your guests, your family, the people you love and have welcomed around your table. It's not about what will look great on Pinterest or Instagram later. It's about loving the people in your life by gathering them close into the private space of your home, about giving them soft places to land in hard seasons, about meeting their needs for food, for listening, for peace, for rest.

WHEN YOU host a gathering, what works for your family? How do you want guests to feel in your home? How do you accomplish that? What are the values in your home, and how do you express them in unspoken ways?

A FORCE FOR GOOD

Suppose a brother or a sister is without clothes and daily food. If one of you says to them, "Go in peace; keep warm and well fed," but does nothing about their physical needs, what good is it? In the same way, faith by itself, if it is not accompanied by action, is dead.

—James 2:15–17

For more than thirty years, our church has been giving food to families in immediate need all over our city. More than eight hundred volunteers serve regularly at the Care Center, walking families through the aisles, helping them choose bread and meat and vegetables that have been grown in our church's Giving Garden.

Maybe it's because I'm a food person. Maybe it's because I'm a mom. Maybe it's because I've volunteered at the Care Center and have looked into the eyes of moms just like me, moms who live in my town, who have come for groceries because without them they can't feed their families. Whatever the reason, hunger moves me. It upsets me and makes me angry. It gets me all wound up and I want to make it right.

I want to make sure the kids I see at the Care Center always have full bellies, that the church community is meeting their needs in daily, practical, immediate ways. The church is at its best, in my view, when it is more than a set of ideas and ideals, when it is a working, living, breathing, on-the-ground, in-the-mess force for good in our cities and towns.

HOW IS your own church a force for good within your community? How would you like it to be one?

October
24

COOKING CLUB GARAGE SALE

If anyone has material possessions and sees a brother or sister in need but has
no pity on them, how can the love of God be in that person? Dear children,
let us not love with words or speech but with actions and in truth.

—1 John 3:17–18

On a clear, cool Saturday morning, the Cooking Club girls arrived at Casey's house. We clutched our coffees, murmured hello, and began sliding folding tables out of the garage. The last several times the Cooking Club has gathered, we've talked about hunger. We're food people, obviously. We're moms and aunts and sisters. We care about hunger, and we wanted to find a tactile, practical way to make a difference in our town.

That's how we arrived at the Cooking Club garage sale and bake sale, with all the proceeds benefiting the Care Center, where our church helps feed needy families in our city. We sold clothes, shoes, toys, books, tables, chairs, lamps, and all manner of kitchen gear. At the end of the day we sat around Casey's kitchen with margaritas, dusty and tired, while she counted out every last quarter. We made over a thousand dollars for the Care Center, which feels like an insane amount when you make it mostly in two-dollar increments. A thousand dollars in the face of a problem like hunger in a city the size of Chicago isn't that much. But it's something. We did something.

WHAT DIFFERENCE are you making in your local community? What's something you could do this season to alleviate suffering or hunger in your neighborhood or town?

WHAT MONEY CAN BUY

Do not forget to do good and to share with others, for with such sacrifices God is pleased.

—**Hebrews 13:16**

Before the Cooking Club decided to hold a garage sale and bake sale for our church's Care Center, we talked about hunger, about privilege, simplicity, waste, and wealth. We talked about how easy it is to settle into a lifestyle of accumulation, to get used to buying and buying and buying, and then living in homes that are bursting with stuff we don't need, can't find a place for, shouldn't have bought in the first place. We want to live simpler, more responsible lives, with less waste and clutter. We want to be thoughtful consumers instead of rabid accumulators.

It's easy to think that because you can't do something extraordinary, you can't do anything at all, that if you can't overhaul your entire life in one fell swoop, then you might as well do nothing. We started where we could, with what we had. I hope it's just the beginning for us. I hope the next time each of us are at Target or Anthropologie, we think a little harder about what that money could buy, about families in our community who need bread, milk, and apples more than we need necklaces, sunglasses, and cardigans.

THINK FOR a moment about your own buying habits. How do you try to be a thoughtful consumer? How much clutter does your house hold, and how many things you never use? What could you do to benefit others with your resources?

GRATITUDE

"For I know the plans I have for you," declares the LORD, *"plans to prosper you and not to harm you, plans to give you hope and a future."*

—Jeremiah 29:11

One of my most cracked-up, errant beliefs is that skinny people are always happy. I think I would be happy all day long if I were skinny. If something upset me, I would just look down at my long, skinny legs—happiness! I know this is crazy talk.

But I found myself believing the same thing about being pregnant— that all my left-out, broken-down, fragile, ugly feelings would vanish the second I saw the all-important line on the pregnancy test. I know it's not true, but I felt it.

It's not wrong to want another baby, but there's a fine line in there, and I've crossed it a few times, and moved over into that territory where you can't be happy unless you have just that thing you want, no matter what else you have. That's not how I want to live.

I want to cultivate a deep sense of gratitude, of groundedness, of enough, even while I'm longing for something more. I'm practicing believing that God knows more than I know, that he sees what I can't, that he's weaving a future I can't even imagine from where I sit this morning.

EVEN IN the midst of whatever you're longing for today, take a moment and acknowledge what you're grateful for.

ON BEING HUMAN

The apostles gathered around Jesus and reported to him all they had
done and taught. Then, because so many people were coming and going
that they did not even have a chance to eat, he said to them, "Come
with me by yourselves to a quiet place and get some rest."

—Mark 6:30–31

When I'm in a really busy season, what I think I need is work. My first impulse is to put my head down and *work, work, work,* treating myself like a robot,
a bad robot, in fact, for daring to be tired, daring to need anything. I get
into this nutty mindset that insists that whatever other things I could be
doing—like seeing a therapist, sleeping, reading—must be put on hold until
the war is over, because I am a soldier.

What I really need, though, is pretty much the exact opposite. I need
self-care. Instead of working like a soldier or a robot, I'm learning to work
like a *human*. Like a tender, loved human being person who needs rest, who
needs downtime, who needs kindness and nurturing along the way. I need
lots of breaks, lots of self-care, lots of space. This kind of stuff doesn't come
naturally to me. I'm good at work, and I'm good at fun/play/planning/host-
ing/keeping *busybusybusy*, but I'm not great at rest or self-care. But I did take
a nap today. Baby steps?

WHEN WE most need rest and self-care is often when we're
least likely to get them. How do you give yourself rest and self-care?

CLINGING

I have been crucified with Christ and I no longer live, but Christ lives in me. The life I now live in the body, I live by faith in the Son of God, who loved me and gave himself for me.

—Galatians 2:20

Food is my thing. What I eat and drink are little moments of joy throughout the day—the things I think about, plan around, daydream about. I love the moment when I open the menu at a restaurant or start prepping to make dinner or uncork the wine. On long writing days, those breaks for bread and cheese or leftover cold pasta or a slice of Emily's poppy seed cake dipped into espresso are the little motivators that keep me writing.

But the very things you think you need most desperately are the things that can transform you the most profoundly when you finally release them. The college I had my heart set on, the boyfriend I believed would be my husband, the job that defined me, the pregnancy I believed would end a season of longing and loss. Each one, pulled from my grubby fists, taught me something fundamental about desire and transformation. Over and over, I learn the hard way that the thing I'm clinging to can be the thing that sets me free.

WHAT ARE you clinging to in this season? What do you think might happen if you released it?

ON SEEING THE IMPORTANT THINGS

I pray that you, being rooted and established in love, may have power, together
with all the Lord's holy people, to grasp how wide and long and high and
deep is the love of Christ, and to know this love that surpasses knowledge—
that you may be filled to the measure of all the fullness of God.

—Ephesians 3:17–19

One month in the fall, we hosted two showers and a rehearsal dinner; I made a job transition; a friend got married, another celebrated her thirtieth birthday, another found out she was pregnant, and another adopted a newborn; and my husband had his wisdom teeth removed.

Aaron needed more gauze. I flew out the door, and raced through the store, throwing things in the cart. When I got home, he told me that I bought the wrong gauze. I stomped out the door, and then I stopped in my tracks. Across the street, one of the tallest trees, twice as high as a two-story house, was the brightest, lit-from-within red I have ever seen. I had not noticed one step of its turning.

I had stopped seeing the important things. I saw the to-do list. I had gifts to buy and people to celebrate. But I wasn't seeing the people or the celebrations. I wasn't seeing anything beyond the chaos of my life.

CHAOS HAS a way of drowning out the quieter, more important things from our awareness. What might you be missing today?

LOVE & SKELETONS

Dear friends, since God so loved us, we also ought to love one another.

—1 John 4:11

My husband and I aren't Halloween people—we're not into tombstone decorations. We don't put cobwebs in our trees or fake spiders on our porch or skeletons holding machetes in our bushes. At least, we didn't until this year.

Our son Henry is six, and this year he asked if we could have decorations. We told him we're not decoration people, hoping he'd forget about it. And then the day before Halloween, he started carrying things out on to the front porch—rubber snakes, pirate hats, fake swords.

"What are you doing, buddy?" I asked.

"I'm making it *spooky*," he said, face lit up with delight.

At a certain point I called my husband. "I give up. I think we need to go to the store and get this kid some spooky decorations."

Aaron agreed, and we spent Halloween morning setting up lights shaped like skulls, cobwebs with huge fake spiders, poison signs, and pumpkins. Henry was beside himself.

At the end of the day, after the chaos and candy eating was over, Aaron and I decided that we're Halloween people. We're Halloween people because Henry's a Halloween person, and more than anything, we're Henry people.

HAVE YOU ever found yourself surprised by a change you're willing to make for someone you love? Are there any changes you could make today that would bring delight to someone you love?

BEING A FRIEND

May our Lord Jesus Christ himself and God our Father, who loved us and by his grace gave us eternal encouragement and good hope, encourage your hearts and strengthen you in every good deed and word.

—2 Thessalonians 2:16–17

My husband and I were talking in the car the other day on our way to a birthday party for me, and he said something about a friend of ours: "She's really good at being a friend."

And in the silence, we were thinking of a couple people we love very much who, frankly, are not so good at being friends. We share history and care about one another and are always happy to see each other, but when it comes down to it, they don't *do* what good friends *do* very often. That led us into a conversation about all the ways we don't always *do* what good friends *do* either.

Because it doesn't matter how you feel in your heart about your friends—what matters is showing those feelings through words and actions.

After dinner, each person toasted my birthday. The not-so-good friend blew my mind, saying something so lovely and sweet and meaningful, something I had no idea she felt about me.

How often is that happening in our lives? The things we feel about one another often go unexpressed because we assume it's clear. But is it?

HOW DO you communicate your feelings about other people? Is there anyone you care deeply about who might not realize it? What could you say or do to show them?

November

1

RADAR

*Finally, brothers and sisters, whatever is true, whatever is noble, whatever
is right, whatever is pure, whatever is lovely, whatever is admirable—
if anything is excellent or praiseworthy—think about such things.*

—Philippians 4:8

I have to remind myself that life is good. There's a radar inside me for the
bad parts of life. I walk into the kitchen and all I see are crumbs on the
counter, and I look in the mirror and don't even see my face, I just see all the
potential wrinkles forming. It's all true. There are crumbs on the counter. I
am getting wrinkles. I just don't want to live in only that reality.

Because there is another reality. Hope, redemption, and change are
real, and they're happening all around me. So I choose to act out of that
reality, because the other one makes life too hard. I've missed whole seasons
of my life. I look back and all I remember is pain. I guess I went to work or
to class during that time, but I don't really remember. I was too busy being
angry about the life I was given. I wanted it to be different. But being angry
didn't change anything. It just wasted time. I can't take away the things that
have happened, but we have today. Today is a gift. And if we have tomorrow,
tomorrow will be a gift.

THERE IS both good and bad all around us. Which do you
tend to notice more? Do you think it's possible to develop a radar
for the good stuff? When you notice anything good today, pause
for just a moment to absorb it and cherish it.

THE SACRED & THE DAILY

He has made everything beautiful in its time. He has also set eternity in the human heart; yet no one can fathom what God has done from beginning to end. I know that there is nothing better for people than to be happy and to do good while they live.

—Ecclesiastes 3:11–12

There's normal life, day-to-day, make-breakfast, do-the-dishes life, but just underneath that, like a throb of bass you feel in your chest, I feel a whole other thing going on. There is something sacred, something special dipping and weaving within that same old thing, like a firefly, like a great song. The sacred mixes in with the daily when you have a conversation with someone you love, or when you read a great book, or when you do something courageous. It's still just a normal day, but there's something bigger, something more compelling going on too.

I live according to my faith when I let the flavor and scent of something fresh from the ground surprise me and bring me back to life. I demonstrate my theology when I dance all night with people I love, because this life is worth the best celebration we can offer up to it. I thank God every time I eat crusty bread and garlicky olives, and when I smell clean laundry and hear that little squeak of fingers on a guitar. For me, what God said when he made the world is a prayer: It is good.

HOW OFTEN do you tell God that his world is good? When was the last time you celebrated your life, or took notice of the sacred woven into everyday life? How could you do that today?

DRAMA & BLAZE

*Every skilled woman spun with her hands and brought what she
had spun—blue, purple or scarlet yarn or fine linen.*

—Exodus 35:25

When you make art, use what you have, what the world gives you. Use the first day of fall: cool nights and the smell of fire. Our kitchens are filled with the smells of apples bubbling into sauce, roasting squash, cinnamon, nutmeg, cider, warmth itself. The leaves as they spark into wild color just before they die are the world's oldest performance art, celebrating one last violently hued hurrah before the black and white and silence of winter. Fall is begging for us to dance and sing and write with just the same drama and blaze.

Use your dreams and your secrets. Write a love song for someone who will never love you back. Write a comedy that used to be a tragedy, because you can create any ending you want for your own story. Write a song that says everything you've ever wanted to say to your father, or fill a canvas with all the things you hope you find out that God is, when you meet him someday. Dance till your feet bleed, sing till you're hoarse, spill out all your stories like pouring wine into thin-stemmed glasses, the liquid rich and blood-red.

USE WHAT you have to make art: your skills, your energy, your passion, your dreams, and what's happening all around you. If you take time to look, there may be more raw materials than you thought.

ON TELLING THE TRUTH &
GOD'S MASTERPIECES

You, LORD, are our Father. We are the clay, you are the
potter; we are all the work of your hand.

—Isaiah 64:8

At a gathering of friends recently, the leader of the group talked about how we are God's masterpieces and how we've been created in Christ.

Then the leader asked one person to come sit in a chair, facing the rest of the group. He said, "This man is a masterpiece—like *David* and *Starry Night*, like Monet's *Water Lilies*. Why don't you all tell him how you see that?"

This guy looked like he was going to die of embarrassment. It was so uncomfortable.

But we did it. We talked about his character, and how he made people feel. We told stories about his honesty, his bravery, his commitment to helping people. Tears began to roll down his face. And all our faces. It was one of the holiest moments I've been a part of in a long time.

What many people in that circle didn't know was that it had been the hardest year of his life. Many of us didn't know that he was feeling so vulnerable and broken down. Those words mattered that day.

WHO ARE the people in your life who circle around you when you need to know the truth? And who are you circling around, especially when they most desperately need to be told the truth?

COMMUNICATING LOVE

This is how love is made complete among us so that we will have
confidence on the day of judgment: In this world we are like Jesus.

—1 John 4:17

Aaron had a college professor who said over and over, "It doesn't matter how much you love your kids. What matters is communicating that love in a way that they can understand and feel that love."

The same is true for friendships and marriages and all relationships.

It's so easy for me to feel warm, loving thoughts about friends or family members…and then go on about my day, never reaching out. I think about them all the time, pray for them, and watch the details of their lives spool out over Facebook—first day of school photos, last moments of summer photos. I feel connected and warm, full of affection for these lovely people.

But how on earth would they know that?

Recently I've made a point to send more texts and e-mails, a couple old-fashioned letters. I've scheduled a walk and a coffee and a dinner. I've looked people in the eye and said, "I love you. I'm thankful for you."

Because at the end of the day, Aaron's professor is exactly right: It doesn't matter how much you love someone. What matters is that they know it.

WHAT CAN you do today, this week, this month, to let your loved ones know how you feel?

CHILDHOOD MEMORIES WITH GRANDMA

She gets up while it is still night; she provides food for her family.

—Proverbs 31:15

When, in the weeks before her death, the cousins shared some of our childhood memories with Grandma Hybels, three things came up over and over: blueberries, cinnamon toast, and beach glass. Grandma made the very best blueberry pie, and we all remember picking blueberries with Grandma at DeGrandchamp's in South Haven, which is widely known as the Blueberry Capital of the World, complete with a Blueberry Festival, Blueberry Parade, and Blueberry Queen.

At Grandma's cottage we ate blueberries straight out of the bowl in the mornings, and in muffins all day long, but our favorite was her fresh blueberry pie, with a scoop of Sherman's Ice Cream. In the mornings, we all loved having cinnamon bread from Bunde's Bakery in the sunroom, the toaster and the butter dish in the corner always ready for us.

One of our favorite things to do at Grandma's cottage was to search for beach glass, because Grandma collected it in jars like a precious treasure. Every few days we'd take out all the pieces and spread them out on the dining room table with her, and she acted as though we'd found gold every time.

IT IS a particularly sweet kind of hospitality to make children feel at home and well-fed and like each one is the delight of your heart.

EXCITED FOR HEAVEN

"Today you will be with me in paradise."

—Luke 23:43

In my last conversation with Grandma Hybels, we talked a lot about heaven. She told me she was so excited to go there and that she felt like it was taking a long time. One of the reasons she was most excited about heaven is because there she'll be reunited with her husband. For a woman who had been widowed for more than thirty years, I can't imagine the sweetness of that reunion. She spoke in great detail about wanting to see her sisters and brothers and looking forward to a time when age and disease and pain are gone.

We'll miss Grandma terribly. But we know, with as much certainty as we know anything, that she is in heaven, free from pain and disease, reunited with Christ, with a husband she's missed for three decades, and with the brothers and sisters she loved dearly. And for that, we're so thankful.

The way to honor my grandma's life, I believe, is to live with her faith, simplicity, prayerfulness, and kindness, by living simply in order to give generously, by serving without wanting recognition, by putting the needs of others above our own, by praying for the people we love.

JOYS WE cannot fully comprehend will be ours in heaven.

GRANDMA'S LEGACY

I am reminded of your sincere faith, which first lived in your grandmother Lois
and in your mother Eunice and, I am persuaded, now lives in you also.

—2 Timothy 1:5

Above all else, what we remember about Grandma Hybels was her faith. She prayed for us consistently and asked us pointedly where we were going to church and what we were learning from our Bible reading. She modeled for us her deep belief that faith is the center of everything.

At the heart of Grandma's faith was servanthood. She didn't want to be the center of attention. Even at the very end of her life, when she needed something from the nurses, she'd ask, "Would that be too much trouble for you?" They teased her and finally started telling her, "Jerry, this is about you!" She never, ever thought it was about her.

On the last afternoon Todd and I spent with her, she told us that all she wanted at the end of her life was to know that each of her children and grandchildren trusted Christ with their lives. I don't think she cared a bit if we went to good colleges, or how we looked, or if we made a lot of money. She cared about our spiritual well-being and prayed fervently and consistently for each one of us.

SINCERE FAITH is not inherited, but a foundation for it can be learned and absorbed from parents and grandparents who teach us about their faith and model it for us. What legacy of faith are you leaving?

PLANTING WORDS

From the fruit of their lips people are filled with good things,
and the work of their hands brings them reward.

—**Proverbs 12:14**

For an embarrassingly long season, I got out of the routine of daily Bible reading. Call it late-stage rebellion or plain old laziness. I just lost track of it as a habit. And then I hit a series of losses—losing a job, losing a friend, losing a pregnancy—and I found that I was desperate for the power and stability of God's word.

What I also found is that even though I hadn't been doing regular personal daily study in quite some time, the words I'd memorized many years ago kept coming back to me. My parents and my church and my own study had planted those words deep inside me, and to my great joy, when I needed them most, I found them on my lips and on my heart.

My friend who teaches yoga says you don't practice yoga for how you feel in the middle of it; you practice it for how it makes you feel the rest of the time. To a certain extent, that's how God's word works: sometimes you read a few verses and nothing earth shattering happens. But maybe it wasn't about that moment. You studied those words so that you'd have them with you when you needed them, maybe even years later.

ARE THERE any sections of scripture that you've memorized that have come to you later, when you've needed them?

AT THE TABLE

"'Bring the fattened calf and kill it. Let's have a feast and celebrate. For this son of mine was dead and is alive again; he was lost and is found.' So they began to celebrate."

—Luke 15:23–24

The most sacred moments, the ones in which I feel God's presence most profoundly, when I feel the goodness of the world most arrestingly, take place at the table. The particular alchemy of celebration and food, of connecting people and serving what I've made with my own hands, comes together as more than the sum of their parts. I love the sounds and smells and textures of life at the table, hands passing bowls and forks clinking against plates and bread being torn and the rhythm and energy of feeding and being fed.

It's not strictly about the food for me. It's about what happens when we come together, slow down, open our homes, look into one another's faces, listen to one another's stories. It happens when we celebrate a birthday, and also when we break out of the normal clockwork of daily life and pop the champagne on a cold, gray Wednesday just because the faces we love are gathered around our table. It happens when we enter the joy and the sorrow of the people we love, and we join together at the table to feed one another and be fed, and while it's not strictly about the food, it doesn't happen without it. Food is the starting point, the common ground, the thing to hold and handle, the currency we offer to one another.

WHEN WAS the last time you felt nourished and seen and known around the table?

EVERY DAY

Blessed is the one...whose delight is in the law of the LORD, and who meditates on
his law day and night. That person is like a tree planted by streams of water, which
yields its fruit in season and whose leaf does not wither—whatever they do prospers.

—**Psalm 1:1–3**

My dad talks about how every Christian needs to spend time alone with God
every day, praying, listening, reading the Bible, letting ourselves be reminded
that we are God's creation, God's children. God wants his people to trust him
daily, to need him and follow him every morning with new faith.

I couldn't live well without regularly reading God's word. It's often
packaged like a commentary book, with footnotes and indexes and really
tiny type. But parts of it are more like a crime novel or a gothic tale of love,
belief, and betrayal—stories about family, fear, animals, and anger, about
blood, bones, midwives, frogs, and fires, about bread, fish, and storms. At
the center of it, we have the story of a baby, a star, of angels and shepherds.
We have the story of who that baby grew up to be, how he sacrificed for us,
and how he wants to transform us.

GOD WANTS us to meet him and trust him over and
over again, day after day. How is your time with God's word
transforming you?

THE PATH OF LIFE

You make known to me the path of life; you will fill me with joy in
your presence, with eternal pleasures at your right hand.

—Psalm 16:11

God made each one of us, and he has designed a path of life for each of us, as distinct as our fingerprints. The pleasure you think you'll get if you buy this or that thing—that pleasure actually comes along the path, with God. The joy you want to feel that makes you run from experience to experience—burning yourself out, missing your own life—that joy is found in God's presence. It was here all along.

I'm learning this firsthand. I thought I knew what would make me happy. And I pursued it. God, in his grace, keeps bringing me back to the path of life that he has chosen for me. The things I thought would make me happy don't. And the things I've been avoiding for years are giving me life, hope, and peace in ways I could never have imagined.

The God who made us, on purpose and for a purpose, with great love, has laid out a path for your life, and for my life. When we live faithfully on that path—small and ordinary as it may be, different than you planned, not at all what you dreamed—we will live with peace, joy, and fullheartedness.

HOW HAS the path God designed for you turned out differently than you hoped or expected? What unexpected sources of life, hope, and peace has he put in your path?

BE HERE

I say to the LORD, *"You are my Lord; apart from you I have no good thing."*

—Psalm 16:2

Be who you are. Be where you are. Contentment can't happen until you decide to be yourself, whatever that means. Being yourself is so much better than being a poor imitation of someone else. When you decide to be someone else, you're saying to the God who created you, *I don't like what you've done here. Bad job.* You dishonor the creator when you pronounce his creation not good enough.

Psalm 16:2 says, "You are my Lord." Another way of saying that: *I believe that you knew what you were doing when you made me, even though some days it makes no sense to me.*

There is a path of life for you, and it's marked with joy and pleasure and God's presence. But you can't walk someone else's path. Not your mom's or your mentor's or your friend's. The God who made us—who made the moon and the stars, who made the ocean—is a God of love. He knows us. He knows what delights us, what makes us mad, what we're great at, what we're terrible at. You are right where you are supposed to be. Be here, and be all here.

HAVE YOU ever tried to walk someone else's path? What was that experience like for you? Is there anything you need to let go of to really be where you are? Talk with God about that, and thank him for the way he has made you.

KNOCKING

"Here I am! I stand at the door and knock. If anyone hears my voice and opens the door, I will come in and eat with that person, and they with me."

—Revelation 3:20

The image from Revelation 3 of Jesus standing at the door of our hearts and knocking is such a beautiful image, isn't it? I wonder sometimes if we make it too narrow. We save that image for the moment of conversion. But what if Jesus is back again every morning, like a kind neighbor, knocking gently, *Can I walk with you today?*

That's the pattern all through scripture. He's always there, knocking, ready to tell a new story—of identity, purpose, love, future, redemption. God changed your story the day you met him, and he's obsessed with life, wholeness, healing, putting broken things back together again. He is obsessed with abundance, abandon, great love, great possibility. So many of us choose to live in darkness, defined by our brokenness, letting our failures hang around our necks like nametags announcing, *This is all I am. This pain is who I am.*

It's not true. Your pain doesn't define you. Your failures don't define you. Your createdness defines you. Christ in his goodness defines you. God loves you, forgives you, and wants to walk with you, through prayer and his word and community.

WHAT IS defining you these days? Is there a story that you're ready to let God rewrite for you?

THE WIDOW'S MITE

A poor widow came and put in two very small copper coins, worth only a few cents. Calling his disciples to him, Jesus said, "Truly I tell you, this poor widow has put more into the treasury than all the others. They all gave out of their wealth; but she, out of her poverty, put in everything—all she had to live on."

—Mark 12:42–44

The story of the widow's mite is about money, but it's even more about faith. The widow gave, and she trusted that even if she gave everything, God would provide what she needed.

In Exodus, when the Israelites were in the desert, God sent manna. Some people didn't believe that there really would be more tomorrow, even though that's what God told Moses. They took more than they were instructed, out of fear, out of a hoarding instinct, but the food they saved became infested with maggots by the next morning. God wanted his people to trust him daily, to need him and follow him every morning with new faith. But they didn't want to have to trust. They wanted to depend on what they had gathered, instead of what God promised to supply. Hoarding is in our fearful nature.

In the Lord's Prayer, Jesus taught us to pray, "Give us this day our daily bread..." We want bread for a month, for a year. We want guarantees and back-up plans. But God promises bread for a day, and then another day, and then another day. And the widow believed his promise.

HOW HAVE you learned to trust or rely on God's provision for you every day? How has he shown his faithfulness to you?

THE PRACTICE OF GRATITUDE

Devote yourselves to prayer, being watchful and thankful.

—Colossians 4:2

I absolutely believe that gratitude is a way of life, a practice as opposed to a feeling, and I want to be the kind of person who chooses to be grateful for what is instead of angry about what isn't.

When I'm feeling stressed or pressed or crazy-brained, I'm learning to take a little mental time-out to practice gratitude. What seems like a monumental catastrophe melts down into minor annoyance in the face of the things I'm thankful for: health, family, sunshine.

I had a few little things shake loose this afternoon—nothing big, just enough to get me feeling a little rattled and breathless, shoulders scrunched up by my ears. I had less than an hour to work, and I didn't want to end my workday all icky and stressed.

So I practiced gratitude: I made a list of the little and big things I'm thankful for right now, and that list, one after another after another, rose up to face my little stresses and problems, and it forced them to back down a little, to recede into the middle distance, where they can't get to me anymore.

WHAT ARE you thankful for today? Take a few moments to name the things you're thankful for. Breathe deeply. Thank God for these things. Allow peace and joy to well up inside you just a bit.

WHO DEFINES YOU?

They loved human praise more than praise from God.

—John 12:43

I have a serious thing for Amazon Prime and the "Buy Now with 1-Click" option—it's so easy. When our son Mac was a baby, I noticed a new thing Amazon started doing. After my package arrived, they would send an email asking me to rate my experience. The first time this happened, I had ordered diapers. I thought, *Rate my experience?* I didn't go to Paris, or a museum, or the opera. I didn't even read a book or eat at a restaurant. I ordered diapers and they came. That's not an experience. That's not something you rate.

But in the world we live in today, it is. Everything is ratable, up for review, open for critique. How many stars, how many likes, how many page views?

This is a seductive game. Letting yourself be defined by anything other than the good God who created you on purpose and for a purpose is meaningless—and dangerous. When you live for the opinions of a crowd, it's all but impossible to stay on course with the calling you've been given. Because God's call on your life doesn't usually have much in common with the parameters of success as our world defines it.

ARE THERE any areas of your life where the opinions of a crowd draw you away from God's call on your life? Whose voices can you invite into your life to counteract the pull of the crowd's voices?

PLANTING SEASON

There is a time for everything, and a season for every activity under the heavens...a time to plant and a time to uproot.

—Ecclesiastes 3:1–2

I find it's helpful to have sort of a theme or focus for each season. What is this season *about*? What are my highest priorities for this segment of time? What do I say yes to, and what do I say no to...and what priorities guide those choices?

There are some things, of course, that are priorities in every season—faith, marriage, parenting, friendship. But it helps me to have a few framing ideas beyond those, ideas that shape how I spend my time and energy for that season.

This is an *inspiration season,* a planting season. I believe that inspiration is something we create, something we're responsible for. I don't believe in waiting for it to show up. I believe that being an artist means you live a life of imagination and inspiration instead of sitting down at your laptop expecting it to show up at just the moment you need it.

It's planting season—a time to plant seeds and sow my imagination with images and themes and ideas, trusting that when it's time to harvest, what I'm planting now will be enough.

WHAT ARE you planting this season? What are you sowing today so that when harvest time comes, something new has been brought to life?

RUNNING THROUGH DINOSAURS

We take captive every thought to make it obedient to Christ.

—2 Corinthians 10:5

For our son Henry's seventh birthday, we loaded up the car with his best friends and headed to the Brookfield Zoo. It has an amazing exhibition of animatronic dinosaurs—machines that look and sound like dinosaurs. You walk through the bears and the tigers and the kangaroos, and then you walk through the dinosaurs, arching their backs, breathing and growling.

Henry had been looking forward to it for ages. When we finally arrived at the dinosaurs, the boys were wriggling with excitement. They sprinted through the exhibition, yelping, dragging one another on to the next one, the next one, the next one. They reached the end in record time.

"How could you be done already?" we asked. "Don't you want to see it again? Or look at each one up close?" They didn't. They were too wound up, too excited about the dinosaurs to actually experience the dinosaurs.

I run through the dinosaurs all the time. I miss things that really matter to me because I'm caught up in my own head, having imaginary conversations, forecasting imaginary disasters. I want to be where I am and be fully there. I don't want to miss any more dinosaurs.

DO YOU ever come to the end of the day and realize you've missed what was going on around you? Acknowledge this to God, and ask him to help you be fully present in your life.

Annette's Fondue

Annette learned this fondue recipe in Switzerland, and she makes it for special occasions—to mark an anniversary or milestone in someone's life. Now we make it at our house, too, and it reminds me how important it is to mark these special moments in the lives of people we love.

• •

½ pound Gruyère

½ pound Emmentaler

⅛ pound Appenzeller
(if you can't find it, you
can substitute Raclette)

1 ½ tablespoons flour

1 garlic clove, crushed

1 cup extra dry vermouth

1 pinch nutmeg

2 tablespoons kirschwasser
(cherry brandy)

• •

» Grate cheese and mix with flour in a bowl, and set aside. Put garlic and vermouth in a saucepan, on the stovetop. Bring the mixture to almost boiling, then add to cheese mixture. Add nutmeg and kirschwasser, and stir to combine well. Once combined, keep over very low heat and dip items into the fondue, or transfer it to a warmed bowl and serve immediately.

» Serve with bread, sausages, and apples...and make sure to serve a shot of kirschwasser midway through to aid digestion.

KEEPING COMPANY

He heals the brokenhearted and binds up their wounds.

—Psalm 147:3

Most of us learn to pray by talking—we learn that prayer is talking to God. And it is. But I'm learning another way to pray, too: more like keeping company, like sitting in silence with an old friend. It's this kind of praying that heals me when my heart is broken, that binds me up when fear has pulled me into pieces.

Sometimes praying by talking to God only gets me more wound up—articulating each fear, naming each anxiety, putting words to every hurt and broken part. Sometimes these days I feel most connected to God in the silence—trusting that he's there, that he's holding me, that I'm safe.

It's in the silence that I find rest and grace and peace. It's in the silence that I remember the promises he's kept. It's in the silence that I sense his presence, like someone who loves me is keeping me company, because that's exactly true.

When my prayers turn into long rantings, rambling diatribes about what I want and what I need and what scares me, I'm learning to close my mouth, and to settle into the silence. That's where I feel his company.

SPEND A few minutes in intentional silence, keeping company with God in prayer. Is silence a part of your spiritual practice?

ON LIVING FOR THE OPINION OF OTHERS

Do not pay attention to every word people say, or you may hear your servant cursing you—for you know in your heart the many times you yourself have cursed others.

—Ecclesiastes 7:21–22

Solomon, the writer of Ecclesiastes, knew what it's like to live for the opinion of others, and he knew that it's as meaningless as chasing the wind—because it doesn't last. What one person loves is what another person hates. What one person thinks is amazing another person calls total failure. So you wear yourself out trying to respond and pivot and change yourself according to every little thing anyone says, and you end up so tired, and so far from your calling, and so far from satisfied.

So much of the biblical narrative is about God calling his people away from idolatry, over and over. And this is one more example. When you allow other people's opinion of you to define you, that person becomes an idol, a substitute for God. God made you, and he defines you. He calls you; he leads you. When you let yourself be led and called and defined by the clamoring voices that have something to say about every little thing, you'll never be satisfied. You'll never feel peace. You'll never be able to rest.

WHOSE OPINION of you matters to you? How do those opinions stack up against God's definition of you? Spend some quiet moments with God, and ask him to center you once again in his love and his calling for your life.

THANKSGIVING

Rejoice always, pray continually, give thanks in all circumstances;
for this is God's will for you in Christ Jesus.

—1 Thessalonians 5:16–18

On a snowy night in December, we hosted house church, and I cooked a Thanksgiving dinner. Even though I had done the meal part of Thanksgiving twice that year, I hadn't yet done the *thanks* part.

We sat in the twinkly, candlelit dining room and ate stuffing, smashed potatoes, and old-school green bean casserole with crunchy onions on top. We talked about gratitude, and how there are things that are easy to be thankful for. Henry is an uncomplicated happiness, as is my family, my marriage, and the house church.

Then we told the stories that no one tells, of the darkest places, the most painful moments, and the ways God has held those moments up and turned them from ash to luminous things, treasures, shards of hope.

When we stood in a circle to close our night together, we practiced Thanksgiving. We thanked God for the uncomplicated happiness of babies and friendship and food, and for the complicated joys that come from loss, from failure, from reaching the bottom and pushing back up to the light.

HOW DO you practice true Thanksgiving? What ways have you found to honor those complicated joys that come from the painful places in your life?

WOUNDING WORDS

Set a guard over my mouth, LORD; keep watch over the door of my lips.

—Psalm 141:3

We all need a small group of people who echo God's love for us and his belief in us. In an ideal universe, these are the people closest to us, our immediate families. But this is not the case for so many people. The wounds so many people carry are not from the opinions of strangers but from the opinions of the people they love most.

If the people close to you are not for you, if they intentionally hurt you, if they consistently speak to you in a way that makes you feel less, or wounded, or unloved, even if they're your family, you need to draw a boundary, and you need to protect yourself from their words.

If that's the case, carefully choose another small circle who can reflect truth to you even when your family or people close to you surround you with hurtful words. We all need face-to-face reminders of God's love and grace. Bring the wounding words to a safe circle, and invite them to help you replace those words with God's truth.

Over time, the messages of pain are slowly replaced with messages of love—that's some of the most sacred work we can do in one another's lives.

ARE THERE people in your inner circle, family or not, who use their words to intentionally hurt you? Are there people in that circle whom you have hurt with hostile or careless words? What would it take to heal those relationships or set new boundaries?

LITTLE TRAVELERS

"You will receive power when the Holy Spirit comes on you; and you will be my witnesses in Jerusalem, and in all Judea and Samaria, and to the ends of the earth."

—Acts 1:8

Sometimes people ask me why I travel so much, and specifically why we travel with Henry and Mac so often. They think it's easier to keep the kids at home, in their routines, surrounded by their stuff. It is. But we travel because Capri exists and Kenya exists and Tel Aviv exists, and I want to taste every bite of it. I want my kids to learn, as I learned, that there are a million ways to live, eat, dress, speak, and view the world. I want them to know that "our way" isn't the right way, but just one way, that children all over the world, no matter how different they seem, are just like the children in our neighborhood—they love to play, to discover, to learn.

I want my kids to learn firsthand and up close that different isn't bad, but different is exciting and wonderful and worth taking the time to understand. I want them to see themselves as bit players in a huge, sweeping, beautiful play, not as the main characters in the drama of our living room. I want my kids to taste and smell and experience the biggest possible world.

HOW DID you learn the scope of the world and of God's story? If you have children, how are you helping them to learn and experience these things?

November

25

BE A GROWER

But the fruit of the Spirit is love, joy, peace, forbearance, kindness,
goodness, faithfulness, gentleness and self-control.

—Galatians 5:22–23

One way to build a stronger marriage is to take responsibility for your own emotional and spiritual health. Be a grower, a person committed to health and wholeness in every part of your own life.

In Mark 10 Jesus describes marriage this way: "But at the beginning of creation God 'made them male and female. For this reason a man will leave his father and mother and be united to his wife, and the two will become one flesh.' So they are no longer two, but one." That's the definition of marriage—two becoming one. But a friend of mine says this: "Two can never really become one if they weren't two to begin with." She's talking about wholeness, about spiritual and emotional health. The number one thing that you can to do build your marriage is take responsibility for your own spiritual and emotional health.

A mentor of ours says a marriage can only ever be as healthy as the least healthy person in the marriage. If addiction or apathy or unhealed pain from your past is ruling your life, your marriage has no chance to be healthy. Pursue personal wholeness, whatever it takes.

ARE THERE any areas of your spiritual or emotional health that have become stagnant? What step could you take toward nurturing new growth?

OUR CLOSEST NEIGHBOR

One of them, an expert in the law, tested him with this question: "Teacher, which is the greatest commandment in the Law?" Jesus replied: "'Love the Lord your God with all your heart and with all your soul and with all your mind.' This is the first and greatest commandment. And the second is like it: 'Love your neighbor as yourself.'"

—Matthew 22:35–39

The command to love is not just about the people who live next door. Your husband is the neighbor that's never moving away, and lives right up in your business. Whatever neighborhoods you live in throughout your life, your spouse will always be your number one neighbor. Marriage is the most intimate, long-term relationship any of us will have. Aaron will spend more time, in his lifetime, with me, than any other person.

I'm starting to understand what a huge responsibility that is. I have the honor of affecting his life more than any other person. What I say to him and don't say to him, what I do and don't do, everything about how I live with him affects him more than any other person on earth will.

It makes me want to do so much better. Aaron's my person, and I get to show him God's great love every day. That's an amazing opportunity. I get to show him how present God is when we need him, how quick to grace he is, and slow to anger. I get to demonstrate God's love in Aaron's life more than anyone else.

HAVE YOU ever thought about your spouse as your neighbor before? How does he need you to show God's love to him?

EXPERT FORGIVERS

Then Peter came to Jesus and asked, "Lord, how many times shall I forgive my brother or sister who sins against me? Up to seven times?" Jesus answered, "I tell you, not seven times, but seventy-seven times."

—Matthew 18:21–22

If you want to be a part of a durable, beautiful, long marriage, you have to be an expert forgiver. You will get hurt in your marriage, in big ways and small ways, and if you hold tightly to a record of wrongs, your marriage will choke. It will die. Resentment and unwillingness to forgive will force you to live in your past—back in the mistakes, in the betrayals, in the mess.

One of my closest friends was betrayed by her husband, in small ways, and then in a big way. She had every right to walk. But she decided that she's the kind of person who forgives, and that what they'd built over the years was worth another chance. She became an expert forgiver. They have a new baby now. More than that, they have a new life together. You can see it on their faces, a depth of understanding, a sober-minded commitment to try again.

It's not always possible. But it's possible more than we tend to believe.

God wants to make all things new. God can make your marriage new if you let him, if you lay down the resentments and learn to be an expert forgiver.

WHO HAS been an example to you of an expert forgiver? What have you learned from that person? Is there anything in your marriage right now that you need to forgive?

WHAT GOD HAS JOINED TOGETHER

"Therefore what God has joined together, let no one separate."

—Mark 10:9

When we were newly married, a mentor challenged me to always communicate with men in such a way that my husband could read every text, listen in on every phone call, read every e-mail, eavesdrop on every conversation and feel great. She encouraged me to communicate with men as though my husband was right there with us. That's a great rule, and it's served our marriage well.

Mark 10:9 says, "Therefore what God has joined together, let no one separate." What this means is that all of us, single or married, have a part to play in helping other people's marriages.

The most seductive, cheap, easy belief is that it would be better with someone else. That's a lie. You think the grass is greener with him?

The grass is greener where you water it.

The beauty you're looking for, the adventure you're craving, the love story you're longing for—it's the one you create in your own home. There is so much beauty and love and redemption and possibility in the marriage you're already a part of. I know sometimes it doesn't seem like it. But it's true.

IS THERE anyone in your life whose marriage you're not supporting, by the way you interact with either the husband or the wife? Would you honor that friend's marriage best by bowing out of that interaction?

November

29

CREATING BOUNDARIES IN MARRIAGE

Your ways are in full view of the LORD, and he examines all your paths.

—Proverbs 5:21

People create boundaries to protect their marriage in all sorts of different ways. Sometimes they seem a little strict. But in a season where it seems like every time I turn around another friend tells me about another affair, those boundaries don't seem so crazy.

I have an old friend who lives in LA, and I hadn't seen him for years. I was going to be out there, and I sent an e-mail—I wanted to see him and his wife and their kids. But his wife and kids were going to be out of town, so if we got together it would be just him and me.

He replied, "Hey, I know this might seem nuts to you. But my wife and I have a deal that we don't meet alone with anyone—even for coffee, even in the middle of the day, even an old friend. That's our thing."

He was willing to risk offending me instead of breaking a boundary he's set with his wife—I respect that. Because his relationship with his wife is so much more important than his friendship with me. I love it when someone chooses their marriage, whatever that means.

WHAT KIND of boundaries have you and your spouse set to protect your marriage? Do they need any readjusting?

FRIENDSHIPS & BOUNDARIES

Drink water from your own cistern, running water from your own well.
Should your springs overflow in the streets, your streams of water in the public
squares? Let them be yours alone, never to be shared with strangers.

—Proverbs 5:15–17

No one sets out to have a relationship outside their marriage. No one, on their wedding day, says, *Several years down the road, I might lie to you about where I'm going. I might text an old boyfriend while I'm sitting next to you on the couch. I might fall in love with someone else, little by little, and you might not even know.* No one thinks that will happen to their marriage. But I'm learning, by watching people I adore live through so much heartbreak, that it happens all the time.

It doesn't have to. The number one best way to keep your marriage from being vulnerable to an affair is to invest in it, and the number two way is to build boundaries to protect you from a relationship that could ruin your marriage.

I absolutely believe men and women can be friends. The men that I walk with—my friends, Aaron's friends, our small group—they're my brothers. They talk to me like I'm a sister. They want our marriage to win. I want theirs to win. I believe men and women can be friends. And I believe those friendships flourish within healthy boundaries.

DO YOU and your spouse have friends who are like brothers and sisters to you? What kind of boundaries do you have with those friendships?

December

1

TO BUILD A BETTER MARRIAGE

When Jesus saw him lying there and learned that he had been in this condition for a long time, he asked him, "Do you want to get well?"

—John 5:6

If you want to build a stronger marriage, ask for help, professional and otherwise. For some people, there's a stigma that goes along with counseling—that there's something seriously wrong if you need to go to counseling. Let's change that stigma. Let's cheer people on when they want to make their marriages better. Let's say "You're so brave!" instead of "You're so screwed up."

Let me clarify one thing. Marriage is difficult, but abuse has no place in marriage. God's design for your life does not include you being abused, verbally or physically. God's call to stay and build marriages does not mean that you stay in a situation where you're being abused.

In John 5, Jesus heals a man. There are lame and diseased men all around, and Jesus comes to one, and asks only one question: *Do you want to get well?* That's the question: Do you want to be well? Don't let pride or fear or worrying about what somebody will think stand in the way of being well, of being healed, of letting God work through a counselor to heal the broken spots in your marriage.

HAVE YOU sought help from a counselor? Do you want a strong marriage enough to ask for help when you need it?

ASK FOR HELP FROM YOUR COMMUNITY

Let us consider how we may spur one another on toward
love and good deeds . . . encouraging one another.

—Hebrews 10:24–25

Marriage doesn't happen in a vacuum. Every marriage needs support. Surround yourselves with people who want your marriage to win. Surround yourself with people who celebrate with you when you grow, and have hard conversations with you when you screw up. And this doesn't mean only other married people.

A friend of mine, many years ago, reached a point with her husband where they decided to separate. She was in a small group, and she was the only married one in the group. She showed up that night and told them about the decision. She wasn't asking for advice, just reporting. *This is what we've decided.* And that group of single men and women looked back at her and said *no. No. We believe that you can make it. We believe that you can try again, both of you, and we're going to help.* That couple has now been married over twenty years, because their community wanted them to win, and wanted to help. They were ready to walk away, but their community nudged them back toward their marriage, toward their family, toward second chances.

Surround yourself with people who, if you said, *I'm out,* would say back to you, *No.*

DO YOU have people around you who want your marriage to win? Do you trust them to tell them the truth about your marriage?

SISTERHOOD

The beginning of wisdom is this: Get wisdom. Though
it cost all you have, get understanding.

—Proverbs 4:7

When I was in high school, a woman named Ann took me out for coffee and shared books with me—Tozer and Chesterton and Lewis. She let me ask her anything and held my secrets close, and she showed me what it looked like to be an adult. In college, a camp director named Diane walked with me and hugged me tight and showed me what it looked like to be an adult. In my twenties, a woman named Nancy met me for breakfast and let me babysit her kids and brought me magazines and ice cream when I was sick and showed me what it looked like to be an adult. Now, in my thirties, Pam and September and Maria and Christine give sage advice and snuggle my kids and show me what it looks like to be an adult.

At every step along the way, women I look up to have given their time and wisdom to me just when I've needed it. They've showed me what's ahead and how to get there. I've needed every bit of the wisdom and direction, and now I'm honored to give it, too, knowing that that's how it works, how this important sisterhood continues—coffee and storytelling and passing on the things that someone taught you all those years ago.

WHO HAS mentored you? Who plays that role now, or do you need to pray for God to lead you to the right person for this season? And who are you sharing your wisdom with?

A LOVE WE DIDN'T KNOW EXISTED

They are fighters, and as fierce as a wild bear robbed of her cubs.

—2 Samuel 17:8

Once Henry was born, the world turned a color I never imagined, and I never dreamed that one little person could capture me so deeply, could change my entire life so completely. That year I lost some things that were very important to me, but as I held his little feet, I knew that I had everything the world could possibly give me, that I was richer than a Rockefeller and luckier than a leprechaun. Life sneaks up on us, every once in a while, and gives us something we didn't even know we wanted, and lights within us a love we didn't even know existed.

I was stunned by the intimacy of this, by the ferocity of feeling. I felt like I could turn inside out if something happened to him, like my mind could melt or my heart stop if he experienced one moment of pain. I wanted to touch him, hold him, protect him with a panicky, fierce love, like a bear or a dog. I had visceral, wordless feelings that woke me up in the night and made me tremble, and other moments when the world seemed so deeply right, so good and perfect I couldn't help but pray.

BECOMING A mother is astonishing. Who knew we could love like this? If you're a parent, or play a nurturing role in the life of a child, spend a few minutes thanking God for that privilege.

December

5

ON MOTHERHOOD

From everlasting to everlasting the LORD's love is with those who fear
him, and his righteousness with their children's children.

—Psalm 103:17

I have seven dear friends from high school. We see each other every year or so for an official gathering, and more often when life allows. In recent years, motherhood has descended upon several of us, with all the hope and love and beauty our hearts can contain, and all the pain and fear our souls can bear.

I'm surprised that the topic of pregnancy and birth and mothering, for every single one of us, has been touched with pain or just a shade of heartache. The odds of that surprise me. Eight women, and eight stories of waiting or yearning, of brokenness mixed in with deep delight.

Our hearts are full, but also a little tender, bruised, tired. Motherhood, and the journey toward it, has battered us a little bit, each in our own ways. From ambivalence to longing to loss, from the anger that our bodies won't do what we want them to, to the consuming, crushing love for a baby that is just hanging on. From the emptiness every month, over and over, to the physical brokenness of our bodies, to the deep questions—*When? When? When? Why? Why not?*

WHAT HAS motherhood and the journey toward it been like for you? Sit quietly, gently with the bruised and tender parts of your heart, and allow God's love to nurture and heal them.

HEADLINES & LULLABIES

Jesus...said to them, "Let the little children come to me, and do not hinder
them, for the kingdom of God belongs to such as these."...And he took the
children in his arms, placed his hands on them and blessed them.

—**Mark 10:14, 16**

When it seems like there's more bad news than good, I gather the people I love around me. Sometimes what it takes for me to really regain a sense of God's hand and presence is to stop the dozens of things I'm doing all at the same time and connect with my son. Everything stops in those moments when I finally stop trying to write one more e-mail or put away a few more dishes, and I really see him. I see the way his mind works and the way he sees the world, and I realize, in those moments, that the world he sees is full of beauty and mystery, that it's waiting to be discovered, new every day.

The headlines don't have nearly as much to say to me as this little person does. The things that matter most are our sons and daughters and the stories we write with them in our own homes every day. Those stories might not make for salacious headlines, but they do make beautiful lullabies, so sometimes the very best thing to do is to turn off the news and keep writng our own stories and lullabies.

TODAY, TAKE a few minutes to intentionally connect deeply with each family member or person in your home. Notice how your day changes when you do that.

December

7

LESS IS MORE

Yes, my soul, find rest in God; my hope comes from him.

—Psalm 62:5

In other months, I spend a lot of time cooking up fun things to do—parties, trips, shopping lists. But December, lovely month, does it all for me. It's all my favorite things coming together—special occasions, traditions, gatherings centered around food and presents. A weekend in the city, a party tonight, a night out tomorrow. Birthday parties and Christmas parties and cookie exchanges and dinners.

But every December, I slip into believing that if one dinner party is good, two is better, that if one caramel is good, four is much better, that if staying up to read for an hour is good, then all night is even better.

I keep coming back to the old cliché *less is more*. I want to really notice each meal, each bite, each conversation, instead of shoving food in my mouth, running out the door, promising someone we'll connect again soon. I have so many intentions and plans, but I lose the ability to listen, to stay, to connect. I'm embarrassed that I fall for it every time. *Less is more* is a great idea, but you wouldn't know that from my calendar.

SOMETIMES SLOWING down and choosing *less* allows us to savor our meals, our conversations, our every moment. How can you choose less today?

PRESENT OVER PERFECT

He makes me lie down in green pastures, he leads me
beside quiet waters, he refreshes my soul.

—Psalm 23:2–3

During Christmastime we find ourselves tempted to abandon Christlikeness in favor of overdoing. The season that centers around the silent, holy night, the simple baby, and the star quickly becomes the season in which we over-everything—overspend, overeat, overindulge, overcommit.

I fall into it every year, and one year, I was falling even a little bit deeper than usual. The stress and chaos were on the rise, and something had to change or I'd miss the loveliness of the season entirely. I stopped myself in the middle of it all—the trips, the wrapping, the cookies, the expectations—and I asked for help. I prayed for new eyes to see, for a way outside myself and my tense, swirling chaos. As I slowed down and listened, three words laid themselves on my worn-out spirit like a blanket: *present over perfect*.

I can show up with my *perfectly* wrapped gift and my *perfectly* baked cookies…and my *perfectly* resentful and frazzled self, ready to snap at the first person who looks at me wrong. Or I can rest my body and nourish my spirit, knowing that taking a grounded, present self to each holiday gathering is more important than the gifts I bring.

GOD DESIGNED us to need rest and nourishment. When we receive them, we are better able to be wholly present. What do you need to cut out this season, in order to be fully present?

CHRISTMAS LOVE

Gracious words are a honeycomb, sweet to the soul and healing to the bones.

—**P r o v e r b s 16 : 2 4**

I'm hit-or-miss on Christmas cards, having totally abandoned the idea these last few years. I know you all sent them out the day after Thanksgiving, and that they had little handmade ornaments inside or something, but some years the idea of all the addresses and the photo and the stamps just puts me absolutely over the edge. However, I do still buy one little box of cards to give to the people I love, and it guarantees that I sit down, right in the midst of the insanity of the season, and tell my family and my closest friends how deeply their love has affected me.

Don't let this season pass without taking the time and energy and creativity and risk to speak plainly with the people you love about exactly what they bring to your life. You may come from one of those families that consider a wink and a handshake true intimacy, but if Christmas hinges on traditions, please consider beginning a new family tradition. You can get away with anything at Christmas—we wear earrings that light up and eat cookies for three meals a day. This is your time to be a little wacky and get away with it.

CHRISTMAS IS a season of opportunity—who can you love through words and gifts and memory-making?

THE ADVENT ALTERNATIVE

All this took place to fulfill what the Lord had said through the prophet: "The virgin will conceive and give birth to a son, and they will call him Immanuel" (which means "God with us").

—Matthew 1:22–23

Advent is about waiting, anticipating, yearning. Advent is the question, the pleading, and Christmas is the answer to that question, the response to the howl. There are moments in this season when I don't feel a lot like Christmas, but I do feel like Advent.

Advent gives us another option beyond false Christmas cheer or Scrooge. Advent says the baby is coming, but he isn't here yet, that hope is on its way, but the yearning is still very real. Advent allows us to tell the truth about what we're grieving, without giving up on the gorgeous and extravagant promise of Christmas, the baby on his way.

Consider Advent a less flashy but still very beautiful way of being present in this season. Give up your false and failing attempts at merriment, and thank God for a season that understands longing and loneliness and long nights. Let yourself fall open to Advent, to anticipation, to the belief that what is empty will be filled, what is broken will be repaired, and what is lost can always be found, no matter how many times it's been lost.

GOD FULFILLED so many promises when Jesus came as a baby in Bethlehem. Dare to hope and trust that he will fulfill his promises to you as well.

December

11

SET FREE

A heart at peace gives life to the body.

—Proverbs 14:30

As the Christmas season unfolded one year, I was given opportunity after opportunity to decide how much to do—or overdo. A new friend invited me to a cookie exchange on the only night Aaron would be home until Christmas. We didn't have plans, per se, but I had a sense we needed to be home together. So I said no, which was hard for me, and our little family did approximately nothing, which was exactly what we needed.

I cohosted a party, and one of the things I brought was frozen meatballs. I love to cook, and I was planning, of course, to make them from scratch. But it was too much for me, too much time and energy I don't have in this time of the year.

And, *of course*, no one cared. That's the lesson in this for people like me who sometimes get wound up about doing things perfectly: 90 percent of the people in your life won't know the difference between, say, fresh and frozen, or handmade and store-bought, and the 10 percent who do notice are just as stressed-out as you are, and your willingness to choose simplicity just might set them free to do the same.

GIVE YOURSELF permission to make choices: yes or no, simple versus complicated, celebration and rest.

SIMPLER THIS SEASON

Now may the Lord of peace himself give you peace at all times and in every way.

—2 Thessalonians 3:16

The irony must not be lost on us: a season that is, at its heart, a love story—about faith and fragility, angels, a baby, a star—gets lost so easily in a jarring, toxic tangle of sugar and shopping bags and rushing and parking lots and expectations.

In our lowest, most fragmented moments, we feel out of control—we feel controlled, in fact, by expectations and to-do lists and commitments and traditions. It's that time of year, we shrug, when things get a little crazy. No avoiding it.

But that's not true. And that's shifting the blame. We have, each one of us, been entrusted with one life, made up of days and hours and minutes. We're spending them according to our values, whether or not we admit it.

My friends from high school always get together at Christmas and build gingerbread houses with all our kids. One year, two of us had sick kids. I had a newborn. One was working full-time in a new position. One was nine months pregnant. As the e-mails swirled around, finally Courtney said, "I love you all so much—enough to let tradition slide this year in order to keep things simpler this season." Ah, yes. Yes. *Yes.*

WE REALLY do get to choose how we spend our time. The most thoughtful gift we can give each other is release from well-intentioned plans that have unexpectedly become burdensome.

A SPACE FULL OF LOVE

Better a small serving of vegetables with love than a fattened calf with hatred.

—Proverbs 15:17

One year when Aaron and I were first married, we had a big Christmas party in our tiny one-bedroom town house. We set up small food and drink stations in every room—ice buckets of champagne and tiny turkey sandwiches and little pots of sweet and spicy mustard on the coffee table and the kitchen counter, with another platter down in the basement studio, next to the drums, and another in the loft.

Even those stations weren't enough, so just before guests started arriving, I took a deep breath, shoved all of our clothes and shoes in the closet, and put a platter of sandwiches and an ice bucket with champagne on the piano in our bedroom. At one point, I found a whole group of our friends lounging on our bed with sandwiches and champagne flutes. Later in the evening I found them trying on all of my shoes.

People aren't craving perfection or longing to be impressed; they're longing to feel like they're home. If you create a space full of love and character and creativity and soul, no matter how small or undone or odd, they'll take off their shoes and curl up with gratitude and rest.

WHEN IT comes to making people feel welcome, a loving attitude matters far more than how fancy your house is. Today, put a date on the calendar to gather people you love in your home, and pray for what God will do in that time.

WHY THE DOOR STAYS CLOSED

"Martha, Martha," the Lord answered, "you are worried and upset about many things, but few things are needed—or indeed only one. Mary has chosen what is better, and it will not be taken away from her."

—Luke 10:41–42

Men, in my experience, don't have the kind of shame about their homes that many women do. Aaron will invite someone into our house and not even notice the cereal-and-milk smears on the table, the socks on the floor, the crumbs on the counter. Meanwhile, I consider lying to the people in our foyer about a gas leak or something, anything to get them back on to the porch so I can sprint around with baby wipes in one hand and a laundry basket in the other.

This is why the door stays closed for so many of us, literally and figuratively. One friend promises she'll start having people over after they remodel. Another says she'd be too nervous that people wouldn't eat the food she made, so she never makes the invitation.

But it isn't about perfection or performance. You'll miss the richest moments in life—the sacred moments when we feel God's grace and presence through the faces and hands of the people we love—if you're too scared or too ashamed to open the door.

UNTIL WE learn to open the door, we have no way of knowing who's outside, just waiting for a chance to be invited inside. Why do you keep the door closed?

WHAT CAN HAPPEN IN A YEAR

And the God of all grace, who called you to his eternal glory in Christ, after you have suffered a little while, will himself restore you and make you strong, firm and steadfast.

—1 Peter 5:10

When things are dark and splintering, I get stuck, believing that it will always be so, that new life will never come, that change will never really break into my life. But this year is all the proof I need. One year ago today, a similarly snowy day, it was all different, and I want to hold this moment like a charm—*remember, remember.* The snow is falling on the evergreen tree in our new backyard, and our cozy little house feels warm and safe. I'm wrapped in a blanket that's been dragged to every home we've lived in since we got married— new couch, new view, same old yellow blanket. A candle flickers on the table, and the steam from my tea smells like cloves. We are a million miles from last December, and I want to keep this moment with me as a reminder of what can happen in a year.

As I look out the window, the snowflakes are bigger now and falling even faster. People are wondering about canceling events for tonight and school closings for tomorrow. That would be just fine with me. I have all I need right here: this evergreen, this tea, this candle, this December.

WHEN WE remember what God has brought us through, it gives us gratitude for where we are and hope for where we will be. Spend a minute thinking through a couple areas of your life, and thank God for what he's done in that area.

VOICES

"I have come that they may have life, and have it to the full."
—John 10:10

Our week was full to bursting with family parties and gatherings with friends, preschool Christmas programs and coffee dates with out-of-town friends just here for the holidays. Our gifts were mostly purchased but mostly not wrapped, and our laundry situation, after a busy weekend, was dire.

When things are too crazy, the only voices I hear are the voices of fear and shame. I stop being able to hear the voice of God, the voice of rest, the voice of hope and healing and restoration, the voice that gives new life to dry old bones. And instead I hear that old song I've heard all my life: *You're not good enough. You're not good enough.*

But that voice is a lie. And it's a terrible guide. When I listen to it, I burn the candle at both ends and try to light the middle while I'm at it. The voice of God invites us to full, whole living—to rest, to abundance, to enough. To say no. To say no more. To say I'm going to choose to live wholly and completely in the present, even though this ragged, run-down person I am right now is so far from perfect.

GOD DOES not require perfection—he receives us just as we are. Let his voice be the loudest in your ears this season.

WHOLLY PRESENT

"Take my yoke upon you and learn from me, for I am gentle and humble in heart, and you will find rest for your souls. For my yoke is easy and my burden is light."

—Matthew 11:29–30

My intention for this season is *present over perfect*. I determined to add nothing to the to-do list. I abandoned well-intentioned but time-consuming projects. And in their place I'm making rest and space priorities, so that what I offer to my family is more than a brittle mask over a wound-up and depleted soul.

Either I can be here, fully here, my imperfect, messy, tired but wholly present self, or I can miss it—this moment, this conversation, this time around the table, whatever it is—because I'm trying, and failing, to be perfect, keep the house perfect, make the meal perfect, ensure the gift is perfect. But this season I'm not trying for perfect. I'm just trying to show up, every time, with honesty and attentiveness.

One thing's for sure: if you decide to be courageous and sane, if you decide not to overspend or overcommit or overschedule, the healthy people in your life will respect those choices. And the unhealthy people in your life will freak out, because you're making a healthy choice they're not currently free to make. Don't for one second let that stop you.

IT'S WORTH giving up the endless, fruitless pursuit of perfection in order to be wholly present. What do you need to give up in this season?

THIN PLACES

The Word became flesh and made his dwelling among us. We have seen his glory, the glory of the one and only Son, who came from the Father, full of grace and truth.

—John 1:14

My mother is Irish, and when I was in college I studied Irish literature and poetry in Ireland for a little while. One of my favorite Celtic ideas is the concept of thin places. A thin place, according to the Celtic mystics, is a place where the boundary between the natural world and the supernatural one is more permeable—thinner, if you will.

Sometimes they're physical places. There are places all over Ireland where people have said, if you stand here, if you face this direction, if you hike to the top of that ridge at just the right time of day, that's a thin place, where the passage between heaven and earth is a short one, a place where God's presence is almost palpable. The boundary between the divine world and the human world becomes almost nonexistent, and the divine and the human can, for a moment, dance together uninterrupted.

Other thin places aren't places at all, but states of being or circumstances or seasons. Christmas is a thin place, a season during which even the hardest-hearted of people think about what matters, in the face of the deep beauty and hope of Christmas. The shimmer of God's presence, not always plainly visible in our world, is more visible at Christmas.

BE WATCHING, be listening for the grace that shines through the Christmas season.

DIVINE FINGERPRINTS

The shepherds returned, glorifying and praising God for all the things
they had heard and seen, which were just as they had been told.

—Luke 2:20

When we find a thin place—one of those places where God's presence is almost palpable—we should live differently in the face of it, because if we don't, we miss some of the best moments that life with God has to offer us. These thin places are gifts, treasures, and they're worth changing our lives for. Reach through from human to sacred every time the goodness of this season moves you. A thin place is an opportunity to be more aware of the divine fingerprints all over this world, and Christmas is one invitation after another to do that.

When you hear music that pierces your spirit, thank God for the gift of music. When you witness generosity that reminds you of the deep goodness of humanity, thank God for the way he created us. When you feel a profound sense of beauty, thank God for it. When the faces of your children or your parents shock you with the love you feel for them, thank God. When the traditions and smells and sounds of Christmas that you love and wait for all year long overwhelm you and you think, *I love this world we live in*, thank God for those things.

DRINK IN the wonder of Christmas, the bounty of God's gifts to us. When you notice God's fingerprints on your world, thank him for his touch.

OUTSHINING THE DARKNESS

The LORD is close to the brokenhearted and saves those who are crushed in spirit.

—Psalm 34:18

Sometimes, our lives and our hearts are broken open. Brokenness has a way of allowing the supernatural into our lives in the same way that deep joy or great beauty do—and maybe, I'm finding, even more.

Let me be clear: brokenness doesn't automatically bring us to the thin place, the sacred place where God's breath and touch are closer than our own skin. Heartbreak brings us lots of places—to despair, to bitterness, to emptiness, to numbness, to isolation. But because God is just that good, if we allow the people who love us to walk with us right through the brokenness, it can also lead to a deep sense of God's presence. When things fall apart, the broken places allow all sorts of things to enter, and one of them is the presence of God.

My prayer is that what you've lost, and what I've lost this year, will fade a little bit in the beauty of the Christmas season, that for a few moments at least, what is right and good and worth believing will outshine all the darkness, within us and around us.

GENTLY CONSIDER whether, alongside the loss in your heart, there is space for the warmth of Christmas to rest. What can you do to create a little space for that goodness?

THE MOST IMPORTANT GIFTS

But Mary treasured up all these things and pondered them in her heart.

—Luke 2:19

During Christmas, God's presence is more palpable than any other time of the year. What we've lost is also more present to us; the pain or the loneliness or the fear are more present than at any other time. It's a glorious, beautiful time and also one in which even the smallest kindnesses can transform us.

If what it takes for you this year to be present in this sacred place, to feel the breath and presence of a Holy God, is to forgo the homemade cookies and the perfect decorations and the cards and the rushing and the lists, then we'll be all right with cookies from the store and a few less gifts. It would be a great loss for you to miss this season, the soul of it, because you're too busy pushing and rushing. And it would be a great loss if the people in your life receive your perfectly wrapped gifts, but not your love or your full attention or your spirit.

My prayer for us is that we would give and receive the most important gifts this season—the palpable presence of a Holy God, the kindness of well-chosen words, the generosity of spirit and soul.

IT TAKES time to give and receive and enjoy the intangible gifts of Christmas, and it's well worth taking that time.

CHRISTMAS VEILED IN LOSS

*This is how God showed his love among us: He sent his one and
only Son into the world that we might live through him.*

—1 John 4:9

For some, Christmas is a season of loss. Maybe it's the first Christmas without a family member or dear friend, and your heart has been so wholly battered that it allows God's presence and voice to seep into it at every turn. Or maybe a relationship broken this year hangs over the season like a veil. You are alone, freshly. A close friend of mine will celebrate her first Christmas alone, because her divorce became final earlier this year, and the man she fell in love with, hard, just after that, walked out of her life as quickly as he walked into it. She says that the loneliness is deafening sometimes.

I don't know what you've lost this year: a life, a friend, a child, a dream, a job, a home. I don't know what's broken your heart this year, but I do know that whatever it is, you may feel the loss of it even more acutely at Christmas.

I believe deeply that God does his best work in our lives during times of great heartbreak and loss, and that much of that rich work is done by the hands of people who love us, who dive into the wreckage with us and show us who God is, over and over and over.

IF YOU are heartbroken or walking through grief with a friend, receive God's presence during this season.

BABY FEET

Our mouths were filled with laughter, our tongues with songs of joy.

—P s a l m 1 2 6 : 2

One snowy Monday after a busy weekend, when he was almost three months old, Henry and I stayed home and wore our pajamas all day. When he was awake, we played together. I'd stick my tongue out, and he'd stick his tongue out, and then he'd smile and laugh, a gurgly drooling laugh, where his blue eyes flashed and I was convinced that he knew a lot more than he let on. He looked up at me with a face that seemed to say, "I hear you. I get what you're saying, Mom." We stuck our tongues out for hours.

When I changed him, I talked with him. Before I put his sleeper back on, I tickled his legs and belly, and I kissed the bottoms of his feet, because they're so soft and perfect and chubby, and before I knew it, there were tears running down my face, and I cried so hard I couldn't keep talking to him.

All alone with my son, in the midst of a frantic holiday season, that moment on a dark Monday afternoon was the merriest Christmas moment for me. The sweetest moment of gratitude and hope happened right then, in our quiet house, with my son, kissing his little baby feet.

WHEN WAS the last time you felt this kind of gratitude and hope? Spend a few moments thanking God for the beauty of those experiences.

A SEASON FOR BABIES

I bring you good news that will cause great joy for all the people. Today in the town of David a Savior has been born to you; he is the Messiah, the Lord.

—Luke 2:10–11

Christmas is, after all, a season for babies. After Henry was born, it made sense to me in a new way that God chose to wrap his divinity in baby bones and baby skin. I always thought maybe it was to demonstrate vulnerability, or to identify fully with each phase of humanity, but now I think it was something else. I think it was because babies make us believe in the possibility and power of the future. We've had regular babies, non-Messiah babies, and when I looked at their sleeping faces, all the world seemed new and possible.

Babies make you believe in God because there's something just beyond understanding about their freshness and fragility. When they take their first breaths, and when they land, floppy and slippery, on your chest under the bright overhead light in an otherwise dim delivery room, when you watch their tiny sleeping selves, when you hear their thin wild animal cries, you know, you just know in your guts that God is real, and that babies have been with him more recently, have come more directly from him than our worn-out old selves have.

BABIES BRING joy and wonder and hope for the future. Spend a moment thanking God for the beauty of the Christmas story, and for what it teaches us about who God is.

December

25

TRULY & DEEPLY IN THE PRESENT

While they were there, the time came for the baby to be born, and she gave birth to her firstborn, a son. She wrapped him in cloths and placed him in a manger, because there was no guest room available for them.

—Luke 2:6–7

Let's be courageous in these days. Let's choose love and rest and grace. Let's use our minutes and hours to create memories with the people we love instead of dragging them on one more errand or shushing them while we accomplish one more seemingly necessary thing. Let's honor the story—the silent night, the angels, the miracle child, the simple birth, with each choice that we make.

My prayer is that we'll find ourselves drawn closer and closer to the heart of the story, the beautiful, beating heart of it all, that the chaos around us and within us will recede, and the most important things will be clear and lovely at every turn. I pray that we'll understand the transforming power that lies in saying no, because it's an act of faith, a tangible demonstration of the belief that you are so much more than what you do. I pray that we'll live with intention, hope, and love in this wild season and in every season, and that the God who loves us will bring new life to our worn-out hearts this year and every year, that we'll live, truly and deeply, in the present, instead of waiting, waiting, waiting for perfect.

WHAT CAN you intentionally leave behind in this season in order to make more space for the new life God wants to bring?

HOLY CURIOSITY

As he went along, he saw a man blind from birth. His disciples asked him,
"Rabbi, who sinned, this man or his parents, that he was born blind?"
"Neither this man nor his parents sinned," said Jesus, "but this
happened so that the works of God might be displayed in him."

—John 9:1–3

Our culture specializes in boxes, in categories, in labels. We think we know all about someone because they send their kids to this kind of school, or because they go to that kind of church. This is sloppy. And this is dangerous.

A wise friend of mine is teaching me to ask this question every time I disagree with someone in a visceral way: "How did that person come to feel this way?" Essentially, he's teaching me to ask: "What part of this person's story do I need to know to understand what he or she is telling me right now?"

Wouldn't that change everything?

When we listen to stories, there's no room for stereotypes. Storytelling and story listening is unfamiliar at first, and scary, but you begin to develop muscle memory for it. You begin to feel a holy curiosity for everyone you see: *What's her story? How did he come to feel this way? What is it that I don't yet know about her story?*

This is a Kingdom way to live, because instead of labels and categories, we begin to dwell in actual humanity, which was the plan all along, of course.

IS THERE anyone in your life that you've put into a box based on one or two facts about them? What do you think might happen if you learned the depth of their story?

OPENING DOORS

He has given us this command: Anyone who loves God
must also love their brother and sister.

—1 John 4:21

Sometimes love asks you to change. Life is full of opportunities to love someone well by loving their thing, not just your thing, by stretching across your preferences and opinions and comforts.

It's so easy to love people who like all the same things you do—who never listen to music that makes you cringe, or who believe all the same things you believe. But love sometimes asks you to lay down your preferences and dive into someone else's world for a little while.

Sometimes that world is the ballet or country music or Russian novels. Sometimes it's staying quiet when you want to talk. Sometimes it's giving space when you want to rush in. Love asks what's best for the person you love, not what's best or most convenient to you.

Sometimes love opens doors for you that you never knew were there. You may dive into someone else's world thinking you're doing them a favor, only to wind up learning something new about yourself. Love will expand your horizons in ways you can't even imagine.

WHEN HAS someone loved you well by doing something outside their own comfort zone? When have you done that for someone else? Who can you do that for today?

THE GIFT

The Spirit of God has made me; the breath of the Almighty gives me life.

—Job 33:4

If I gave you a sweater, and you loved it, I would know because you would wear it so much you'd be on the verge of wearing it out. It would be the sweater you wear to get coffee and that you sleep in sometimes and that you drag around in the back of your car and tie around your waist. It would start to smell like you, and it would get snags and get all stretched out, and just looking at it would make you tell a thousand stories of where it's been and who you've been in it.

That's what I want my life to be, like a well-loved gift. I think life, just life, just breathing in and out, is a great gift. God gives us something amazing when he gives us life, and I want to live with gratitude. I want to live in a way that shows how much I appreciate the gift. If life were a sweater, I would wear it every day. I wouldn't save it or keep it for a special occasion. I would find every opportunity to wear that sweater, and I'd wear it proudly, shamelessly, for days on end.

HOW ARE you living the gift you've been given? When was the last time you expressed gratitude for the gift of life?

WHERE TIME STOPS

The ear tests words as the tongue tastes food. Let us discern for
ourselves what is right; let us learn together what is good.

—Job 34:3–4

Sit down at the table and offer the people you love something humble and nourishing, like soup and bread, like a story, like a hand holding another hand while you pray. We live in a world that values us for how fast we go, how much we accomplish, how much life we can pack into one day. But it's in the in-between spaces that our lives change, and that the real beauty lies.

Most of the time, I eat like someone's about to steal my plate, like I can't be bothered to chew or taste or feel, but I'm coming to see that the table is about food, and it's also about time. It's about showing up in person, a whole and present person, instead of a fragmented, frantic person, phone in one hand and to-do list in the other. Put them down, both of them, twin symbols of the modern age, and pick up a knife and a fork. The table is where time stops. It's where we look people in the eye, where we tell the truth about how hard it is, where we make space to listen to the whole story, not the textable sound bite.

HOW OFTEN does your family eat with phones and laptops and TVs and video games? What would it be like to make space to listen to the whole story around the table?

COME TO THE TABLE

Six days before the Passover, Jesus came to Bethany, where Lazarus lived, whom Jesus had raised from the dead. Here a dinner was given in Jesus' honor. Martha served, while Lazarus was among those reclining at the table with him. Then Mary took about a pint of pure nard, an expensive perfume; she poured it on Jesus' feet and wiped his feet with her hair. And the house was filled with the fragrance of the perfume.

—J o h n   12 : 1 – 3

This is what I want you to do: I want you to tell someone you love them, and dinner's at six. I want you to throw open your front door and welcome the people you love into the inevitable mess with hugs and laughter. I want you to light a burner on the stove, to chop and stir and season with love and abandon. Begin with an onion and a drizzle of olive oil, and go from there, any one of a million different places, any one of a million different meals.

Gather the people you love around your table and feed them with love and honesty and creativity. Feed them with your hands and the flavors and smells that remind you of home and beauty and the best stories you've ever heard, the best stories you've ever lived.

I want you to invest yourself wholly and deeply in friendship, God's greatest evidence of himself here on earth. More than anything, I want you to come to the table.

COME TO the table, and bring the people you love with you. Create space for friendship to bloom and flower and make all your lives richer and sweeter.

December

31

A PLACE OF REST

"Come to me, all you who are weary and burdened, and I will give you rest."

—Matthew 11:28

We don't come to the table to fight or to defend. We don't come to prove or to conquer, to draw lines in the sand or to stir up trouble. We come to the table because our hunger brings us there. We come with a need, with fragility, with an admission of our humanity. The table is the great equalizer, the level playing field many of us have been looking everywhere for. The table is the place where the doing stops, the trying stops, the masks are removed, and we allow ourselves to be nourished, like children. We allow someone else to meet our need. In a world that prides people on not having needs, on going longer and faster, on going without, on powering through, the table is a place of safety and rest and humanity, where we are allowed to be as fragile as we feel. If the home is a body, the table is the heart, the beating center, the sustainer of life and health.

Come to the table.

WHEN WAS the last time someone met your need at the table? When was the last time you met someone else's need at the table?

ACKNOWLEDGEMENTS

The idea for this book was born around the table, over goat cheese and cherry ice cream, which is where all the best ideas begin, I think. A thousand thanks to Rebecca Warren, Molly Hodgin, Laura Minchew, and Carrie Marrs for dreaming over ice cream with me. And love and thanks to Chris Ferebee and Carolyn McCready—we make a good team, and I'm so grateful for you. Very special thanks to my friend Lindsay Sherbondy, for making it pretty. Thanks to dear friends who allowed me to share their delicious recipes: Sara Close, Heather Larson, Melody Martinez, Annette Richards, Monica Robertson, Jennifer Van Beek, and Lindsay Todd (shelikestoeat.com). And thanks to all the people we love who have gathered around our table over the years—these ideas and prayers and recipes and stories are not just mine, but all of ours. Most of all, thanks to Aaron, Henry, and Mac, who make my life infinitely richer—louder, messier, wilder, sillier, better in every way. I love you with my whole heart.